Stress, Trauma, and Posttraumatic Growt

What happens in trauma's aftermath? How do its effects manifest differently on the individual, family, and community-wide levels? *Stress, Trauma, and Posttraumatic Growth: Social Context, Environment, and Identities* explores the way traumatic events are defined, classified, and understood throughout the life cycle, placing special emphasis on the complex intersections of diverse affiliations and characteristics such as age, class, culture, disability, race and ethnicity, gender identity and expression, immigration status, political ideology, religion, sex, and sexual orientation. The book gives its readers a solid basis for understanding traumatic events and treating their effects and also shows the varied ways that trauma is conceptualized across cultures. Both new and seasoned clinicians will come away from *Stress, Trauma, and Posttraumatic Growth* with a deep understanding of the principles that guide successful trauma treatment.

Roni Berger, PhD, LCSW, is professor of social work at Adelphi University School of Social Work.

Stress, Trauma, and Posttraumatic Growth

Social Context, Environment, and Identities

Roni Berger

Routledge
Taylor & Francis Group

NEW YORK AND LONDON

First published 2015
by Routledge
711 Third Avenue, New York, NY 10017

and by Routledge
27 Church Road, Hove, East Sussex BN3 2FA

Routledge is an imprint of the Taylor & Francis Group, an informa business

Library of Congress Cataloging-in-Publication Data
Berger, Roni.
   Stress, trauma, and posttraumatic growth : social context,
environment, and identities / by Roni Berger.
      pages cm
   Includes bibliographical references and index.
   1. Stress (Psychology)   2. Post-traumatic stress disorder.
3. Cognitive-behavioral therapy.   I. Title.
   BF575.S75B395 2015
   155.9'3—dc23
   2014032809

ISBN: 978-0-415-52780-4 (hbk)
ISBN: 978-0-415-52781-1 (pbk)
ISBN: 978-0-203-11879-5 (ebk)

Typeset in Baskerville
by Apex CoVantage, LLC

Printed and bound in the United States of America by Publishers Graphics,
LLC on sustainably sourced paper.

Contents

Acknowledgments

While my name is on the cover, this book has many parents to whom I am very grateful: My students at Adelphi University in New York and in Bob Shapell School of Social Work in Tel Aviv University, who taught me so much about effective ways to teach trauma content. My friend and colleague Professor Ellen Rosenberg, whose question, "if you cannot find a book on trauma that you like to assign to your students, why don't you write one?" inspired the creation of this book. The Dean, colleagues, and leadership at Adelphi University, who always provided me with resources and support for the researching and development of the manuscript. My clients, whose courage and creativity in battling a wide and diverse array of personal and collective stressors taught me humility and endurance. My friend Professor Michal Shamai of Haifa University in Israel, who shared with me over the years her wisdom regarding collective trauma. The reviewers, publishers, and editors at Taylor & Francis, who provided ongoing advice, guidance, and feedback that helped bring the book from an idea to a complete project. My supportive partner Bob who never ceased to encourage me and believe in me. Finally, my beloved son Dan who was my companion and co-traveler through many of the stressful events of my life and who shared my struggles to come together stronger on the other side.

Introduction

The goal of this book is to provide a comprehensive resource on the exposure of individuals, families, and communities in various phases of the life cycle to diverse types of stressor events, in various socio-cultural contexts, the negative and positive effects of such exposure, and ways to address them. Stress, crisis, and trauma have been studied for at least a century and their study has expanded in scope from physiological study of sympathetic responses, to cellular mechanisms, gene expressions, animal models, and human experimental and intervention studies. Capturing these multiple dimensions is challenging given the amount of relevant knowledge and the complexity of the issues. An internet search yields more than 10,000,000 hits for "family stress" and 9,000,000 hits for "trauma" and these numbers are increasing exponentially. Furthermore, definitions of and criteria for what constitutes stress and trauma are constantly changing as reflected in the relevant sections of the DSM-V (APA, 2013) and the forthcoming 2015 ICD-11. Clearly, no book can report about all that has been written in the field. Most available books have focused on a specific population group (e.g. children), a specific type of stressful event (e.g. disaster) or a specific type of intervention. The main principle that guided me in developing this book was an effort to present in a reader-friendly manner a picture of what we know to help practitioners navigate the overwhelming amount of theoretical, empirical, and clinical knowledge available.

Exposure to highly stressful events is a common experience for adults and children, men and women, in all cultural contexts. That stress is part of our lives and influences individuals and communities is well established. It has been estimated that around 82 to 90 percent of the general population is anticipated to be exposed to some type of a traumatic event at some point in their lifetime (Breslau et al., 1998; Powers et al., 2010). Some traumatic events are very common, such as a sudden death of a relative or a friend, school violence, or a serious car accident, whereas others are quite rare, such as being kidnapped or tortured, terrorist acts, or mass shootings in the workplace. These prospects vary depending on who people are (e.g. their gender, socioeconomic status, and race), where they live, and their personal, family, and work circumstances. Thus, living in areas prone to natural disasters – such as earthquakes in Japan or Turkey, tsunamis in South East Asia, or bushfires in Australia – or in a war zone – such as in parts of the Middle East and Africa – increases the likelihood of traumatic exposures and living in poor communities increases the prospects of dire consequences of such exposure.

I was born and grew up in Israel, where living with constant traumatic exposure is part of the national DNA. Having spent sleepless nights in shelters and when they were not available in dark stairwells, completed three years of military services and practiced social work for over two decades before immigrating to the US, experiencing both divorce and the death of loved ones as well as the terrorist attacks in New York on 9/11, I have had my personal and professional share of stress exposure. In fact, I suspect that like many I experienced an acute stress disorder as a young officer during the Six Days War. I served in an emergency room of a hospital that received many with head injuries, working day and night to register the wounded, listen to their stories, accompany them to operation rooms, communicate with their families, and comfort their girlfriends. I experienced numerous symptoms such as the inability to eat, sleep, focus or concentrate and I stayed mostly alone in a closed room, not noticing as the hours and days disappeared. However, because we knew much less about trauma in those days, I received no diagnosis or treatment except the loving embrace of my family and bounced back after a couple of months.

For years I focused my interest on stressful and potentially traumatic experiences close to my heart – such as growing up without a father and immigration – and, like many, the conceptual framework that guided my work was mostly focused on understanding problems and negative effects. However, a little over a decade ago, I developed a growing interest in the emergence of models that adopted a resilience perspective. This book reflects this combined lens of looking at negative and positive effects of the exposure to highly stressful and potentially traumatic events.

The book is organized in four parts. The first part (chapters 1–3) introduces relevant concepts, classifications and theories. The second part (chapters 4–6) reviews current knowledge about negative and positive effects of exposure to stress on individuals, families, and communities. The third part (chapters 7–8) focuses on developmental and cultural contexts of stress, crisis, and trauma. The last part (chapters 9–11) discusses intervention strategies for addressing the effects of exposure.

Part I

Mapping the Arena
Concepts, Definitions, Classifications, and Theories

Some traumatic events are common and anticipated, such as the death of an older parent, the birth of children, or school violence; others are possible though not unavoidable, such as a serious disease, a road accident, or an earthquake; yet others are quite rare, such as being kidnapped or tortured, terrorist acts, or mass shootings in the workplace. The prospects for exposure vary depending on who people are (e.g. gender, socioeconomic status, race), where they live, and their personal, family, and work circumstances. For example, living in areas prone to natural disasters or in war zones increases the likelihood of traumatic exposures and living in poor communities increases the prospects of dire consequences of such exposure. Such encounters may become stressful or even traumatic when the amount of coping they demand exceeds the resources available for managing them.

This part of the book introduces the map for understanding stress and includes three chapters. The first offers definitions and explanations of main concepts; the second reviews diverse classifications of stressful events; and the third presents a concise overview of leading theories relating to stress, crisis, and coping of individuals, families and communities.

1 Concepts and Definitions

What is a stressor event? How does it compare to a traumatic event? What is the difference between stress, crisis, and trauma? Concepts and their definitions can be confusing. The following section presents core concepts in the field of stress, crisis, and trauma, some of which will be further developed in later chapters. These concepts refer to individual, group, and protective aspects.

Individual Aspects

Stressor Event

A stressor event is a life situation which places a demand or pressure on an individual, a family, or a community that produces, or has the potential to produce, a major change from the previous state so that regular responses cannot effectively address it. Bonanno and Mancini (2008) suggest that highly aversive events that fall outside the typical range of normal everyday experience should be viewed as *potentially* traumatic because not everyone experiences them as such. The source of a stressful event can be physical, psychological, financial or social, or a combination of these. The event can be normative – such as marriage, launching an adolescent, retirement, or relocation – or non-normative – such as an accident, divorce, an untimely death, or the birth of a child with a disability. All stressor events are complex, and made up of different traumatic moments, which include varying degrees of threat. While the original event may be a one-time occurrence, it often generates additional challenges and may have ripple effects that can last a long time.

Pile Up of Stressors

This concept, sometimes referred to as cumulative stress, was coined by McCubbin and Patterson (McCubbin, Thompson & McCubbin, 1996), and refers to the build-up of multiple stressful situations, which occur simultaneously and may lead to stress becoming a chronic condition in the life of the individual, family, or community. Stress pile-up can occur as a result of a continuous problem in the social environment (such as the decades of war in Afghanistan) or a single underlying ongoing stressor (e.g. a chronic illness) which produces ongoing stressors such as negative side effects, the appearance of various symptoms and challenges in functioning, or a series of unrelated events which occur immediately after each other leaving no chance to success-fully address one stressor before the next one hits – for example, a child being injured a week after their grandmother has died. Any of these multiple stressor combinations may reduce the ability of those exposed to cope and function because of increasing demands and vulnerability. An example would be an original stressor event of a spouse's prolonged battle with cancer, which may include multiple serial and cumulative stressor events such as repeated negative tests results and side effects of treatment, followed by their death, which may lead to numerous sequential stressors such as loss of income, or relocation that involves loss of friends, peer groups and neighborhood support systems.

Sometimes the effort to cope with and manage the original stressor event creates an additional stressor. For example, when women responded to their husbands' absence due to military service in the Vietnam War by taking on roles traditionally fulfilled by men, disapproval from in-laws and other mem-bers of the extended family became an additional source of stress.

Stress

After years of debate as to whether stress is the function of individual traits, an objective characteristic of the environment or a result of the interac-tion between the two, currently dominant is the acceptance of the people–environment transactional model. While definitions of stress vary, most share at least three core elements. First, that a situation occurs which disrupts the usual stream of life and creates a state where the "normal" way of doing things does not work or is insufficient. This situation can originate from internal or external sources, be they major (e.g. being injured in an accident) or minor (e.g. failing a test), positive or eustress (such as winning the lottery, a promotion at work) or negative (e.g. loss of a loved one, being fired). A second major element across definitions of stress is that the situation is overtaxing because it demands resources that exceed those available for addressing it and thus a disparity is developed between the demands of the situation and the means for responding to it. Third, is whether the disparity is appraised by the exposed individual or system as strenuous, emotionally disruptive, endangering their well-being, and creating tension or as an opportunity for change and development.

Stress is an ongoing process rather than a stable state. Some amount of stress is part of the normal course of everyday life and its total absence may lead to boredom while excessive, unrelenting stress may become a burden and lead to difficulty in functioning. The normal amount of stress varies by profession and life circumstances. Thus, emergency work, military service, or parenting a child with special needs, for example, are characterized by a higher level of routine stress than is experienced by most people. What constitutes stress is somewhat subjective and there is no "optimal" amount of stress for individuals, families or communities as the threshold of tolerance varies by personality and the unique characteristics of those exposed. Some people thrive on an intense and demanding schedule with many unanticipated events whereas others experience as stressful even minute changes to their routine. The occurrence of a stressor event stimulates a chain of physiological-neurochemical reactions, increased heart rate and blood pressure, and a sense of alertness. Stress has been documented as being associated with increased susceptibility to health issues such as coronary ailments and the immune system's reduced ability to fight disease. In families, groups and communities, it triggers a parallel chain reaction of systemic dynamics such as inter-subsystems relationships. For example, Berger (2010b) identified processes of splitting, and projection of anger, guilt, and shame in a group of Black, Latino and Caucasian students during a stressful visit to the torture slave castles in West Africa.

Distress

Although definitions vary and are often vague, there seems to be consensus that distress (often called psychological distress to distinguish it from biological distress) is a combination of negative feelings of being easily annoyed or irritated, emotional pain, sadness, anxiety and fearfulness, and having uncontrollable temper outburst as a result of a subjective sense that something is wrong, whether or not that feeling is associated with actual impairment in any area of functioning. Distress is typically the outcome of exposure to highly stressful events which is not successfully decreased, controlled or eliminated (McCubbin, Thompson & McCubbin, 1996). It may include cognitive, somatic, and affective components. Psychological distress is considered a normal reaction to internal or external stimuli which are perceived negatively and it only becomes pathological when the response is disproportionate to the circumstances (Horwitz, 2007). Manifestations of distress may be somatic (headaches, neck and back pain, gastrointestinal problems, loss of hair and of weight, and heartburn), emotional (sadness, anxiety, depression, anger), cognitive (e.g. difficulty concentrating) or social (withdrawal, combativeness and difficulty in intimate relationships).

Crisis

Definitions of crisis also vary. Hill (1949), in his seminal work on separation and reunification during and following the Second World War, defined it as a sharp or decisive change or life event which renders old patterns inadequate, with a resulting state of disorganization. In a family, a crisis is what happens when an unanticipated event reveals a failure of the rules, norms, behavior, or infrastructure used to handle it. An analysis of crisis literature suggests that most definitions of crisis include several core elements: 1. a *disruption* of normal life conditions or the steady state of an individual, a family, a group, or a community; 2. the *abrupt* or hazardous nature of the disruption; 3. perception of the disruption as a cause of considerable disturbance that compromises normal stability; 4. viewing the situation as insurmountable because regularly used coping strategies and resources that are usually helpful in managing issues are found to be *insufficient* or *ineffective* for resolving the problem; 5. possible development of the extreme response of distress, disorganization, disequilibrium, and impairment of the ability to function or cope with the situation and rectify it. Most crisis literature emphasizes its time-limited nature (4–6 weeks).

Crises may have situational, developmental, or social/cultural origins. A *situational* crisis results from an extraordinary and unanticipated event – such as war, a sudden death, a diagnosis of a life-threatening disease, or a natural disaster – which challenges the fundamental assumptions of one's life. *Developmental* or *evolutional* crises are normal stages of development. The concept originated in ego psychoanalytic developmental psychology, particularly the work of Erikson (1963), who identified eight major phases in a person's life. Each chronological phase presents a dominant age-specific developmental task or crisis. Successful accomplishment of the task and resolution of the crisis allows moving forward to the next phase whereas failure to do so may lead to getting stuck or regressing. Such developmental crises are normative and tend to be universal. The same idea has been applied to families and their transitional crises around diverse phases in their life span such as marriage, the birth of a first child, raising children, launching an adolescent, and so forth. The origins of a *social/cultural* crisis are discriminatory norms such as racism, sexism, and homophobia. While some have seen stress and crisis on a continuum, others have attempted to distinguish them as discrete separate entities. In this book I take the former approach, based on my scholarly knowledge and clinical experience.

Trauma

The word trauma originates from Greek, literally meaning a wound or injury. The definition of this often-used and seemingly clear concept is challenging as it has been used interchangeably to describe not only horrific, often potentially life-threatening events, but also the experience of those exposed to the event and responses to the experience. It is often claimed that trauma is in the eyes of the beholder. The definition of trauma in the DSM-V (2013), the bible of mental health clinicians in the US for the diagnosis of mental health disorder, is:

> direct personal experience of an event that involves actual or threatened death or serious injury, or other threat to one's physical integrity; or witnessing an event that involves death, injury, or a threat to the physical integrity of another person; or learning about unexpected or violent death, serious harm, or threat of death or injury experienced by a family member or other close associate (Criterion A1) others.
>
> (APA, 2013, p. 274).

Similarly, in the European parallel of the DSM, the International Statistical Classification of Diseases, and Related Health Problems 11th Revision (ICD-11), trauma is viewed as resulting from an encounter with an overwhelming, negative, and extremely painful experience that is incongruent with the existing repertoire of perceptions, interpretations and coping strategies, and is likely to create distress. While loss and trauma are different, grief over the loss of people, objects, ideals, and beliefs is often central to the experience of trauma.

In agreement with Freud's view of traumatic events as potent enough to penetrate the protective shell of the ego, there is consensus among scholars and practitioners that trauma challenges the natural need of people for the world to be predictable, just, orderly, and controllable such that they can anticipate the sequence of events in their life, know what will most probably happen at certain times, and plan with some safety. Such challenges may have psychological and neurological aspects and both short- and long-term impact to various degrees on diverse aspects of feelings, thinking, behavior, social relationships, and self-perception.

Complex Trauma

This describes a unique type of trauma characterized by its timing at critical developmental phases and its destabilizing of core elements of the self and one's interpersonal relationships. It refers to extended exposure to multiple simultaneous, sequential, or prolonged traumatic events, most often in the context of interpersonal relationships (such as intimate partner violence), placing the person at risk for severe health and mental health problems (van der Kolk et al., 2005). The term emerged in the 1990s when researchers and practitioners began to realize that some forms of trauma were much more pervasive and complicated than others (Courtois, 2008). In children it typically involves the continuous experience of abuse and/or maltreatment, often in the context of an unsafe community. Complex trauma is viewed as altering basic self-structure, attachment, and relational systems (e.g. with family), and connections with broader communities.

Retraumatization

Retraumatization may occur when the report of a traumatic experience by the victim meets reactions of disbelief, minimization, and pressure to keep it a secret and go on with life as if nothing happened. Some types of stressful experiences such as rape and childhood sexual abuse are especially vulnerable to retraumatization. Thus, a victim of domestic violence in a conservative cultural context who escapes the abuser to seek shelter with her family of origin but is told "go back to your [abusive] husband" may be retraumatized. Some practitioners have been concerned that the use of intervention strategies that require revisiting the traumatic event, such as exposure therapy (discussed in

Chapter 9), may have negative effects of retraumatization. Retraumatization has rarely been presented as an issue in treatment (Karlin et al., 2010).

Vicarious (Secondary) Traumatization

Diverse and somewhat different though closely related concepts have been used to describe indirect impacts of trauma exposure on those who experience it second hand via intensive personal or professional relationships with direct victims. They include compassion fatigue, secondary traumatic stress (Figley, 1995), vicarious effects (McCann and Pearlman, 1999), empathic strain, secondary traumatization (Rosenheck & Nathan, 1985), and co-victimization. The phenomenon of a contagious trauma was originally identified in family members of combat veterans and survivors of sexual assault. Following Carl Jung's idea of the "wounded healer" to connote the pain of therapists caused by interaction with the pain of those they treat, it was later expanded to professionals who provide services to trauma survivors, such as police officers, nurses, social workers, psychologists, psychiatrists, and clergy (Figley, 1995; Killian, 2008). It involves a caregiver's pain and identification with the direct victim's suffering, and its manifestations resemble those of direct victims (Ellwood et al., 2011). Increasing recognition of secondary traumatization led to the journal *Traumatology* dedicating its December 2011 issue to it.

Group Aspects

Concepts with nuanced differences have been used to describe exposure to a common stressor event of a group of people who share a characteristic or an affiliation, such as religion, racial/ethnic background, profession or sexual orientation, or living in the same place (Wieling & Mittal, 2008). It has been defined as the "cumulative emotional and psychological wounding over the lifespan and across generations, emanating from massive group trauma experiences" (Yellow Horse Brave Heart, 2003, p.7), and its effects can reverberate through and be transmitted from one generation to another by the process of *transposition.*

Collective or Mass Trauma

An immense trauma experienced simultaneously by a large number of people can be an isolated event or an ongoing series of circumstances such as the decades of exposure to civil wars and armed conflicts in Liberia, Sudan, and the Middle East. When such a shared and widespread exposure to radical technological, political, economic, or physical changes is experienced by members of a certain group and is interpreted as fundamentally incongruent with core values and identity, it may lead to the demise of a previously orderly and taken-for-granted universe. This type of trauma is viewed as the most threatening, with the longest endurance in the collective memory or subconsciousness

(Alexander et al., 2004; Sztompka, 2000). While some claim that the concept of historical trauma should be limited to events created by people rather than natural disasters, often a more inclusive view is used. Examples of such trauma include major political reform – such as recent revolutions in the Arab world – war and terror, genocide, ethnic cleansing or persecution of an indigenous religion – such as the destruction of the Aztec empire by the Spanish invasion – a natural or human-made disaster – such as the atomic catastrophes in Chernobyl and Fukushima – an earthquake, a tsunami, or a famine. The trauma becomes part of the collective narrative and changes the collective identity as manifested in Native Americans, Jews, African Americans, Khmer, and Armenians.

Community Disaster

This has been suggested as a more specific concept in that it excludes chronic environmental hazards, ongoing community and political violence, war, and epidemics, instead focusing on acute events. This focus is evident in the commonly used definition by McFarlane and Norris of a community disaster as "a potentially traumatic event that is collectively experienced, has an acute onset, and is time delimited; disasters may be attributed to natural, technological, or human causes" (2006, p.4). However, in reality, the distinction between a community trauma and a disaster is challenging. For example, the August 2005 breaking of the levees in New Orleans met the narrow definition of a disaster. It was sudden, unanticipated, and affected numerous individuals and families across many neighborhoods and communities. However, the lack of employment, housing, and safety that resulted, and became chronic stressors, lasted in the most badly affected neighborhoods for years – the same is true for contamination and health hazards that sudden technological disaster can breed. Similarly, the brutal forced relocation of Navajos by the US army in the 1860s in the Long Walk to Bosque Redondo caused suffering and death during the torturous 500-miles march and stay in camp and also left long-term stressor events by considerably heightening the prospects for fatal genetic diseases. The Māori in new Zealand, the "stolen generation" of outcast Aboriginals in Australia, the mass killing of those defined as enemies of the people by the Khmer Rouge regime in Cambodia, the genocide of Tutsis by the Hutu in Rwanda in the 1990s, the Armenian genocide by the Turks, and the 1950s great famine in China, caused by the agricultural policy of the Maoist regime, are just a few of numerous community disasters across the globe.

Cultural Trauma

Cultural trauma is defined as incidents perpetrated by an external source intending to harm a group of others, such as the enslavement of Africans, the colonization and destruction of the indigenous nations of South America mostly by Spaniards, and the execution of Jews, Roma, and gay people by the

Nazis during the Holocaust. The number and frequency of community disasters has become so alarming that the journal *Social Forces* dedicated a special section in its December 2008 issue to the discussion of their anticipated social aspects in the twenty-first century. Brunsma and Picou (2008) reported that in the first eight years of this century, 422 disaster declarations had been issued in the United States alone, and the number of affected people and communities globally reflects intensification of death and destruction. Media coverage and social networks that make information about such disasters available in real time further exacerbates awareness of them.

Protective Aspects

Social Support

Although social support does not intuitively appear to be part of the main concepts related to stress, crisis, and trauma, because of its centrality in many stress, crisis and trauma theories, models, and studies, it should be part of the discourse. Social support refers to interpersonal interactions among individuals, families, and groups through which people help each other. Such help can be instrumental, informational, or emotional. *Instrumental* support includes providing tangible goods such as shelter, food, clothes, and other items to substitute for those lost in a disaster, or supplying what never was available. *Informational* support means sharing of knowledge about where help can be received, which agencies provide what type of assistance, the procedures for seeking this help, who are the key people, and what are good times and locations. For example, a pregnant teen may benefit from information about her options, the pros and cons of each option, good and friendly physicians, and medical facilities. *Emotional* support can include listening in a non-judgmental manner, expression of acceptance, and offering encouragement. For example, lending a helping hand is a major component in twelve steps programs for people struggling with addictions, where mutual help groups and mentors are available unconditionally to reinforce staying free of the addictive substance or behavior.

Social support has been differentiated by its sources and whether it is perceived or received. Sources may be informal or formal. *Informal* sources include immediate and extended family, friends, neighbors, and social affiliation groups such as churches and clubs. *Formal* sources include welfare agencies and psychosocial counseling. *Perceived* support reflects a person's view of who may be available to help if the need arises, and *received* support refers to help actually provided. Three core components of social support are the network of support resources, supportive behavior, and the subjective appraisal of support (Hobfoll & Vaux, 1993).

Coping

Coping is a multidimensional and dynamic concept that includes cognitive, emotional, and behavioral components, all of which are personal or collective strategies used to address and manage hardships associated with a stressor event and aimed at mastering, reducing, overcoming, or learning to tolerate the demands it creates. Coping is the product of genetic, early, and current environments. As the concept has been developed, diverse classifications of coping strategies emerged, all of which co-exist in current coping literature. Coping can be geared towards changing the situation that created the stress, changing the effects or consequences of the situation even if the situation itself cannot be changed, or changing one's perception of or reaction to the situation. Rather than being unidirectional, it is a recursive process that unfolds over time and is shaped by the circumstances and the characteristics of the people involved. In coping those affected may use diverse personal, familial, and social resources such as aptitudes, physical characteristics, knowledge, time, organization, support, cohesion, and trust. Coping strategies can be active or passive, prosocial or antisocial, functional and positive or dysfunctional, such as substance abuse, obsessive shopping, and violence, which may relieve distress in the short run but rather than resolving the situation, exacerbate it and create negative side effects. However, even positive coping strategies may have some negative effects.

Resilience

Resilience reflects the recognition that positive effects can co-occur with negative outcomes of exposure to a highly stressful event. While different definitions and measures of resilience exist, there is a consensus that it does not mean invulnerability to stress. Rather, originating from the Latin word *resilire*, which means "to spring back", it refers to the ability to withstand and respond to a stressor event, traumatic exposure, or crisis in a constructive way and bounce back from adverse experiences and circumstances quickly and effectively. It is the reparative potential (Walsh, 2003) and capacity for recovery and sustainability which may develop in individuals or systems as the product of the interaction among developmental processes and environmental factors. Resilience may be multilayered, i.e. reactive, which is the capacity to cope with and adapt to adverse conditions, and proactive, which refers to seeking and creating options (Obrist, Pfeiffer & Henley, 2010). Research on resilience included efforts to measure it, identify what differentiates those who succeed from those who do not in the context of adversity, and understand processes that might lead to resilience and interventions to foster it. A recent development in the field of resilience is the concept of *hidden resilience* (Ungar, 2004), which means patterns of coping seen subjectively as successful whether or not others from different cultures or contexts view them as such.

Posttraumatic Growth (PTG)

Benefits (growth) or positive changes that can be gained from struggling with a highly stressful event include strengthening of individuals, families and communities, discovering abilities and talents not previously recognized, and tightening relationships and solidarity. Such benefits have been conceptualized as adversarial growth, stress-related growth, benefit finding, thriving, blessings, changes in outlook, positive by-products, transformational coping, and positive psychological change (Aldwin, 1994; Calhoun & Tedeschi, 2006; Weiss & Berger, 2010), and they go beyond mere survival, resistance to damage, adaptation, or simply returning to the pre-stress baseline. It implies that those exposed to trauma undergo a transformational change *beyond* pre-trauma levels. PTG is universal (Weiss & Berger, 2010) and can change over time (Dekel, Ein-Dor & Solomon, 2012). However, there is still debate as to whether finding benefits from the struggle with a highly stressful and potentially traumatic event is a coping strategy, a personality trait, or a manifestation of a verifiable change (Weiss & Berger, 2010).

2 Classifications of Stressful Events

Scholars vary in their emphasis on the importance of the nature of the stressor event in determining and shaping people's reactions and the ways they cope with it. For example, Hill (1949), who developed one of the first models for understanding coping with stress on the basis of his work with American families who experienced the drafting to and release from military service of men in the Second World War, identified diverse responses to stress based on its source, whereas Calhoun and Tedeschi (2006) posited that the effects of the event on people's assumptive world rather than the characteristics of the event itself are the key to understanding responses to stress. The nature of stressful events can vary greatly as do the ways for classifying them. Dimensions typically used for the classification of stressor events include their source, nature, severity, intensity, duration, and controllability. The following sections address commonly used dimensions to classify stressor events. For clarity, these dimensions are presented as a dichotomy although in reality the picture is more complex.

Internal or External?

Stress can originate from an internal or an external source. Internal stress – such as incompatibility of values, goals, attitudes, needs, or desires – originates from within the individual, the marital dyad, or parent–children or siblings relationships. Externally triggered stressors are those originating from the workplace, social and environmental circumstances such as a financial national crisis, a social environment characterized by discrimination, a poor neighborhood, or issues in the extended family. Differentiating the stresses that are inflicted from *within the family*, such as domestic violence, versus trauma that originates from *outside the family* is particularly important for children (e.g. Sagi-Schwartz, 2008). However, because of the circular nature of events in human life and the interdependence among elements in social systems, it is not always clear whether stress is related to sources external to the individual or the family or is internally generated. Examine the following scenario. Mr. Jones has been a successful hi tech engineer in a startup company. The family lived comfortably, supporting two young adult children in private colleges. Mrs. Jones, who was a stay-at-home mom while her children were growing up, has been active in diverse charities in their affluent suburban community. When his company encountered financial troubles because of the recession and Mr. Jones lost his job, the family was able to maintain its lifestyle for several months by relying on the exit package provided by Mr. Jones' previous employer and by using their savings. However, as the months went by and Mr. Jones failed to find employment, tensions between the couple started to mount. They were forced to sell one of their cars, cut down on expenses and eventually move to a more modest house. Mr. Jones became depressed and required psychiatric treatment to which his wife reacted by developing anxiety symptoms. Consequently, their son dropped out of school and became estranged from the family.

What in this sequence of events can be identified as the stressor? The answer is neither clear nor simple. Some may point to the economic recession or the loss of employment, i.e. external sources; however, not all who experience similar economic conditions and forced unemployment necessarily view it as equally stressful, neither do all respond with the same reactions. Others may view the tension between the spouses as the source – an internally generated stress. Furthermore, the tendency to blame forces that are intrinsic or external is affected by cultural norms as well as one's locus of control. Some cultures tend to relate stressful events to divine punishment or unnatural evil spirits whereas other cultures view them as accidental arbitrary occurrences. On the individual level, some people believe that they can control events that affect them and thus view their own actions or lack thereof as responsible for what happens to them (internal locus of control), whereas others view their life as controlled by powers in the environment and by others (external locus of control) and therefore view themselves as subjects of acts done to them rather than their own actions. Whereas external sources of stress are beyond the control of both individuals and families, perceptions of sources of stress as internal may create blame ("I should have . . .") and may lead to friction, tension, and blame among family members.

Human-Made or Natural?

Stressor events can be classified according to social or natural causes. The former include events created by negligence, error, or intent. Examples of human-made stressor events are wars, acts of terrorism, abuse, genocide, large-scale industrial and technological accidents, mass violence, and civil disturbances. Natural disasters tend to be more impersonal and include floods, earthquakes, wildfires, volcano eruptions, typhoons or hurricanes, landslides, drought, and tsunamis. However, sometimes the boundaries between the two are blurred, such as the collapse of a neglected levee system (human-made) due to a major hurricane (natural). Some natural stressor events (such as earthquakes or floods) are more readily predictable than human-made ones (such as a mass casualty in an airplane crash).

Research has consistently shown that human-made stressor events tend to have more negative effects than natural ones (McMillen, Smith & Fisher, 1997;

National Institute of Mental Health, 2002; Neria, Nandi & Galea, 2008; Norris et al., 2002). Interpersonal trauma (e.g. rape or intimate partner violence) leaves more emotional scars than non-interperonal trauma (e.g. accidents). This is particularly true when the trauma is perpetrated by somebody with whom the victim is close and who they are dependent on, conceptualized also as *betrayal trauma*. North and colleagues (2002) found that kidnappings and torture were associated with the highest rates of traumatic reactions whereas flooding had the lowest. In a comprehensive review of reports on the effects of 130 disasters, Norris and colleagues (2002) found that technological disasters in the US (which include human contribution) created more stress than natural disasters.

Halpern and Tramontin (2007) suggested that one reason for this difference is that people view nature as powerful and unexpected and thus natural disaster as the act of a superior power whereas there is a built-in expectation for fairness and caring in interpersonal relationships. Thus, traumatic exposures inflicted by people are often accompanied by a sense of betrayal (how can he/she/they do such a thing?) and are more likely to be viewed as representing the malevolent response of others. Consequently, interpersonal violence such as physical or sexual assault increases the risk of trauma-related negative effects. Technological disasters often involve conflicts, creating a ripple effect related to ecological exposure to dangerous substances, begetting competition among agencies and organization and the affected communities (Picou, Marshall & Gill, 2004).

Developmental or Circumstantial?

Stressors can be developmental (universal) or circumstantial (idiosyncratic). Developmental stressors are common, anticipated as part of the regular course of life, and experienced by most people and families. These include events such as marriage, the birth of a child, graduation, or retirement. Examples of situational stressors are unemployment, homelessness, or accidents. In individuals, developmental stress is normally related to transition between phases in the life cycle. In families, Hill (1949) differentiated dismemberment (e.g. loss of a family member), accession (i.e. addition of a family member), demoralization (e.g. loss of family unity), or some combination of these. Stressor events may also (a) be anticipated but occur at an unpredictable time, such as teen pregnancy or an early death; (b) be predictable but occur in an unanticipated fashion, such as the birth of triplets; (c) not be anticipated as a normal part of life but have the probability to occur based on a geographical or social position (e.g. divorce, a diagnosis of a life-threatening disease, or an earthquake); (d) involve the absence of an anticipated event, such as a couple expecting to raise a family encountering a diagnosis of infertility.

Normative or Stigmatizing?

Stressor events also vary by their social connotations. For example, diseases such as HIV/AIDS, suicide, incarceration of a family member, legal troubles, and unemployment, and in some population groups divorce, gay or lesbian sexual orientation, and infertility carry a social stigma, which may affect the self-perception, emotional reactions, and behaviors of those involved. In contrast, other events are associated with a positive hallow of heroism; thus, those who are injured or die while performing rescue actions or in combat receive public recognition, respect and often financial and additional benefits (Mannarino & Cohen, 2011).

When, How Much, How Close, and How Fast?

The severity of the event, the degree to which it disrupts normal ways of doing things, and the demand it puts on those exposed are important factors in determining which life domains are affected (such as emotional, social, financial, professional or vocational, health, and/or a combination of these). Stressor events are also classified by their predictability, severity, frequency, and duration. Events may be acute and temporary or chronic and long-lasting, repeated (e.g. living in Israeli border towns constantly attacked by missiles and rockets) or isolated (such as living near the World Trade Center in New York during the terrorist attack on 9/11). Some stressor events last for months, such as the 1994 Rwandan Genocide; others exist for years, such as the extermination of Jews during the six-year Holocaust in Europe, or even generations, such as slavery and the lynching of African Americans in the US. In an effort to classify traumatic events by their duration, Terr (1991) suggested differentiating between Type I (a single unexpected event) and Type II (repeated exposure to extreme events) trauma. Solomon and Heide (1999) added a third type – multiple, pervasive, violent events that last from an early age over a long period of time. While chronic events do not necessarily lead to crisis, they make people more susceptible and therefore more likely to experience a crisis.

Whether a stressor is isolated or involves a chain of events shapes the nature of the experience and its aftermath. However, for most stressors this is an artificial and inaccurate distinction as each stressor tends to create rippling of additional stressors following the original event. Thus, it is more accurate to think about a continuum of accumulation rather than distinct solid entities of isolated or chronic stressors. For example, the effects on Japanese society of the 2011 earthquake, nuclear disaster, and tsunami that followed each other will likely be shaped by the piling up of the disasters combined with a history of growing up in the shadow of the disastrous long-term effects of the Hiroshima and Nagasaki bombing during the Second World War. Similarly, Dohrenwend et al. (2006) found that the percentage of Vietnam War veterans diagnosed with chronic posttraumatic stress disorder (11 to 12 years after the war) increased as combat exposure was prolonged.

Direct or Secondary?

A stressful event may have both direct effects on those exposed and indirect effects on those who are not exposed but are affected by constant interaction with, witnessing of, or caring for trauma victims with whom they have a close relationship (Pearlman & Mac Ian, 1995; Yahav, 2011). Vicarious traumatization is manifested in symptoms that are similar to the symptoms found in direct victims (Adams, Boscarino & Figley, 2009; Darling, Hill & McWey, 2004). Contributing to the occurrence of vicarious trauma, its nature, and its shape are characteristics of the individual such as personal history (for example, a survivor of rape who volunteers to help others with similar experiences), modes of coping with challenges, and current life circumstances, specifically the presence of other stressors.

Indirect effects may also occur through media and the climate of threat that it induces in the public (Comer & Kendall, 2007). Based on a longitudinal study of communities in rural Appalachian Kentucky that were affected by the 1981 and 1984 floods, Norris, Phifer and Kaniasty (1994) suggested a differentiation between primary victims (i.e. people who experience a personal loss), secondary victims who live in the affected community and witness losses experienced by others in the community (such as family members, neighbors and friends), and non-victims, who do not live in the affected community and are exposed to the disaster and its aftermaths through media.

Controllable or Not?

The degree of choice associated with a stressful event varies and may affect its outcomes. Whether people believe that they have some control over the situation may affect their emotional reactions (such as feeling less guilty if the stressor is viewed as beyond one's control), behavior, and coping strategies (Gamble, 1994; Thoits, 1983).

While the above classifications are helpful in creating an organized structure to conceptualize potentially traumatic events, none is easily applicable in real life. Events are often complex and involve diverse aspects and characteristics. For example, Native Americans experience traumatic events which are interpersonal, accumulative, and prolonged, positioning them at the intersection of three risk factors. Almost no stressor event is an isolated, one-time occurrence. Typically, such an event is the start of a string of consequential chain reactions and each of these reactions may become a stressor event in itself. For example, if as a result of exposure to a stressor event a family loses resources, this loss itself may become a stressor event.

3 Leading Theories

Numerous theories have been developed to conceptualize the nature, processes, factors involved, and outcomes of exposure to highly stressful events. These theories vary in complexity, breadth, and the frameworks on which they rely. Some are comprehensive and others have a relatively narrow focus. Most came from psychobiology, psychology, sociology, psychiatry, social work, and anthropology. This chapter presents a review of leading theories that have informed the understanding of stress and its aftermath in individuals, families, and communities. It is divided into two parts. The first reviews theories with individual focus and the second theories with systemic focus, particularly in relation to families. This distinction is somewhat artificial because some theories were originally developed relative to individuals and expanded to families whereas others developed as universal, all-encompassing frameworks that apply to individuals and systems of all sizes. To help the reader navigate this complex terrain, theories are presented according to their main focus and, when applicable, both individual and systemic versions are introduced.

Individual Theories

Many classical individual trauma theories originate from Freud's concept of repression of experiences that were intolerable in an effort to lessen the anxiety that they provoked, which serves as the springboard for later approaches focusing on dissociation; other theories rely on bio-psychological theories such as those of Selye (1976).

Selye

A pioneer in conceptualizing stress was Hans Selye (1976), the Austro-Hungarian who founded the International Institute of Stress in Montreal and has been hailed as the "father of stress". He started his work in the 1930s and, having been trained in endocrinology, focused on biological aspects of stress. Based on observation of laboratory rats, Selye identified various alterations in adrenalin production and cortisone levels, allergies, and weakened immune systems in response to stress. He recognized that similar reactions may be triggered by emotional, physical, and environmental events which disturb the existing status quo and require alteration; defined stress as a general non-specific reaction of an organism to environmental demands; conceptualized this response as the *General Adaptation Syndrome* (GAS); and developed a three-stage model of this reaction. The first stage is the alarm reaction that includes the experience of a shock followed by counter shock, which is an initial effort to recruit the body for self-defense against the stressor event and its effects. This stage reflects what the Harvard physiologist Walter Bradford Cannon described as three possible reactions to threat: fight, flight, or freeze. If the initial efforts fail, a second phase of resistance occurs and symptoms of alarm disappear, indicating adaptation to the new situation. If the stressor continues, the third phase is exhaustion, inability to cope and giving in. Selye's theory has been criticized for failing to recognize cognitive aspects of stress in humans and the involvement of coping mechanisms (Thoits, 1983).

Selye's work influenced a generation of stress researchers. For example, based on his conceptualization, the psychiatrists Holmes and Rahe (1967) developed a scale of the amount of stress caused by various positive and negative life events. Informed by interviewing hundreds of people from diverse backgrounds, they created a ranking of the relative stress associated with personal and familial potentially stressful events. Although the scale has significant methodological problems and has been criticized for clouding the relationships between stressful events and outcomes by mixing positive, negative and ambiguous changes (Hobfoll & Lilly, 1993), it has been consistently used to assess stress related to phenomena such as physical and mental diseases (e.g. depression and anxiety), changes in the family (e.g. divorce, death of a spouse, remarriage), employment status, financial circumstances, and a wide array of other life situations. Additional scales have been developed to assess individual and family stresses associated with diverse life events in various phases of the life span.

Lindemann, Caplan, and Rapoport

Erich Lindemann (1944), a Boston-based physician, and his colleagues developed one of the first theories of crisis and principles of crisis interventions. His classic paper, "Symptomatology and management of acute grief", was based on observations of acute and delayed reactions in hundreds of those injured in a 1942 fire in the Coconut Grove nightclub in Boston, as well as the families and surviving relatives of the 493 people who died in the fire. Lindemann later established, in collaboration with Gerald Caplan, the first community mental health centre in the US. The group identified five clusters: preoccupation with the event, guilt, hostility, changed behavior patterns, and somatic distress. They further introduced the concept of grief work for the process of mourning the loss and adapting to its consequences, and posited that the ability to recover depended on the ability of those exposed to the stressor event to gradually come to terms with the losses involved and make life changes, to move forwards.

Gerald Caplan (1964, 1970), a child and community psychiatrist, built on Lindemann's work and expanded it to develop and refine models for understanding crisis and planning interventions. Based on his work in residential care in Israel in the early 1950s, where tens of thousands of Jewish immigrant adolescents, many of whom were child survivors of the Holocaust, lost family members and experienced horrific traumatic events, he was a pioneer in relating mental illness to crisis experiences and became the "father of mental health consultation." Caplan studied reactions to diverse developmental stresses in childhood and adolescence and events such as illness or premature birth. His model applies more to a crisis that occurs gradually than to a catastrophic disaster. He conceptualized a crisis as a disruption to the existing balance of a person or a system. When an event threatens homeostasis and traditionally effective patterns of problem solving responses fail to address the unusual situation, the system's ability to function is compromised and negative emotional feelings emerge. He identified four stages in the process of a crisis: *Rise of tension*, when cognitive, emotional, and behavioral changes occur and the individual seeks to escape the stressor or reduce its impact; if these efforts fail, the second stage of *disruption to routine life patterns* develops, followed by phase three of *exacerbation of the tension* when efforts to resolve fail, and, finally a *mental collapse* or a partial resolution of the situation by using different coping strategies. In his work, informed by psychoanalytic thinking, he argued that life crisis can lead to personal changes, which equip the individual with better skills to cope with future crises. This can be viewed as the impetus for the theories of resilience and posttraumatic growth discussed later. Caplan emphasized the importance of cognitive interventions and providing appropriate supports to increase the likelihood of resolution and offered principles for intervention.

Lydia Rapoport (1962) built on the work of Lindemann and Caplan and introduced the idea that an event that upsets the status quo may create a problem, which can be perceived as a threat, a loss, or a challenge. This idea was later developed by Lazarus and Folkman (1984). Rapoport named three factors that create a state of crisis and are interrelated: the occurrence of a hazardous *event*, the *perception* of the event as threatening life goals, and the *inability to cope adequately*.

Lazarus and Folkman

A leading theoretical framework for understanding reactions to stress is the seminal work of Lazarus (1966). In the transactional model he developed with Folkman (Lazarus & Folkman, 1984), stress has been conceptualized as a complex process occurring in the context of dynamic, reciprocal, and bi-directional transactions between people and their environments. The main assumption of this model is that how people appraise an event can influence its potential to evoke negative or positive reactions as well as shape the coping strategies used. Central concepts of the theory are *cognitive appraisal* and *coping.* Encountering a stressful event, one cognitively evaluates the significance of what is happening for one's well-being. *Primary appraisal* is the evaluation of the meaning of the situation and if anything is at stake or anybody important is at risk because of the event. The situation may be appraised as *benign*, presents *harm* (i.e. a damage or loss that has already occurred), a *threat* (i.e. something that could potentially produce harm or loss), or a *challenge* (i.e. something that one feels confident about mastering, and has the potential to present an opportunity for positive outcomes or gain). In later versions, possible appraisal options include also *benefit*, i.e. the view of a stressful situation as potentially producing positive emotions. Components of primary appraisal are the degree to which the issues involved are important to and impact the appraiser (*goal relevance*), their compatibility with personal goals (*goal congruence*) and their implications for self-esteem, moral values, and identity (*ego involvement*).

Secondary appraisal is the evaluation of what, if anything, can be done to overcome or prevent harm caused by the event – i.e. assessing coping options, the availability of resources for addressing the event, and the probability of their success. Its components include: *blame or credit* based on who is viewed as responsible for the event and its outcomes; *coping potential* (i.e. the evaluation of actions potentially effective in addressing the event and minimizing its negative effects); and *future expectations* (i.e. expected implications of the event on one's goals). Ideas have begun to evolve regarding *tertiary appraisal*, i.e. reflecting back about the meaning and effects of a past situation.

How a situation is appraised depends on personal factors such as goals hierarchies, values, commitments, beliefs about self and the world, general expectations, and situational factors such as predictability, controllability, and imminence. Thus, similar situations may mean different things for different people and therefore those encountering them may appraise them differently.

Based on the appraisal, a person develops a mode of *coping*, i.e. cognitive and behavioral efforts to master, tolerate or manage the stress. Three types of coping have been identified. *Appraisal-focused coping* involves modifying thinking about a stressor; *Problem-focused coping* is an effort to change the reality of the situation that creates the stress; *Emotion-focused coping* is an attempt to change the ability to tolerate and regulate feelings related to the stress and minimize its negative effects although the situation itself remains the same. For example, parents waiting for biopsy results of their child may seek aggressive treatments from the best experts (problem-focused) while attempting to curb their anxiety (emotion-focused). Problem-focused coping is likely to be used when appraisal leads to the conclusion that the condition can be changed, whereas emotion-focused coping is likely to occur when the appraisal is that nothing can be done to modify the harmful or threatening condition (Folkman & Lazarus, 1980). Environmental pressures, opportunities, constraints, and culture affect the choice of coping strategies. How a stressor event is appraised and coped with affects the emotional reaction to it. Lazarus identified nine negative emotions, including anger, anxiety, guilt, shame, envy, and jealousy, four positive emotions: happiness, love, relief, and pride, in addition to hope and compassion, which have a mixed valence.

The theory has undergone several revisions, the latest of which (Lazarus, 1991) defines stress as a transaction between individuals and their environment. One addition in this revision was the identification of eight types of coping strategies or behaviors: confrontational, distancing, self-controlling, seeking social support, accepting responsibility, escape-avoidance, planful problem-solving, and positive reappraisal. Another development was the distinction between coping as a personality trait or style versus coping as a process designed to manage stress. This process constantly changes to fit the situational context in which it occurs (Lazarus, 1993).

An expansion of this theory is the integral model of meaning making and coping (Park, Riley & Snyder, 2012), which differentiates global and situational meaning making. The former refers to the broad beliefs, worldview, valued goals, and orientation systems (also called schemas) that inform individuals' understanding of themselves and the world and guide the way they live, behave, and make decisions; the latter is meaning assigned to a specific circumstance. Discrepancies between the two levels of meaning create distress; thus, when an event is viewed as violating the global meaning, one's well-being may be affected negatively. For example, the death of a young person is more incongruent with assumptions about the fairness of the world and age-appropriate goals than that of an older adult. Congruency between the global and the event-specific meaning can be restored by coping. The revised model also added the idea of meaning-focused coping, which can be achieved by changing the meaning attributed to the specific situation ("the college where I was accepted is good, though it was not my first choice"), global beliefs ("where you go to college is not so important"), or their combination. This change can be achieved by making sense or finding benefits. To make sense of a situation (also called comprehensibility and account making) one addresses questions such as: why did it happen to me? This helps rebuild and modify the worldview that was shattered by the stressor event and thus reconcile the event-specific meaning with the global meaning – e.g. "I got sick because I ate too much bad stuff," which is compatible with a global belief that it is possible to control health by mastering one's diet Finding benefits is a possible outcome of making sense by reevaluating events and identifying positive aspects in adversity, which will be discussed later in the context of resilience.

The theory was criticized as lacking a solid conceptual foundation (Krohne, 1996). Research mostly supported the role of cognitive appraisal in responding to stress but was inconclusive relative to the process of making meaning. For example, in a study of 385 athletes in challenging fields such as triathlon and marathon running who were about to take part in a pressure-producing important competition, Hammermeister and Burton (2001) found that an athlete's anxiety level was determined by how they perceived the event, the resources available to them and their coping. Similarly, Gabert-Quillen, Fallon and Delahanty (2011) found that subjective perception rather than objective measurement of injury severity predicted the development of posttraumatic symptoms of PTSD in victims of traumatic injury and an Israeli group of researchers

(Musallam et al., 2005) showed that primary appraisal and emotion-focused coping contributed to the level of acute stress disorder and psychiatric symptoms in Palestinian-Israeli students who were exposed to terrorism and political violence. The picture relative to meaning-making coping is less clear as findings are mixed. Some studies found it to be associated with better adjustment and less distress, especially when the process led to achieving a sense of meaning, whereas other studies reported adverse or no effects of meaning-making coping on well-being outcomes (e.g. Tomich & Helgeson, 2004). It is possible that different strategies of making meaning vary in their impact on outcomes. There is some evidence that coping strategies, especially positive reframing, social support, and spiritual beliefs associated with benefit finding; however, clear and nuanced knowledge about what works for whom under which conditions is yet to be developed.

Studies have also shown that internal and external factors moderate the effects of the stressful situation on individuals. *Internal factors* include personality traits of optimism, a sense of mastery, competence and self-efficacy, interpersonal trust, hostility, differentiation of self, and religiosity; *external factors* are the availability of instrumental (such as help in care giving), informational (such as advice about relevant issues), and emotional social support. In particular, numerous studies found that the availability of social support decreased the likelihood of distress and other negative effects of traumatic exposure to various stressor events and in diverse population groups in diverse cultural-contexts including parents of children of all ages diagnosed with developmental delay or mental illness, combat veterans, victims of violent crime or abuse, and AIDS orphans (e.g. Culver, Fincham & Seedat, 2009; Greenberg et al., 1997; Trickey et al., 2012).

Many of these studies looked specifically at the effects of stress on physical and psychological reactions and documented negative effects of nearly all aspects of human functioning including the immune, cardiovascular, respiratory, cognitive, emotional, and interpersonal systems. For example, Rhodes, Harrison and Demaree (2002) found that one's hostility level affects physiological reactions to stress-inducing situations, and Gerin and colleagues (1995) showed in a study of 26 women that negative effects of stress were buffered by the availability of social support. Furthermore, the availability and use of social support have been repeatedly found as major facilitators of the recovery from trauma (Litz et al., 2002). Women appear to prefer emotional support such as sharing feelings related to the experience and ways to combat its negative effects, whereas men tend to use more informational support, i.e. practical advice relative to "how to's" (Forbes & Roger, 1999). Summarizing the tremendous body of knowledge about positive effects of social support in combating stress and trauma, Hobfoll and colleagues (2007b) stated that social connectedness increases opportunities for sharing practical knowledge about resources, problem solving, processing traumatic experiences, and normalizing reactions. The role of social support as a protective factor applies across all age groups. Thus, Culver, Fincham, and Seedat (2009) found that AIDS-orphaned children exposed to high levels of trauma who perceived that social support was available to them did better than their counterparts who lacked such perception.

Resilience

Resilience theory started to develop in the 1970s out of the study of children at risk, later expanding to additional age groups. It focuses on an effort to understand how some individuals defy the odds, thrive, and become successful in spite of adverse personal, familial, and environmental circumstances whereas others do not (Haggerty et al., 1994; Garmezy, 1994; Howard, Dryden & Johnson, 1999; Luthar, Cicchetti & Becker, 2000; Rutter, 2007). For example, how in the same poor, dysfunctional, immigrant, abusive or neglecting family, one child prospers, adjusts well, succeeds academically and later on professionally, while other siblings abuse drugs, drop out of school, and get in trouble with the law.

This development represented a paradigmatic shift from the traditional pathology-focused theoretical perspectives of trauma. Whereas for decades the emphasis was on understanding what puts people exposed to stressful experience at risk for bad outcomes, the resilience approach began to pay attention to the route to recovery and well-being and the factors that contribute to it. Two seminal studies of resilience were conducted by Werner and Smith (1992) and Garmezy and Rutter (1983). Werner and Smith followed 698 individuals born in 1955 on the island of Kauai, Hawaii from birth to adulthood and Garmezy and Rutter followed over 200 children in urban environments. They found that most children became healthy and successful despite growing up in dire conditions. In the last two decades numerous studies have been conducted to identify conditions that enhance resilience, i.e. differentiating children who make it in spite of adverse conditions from those who do not, and identifying the mechanisms by which they do so with special emphasis on relational aspects of resilience. Various studies address resilience in conditions of socioeconomic disadvantage, community violence, parental mental illness, chronic illness, maltreatment, and catastrophic exposure (Garmezy, 1994; Masten, Best & Garmezy, 1990; Luthar, Cicchetti & Becker, 2000; Luthar, Sawyer & Brown, 2006; Luthar & Brown, 2007).

Models that reside under the resilience umbrella share three common assumptions. First, resilience is different from recovery; second, it is a common phenomenon; and third, there are many paths to resilience (Mancini & Bonanno, 2006). One early model was Antonovsky's *Sense of Coherence* (SOC). Antonovsky (1979), a pioneer in viewing the of effects of traumatic exposure on humans' well-being on a continuum rather than dichotomy, asserted that stressful events may have positive outcomes and searched for factors that may contribute to the shift of people from the disease to the positive end. He posited that people have general resilience resources and proposed the concept of *sense of coherence* to connote a global, stable, long-lasting ability to see the world as comprehensive and under control, balance independence with trusting others, use external and internal resources to address stressful challenges, and be confident in one's own ability to understand, address, and make meaning of life events.

Antonovsky identified three components in SOC. *Comprehensibility* is the belief that life events are mostly predictable, structured, ordered, and explicable rather than chaotic or random. *Manageability* describes one's belief in having the internal and external resources necessary to address stressful events and their implications rather than feeling victimized. *Meaningfulness* is the general sense of purpose and the belief that life events are understandable. Because of their tendency to perceive the world as meaningful and manageable, those with a higher SOC are better equipped cognitively and emotionally to grasp the nature of problems and confront them, are less likely to interpret stressful situations as threatening and anxiety provoking, have greater stress-resistance, and perceive themselves as having the necessary internal and external resources to deal with different situations. Individuals with a high SOC are also more flexible and resourceful and thus more inclined to employ effective coping strategies; consequently, they are physically and mentally healthier with fewer symptoms of anxiety or anger.

Antonovsky (1998) viewed the SOC as dynamic and shaped by life experiences until it becomes a relatively stable personality disposition around the age of 30, although it may fluctuate slightly in reaction to later experiences. A strong SOC is created by consistency, load balance, and participation in shaping outcomes. *Consistency* refers to an environment characterized by order and structure rather than chaos; *load balance* means the absence of demands that significantly exceed resources; and *participation in shaping outcome* connotes having an opportunity to have input into decisions regarding one's life rather than being an object at the whims of arbitrary others. Childhood living conditions, education, wealth, work-related factors, social support, and cultural stability are critical in determining the SOC that a person develops. A recent review of the literature suggested that Antonovsky's model continues to inform research around the globe (Hicks & Conner, 2014).

Kobasa (1979) offered another early model of resilience that was anchored in existential psychology and focused on *hardiness*, a personality characteristic that combines cognitive and behavioral aspects of courage and motivation to create a predisposition to resist negative effects of the encounter with highly stressful events, shake off setbacks and continue the struggle in spite of impediments in circumstances where others tend to give up (Maddi et al., 2010). It has been conceptualized as consisting of three integrated elements – the three C's – which are somewhat similar to the elements in Antonovsky's SOC: Commitment, Control, and Change. Individuals with high commitment tend to be actively involved and find meaning in all aspects of their life, and manifest a strong sense of purpose, optimism, and curiosity (Maddi et al., 2010). Those with personal control have a sense that they are in charge of their experiences and believe that people have a considerable amount of influence on their own life and what happens to them (somewhat similar to the concept of internal locus of control). Hardy people perceive Change as a normal part of life representing an opportunity for growth rather than a threat to security and stability.

Hardiness may affect one's life in three ways: directly such that hardy individuals are less affected negatively by exposure to highly stressful event; indirectly such that hardy people cope better with stress and achieve better outcomes; and as moderators by buffering potentially negative effects of stressful exposure. Consequently, hardy individuals view stressful situations as less distressing and are more able to endure them. Studies in various population groups have shown that hardy individuals are more confident and better able to use active coping. Hardiness was associated with less psychological distress and physical and psychiatric symptoms (including PTSD, depression and anxiety) and better performance, and has been considered a path to resilience (see review by Erbes et al., 2011; Florian, Mikulincer & Taubman, 1995; Maddi et al., 2010).

The concept of resilience has been expanded to include adults of all ages (Hicks & Conner, 2014). Different models have focused on resilience as an adaptive, intrapersonal, interpersonal, or social process (Kent, Davis & Reich, 2014). Michael Ungar (2013), a professor of social work from Nova Scotia, has challenged definitions of resilience as the capacity of individuals to do well and advocates placing greater emphasis on the role that social and physical ecologies play in positive outcomes following encounters with highly stressful events. Supported by research in various countries, he offered a model of ecological resilience built on four principles. In the principle of *decentrality*, resilience depends on the availability and accessibility of culturally relevant resources and the capacity of informal and formal social networks to facilitate positive development. The principle of *complexity* suggests that resilience is dynamic and trajectories to achieve it vary, requiring models to be contextually and temporally specific. *Atypicality* is the idea that a population experiencing increased exposure to risk may develop alternative functional though culturally non-normative coping strategies. *Cultural relativity* underscores the impact of culture on the process of resilience. According to Ungar's model, resilience is relative and pathways to achieve it are differential, context-dependent and shaped by the interaction among individuals' strengths, including ability to navigate and negotiate the environment (S) and challenges (C) with environmental aspects of opportunity structure (O), which includes the availability (AV) of and accessibility (Ac) to resources and their meaning (M) within one's culture and context.

The field of resilience is peppered with debates. For example, no consensus exists as to whether it is a trait, a process, a state, or an outcome (Fraser, Richman & Galinsky, 1999; Glantz & Johnson, 1999; Lepore & Revenson, 2006; Norris et al., 2008), or on how it differs from positive adaptation. Bonanno (2004), a leading voice in conceptualizing resilience, differentiated recovery from resilience trajectories. He views recovery as a gradual return to pre-event functioning after a period of dysfunction whereas resilience involves a stable trajectory of healthy functioning, sometimes after a brief period of transient distress. However, functioning following the exposure may be different than before as a way of adapting to challenges presented by the exposure.

This new way of functioning is not necessarily better or more effective than the previous functioning and therefore, Norris et al. (2008) view resilience as a difference rather than as growth. Masten, Best & Garmezy (1990) conceptualized three types of resilience: the personal ability for enduring adversities, the ability for coping with highly challenging situations, and the ability for recovering from traumatic experience. Additional controversies relate to criteria for defining situations as adversity and the question as to whether to be considered resilient one must demonstrate thriving in one salient domain or in multiple aspects. In spite of such disagreements, resilience scholars and researchers tend to focus on three main core aspects of the theory: *risk factors, protective factors*, and *resilience*.

Risk Factors

Risk factors are contextual circumstances that increase the likelihood for the development of a problem at some point. They can be proximal or distal. Proximal factors include adverse conditions in the immediate environment such as a poor or dysfunctional family, neglect, abuse and maltreatment, parental divorce, or bereavement. Distal factors are situations in the broader community which may present a threat, such as a social environments characterized by racism or violence. All risk factors can individually or in combination increase the prospects for exposure to a highly stressful, potentially traumatic event or exacerbate the ill effects of the exposure (Evans, Marsh & Weigel, 2010; Luthar & Brown, 2007). Relative to children, harsh early environments have been considered risk factors as they may have long-lasting negative effects on brain structure and on neuroendocrine functioning and genetics, which eventually may exacerbate vulnerability to future psychopathology and coping (Luthar & Brown, 2007).

The concept of risk factors was later expanded to include stress or adversity in general throughout the life span. For example, conditions such as living in Japan during an earthquake or an atomic disaster, living in lower Manhattan at the time of the terrorist attacks of 9/11, or living around the Gaza strip during the Palestinian Intifada are risk factors. Thus, the concept is viewed as dynamic and may change as time passes and new circumstances develop such that risk factors may turn into protective factors and vice versa, or some factors may be protective in some areas and risk in others.

Protective Factors

Protective factors are external and internal facets that can shape the effects of risks on one's outcomes and modify them in a positive direction (Luthar, Sawyer & Brown, 2006). They include personal characteristics and external-environmental conditions. Protective personal characteristics include agency, social competence, interpersonal communication and problem solving skills, high motivation, autonomy, independence, self-esteem and self-efficacy, pragmatic coping, internal locus of control, temperament, intelligence, assertiveness, good impulse control and self regulation, sense of humour, flexible adaptation, and a sense of purpose (Bonanno & Mancini, 2008; Garmezy, 1994; Masten, Best & Garmezy, 1990; Rutter, 1987). Current studies suggest that some individuals are genetically more resilient and better protected from the effects of stressful events (Almli et al., 2014).

Environmental conditions come from the family, school, religious organizations, and the community. Familial protective factors are socio-economic status (though there is some debate about this), social positioning (such as immigration or citizenship status), consistency and quality of care for children as they grow up, effective parenting practices and parental involvement, a structured, close, warm, stable and cohesive, non-conflictual family with good relationships, and a supportive, multigenerational extended family. Specifically, early caregiving environment and strong attachment relationships have robust effects (Luthar & Brown, 2007). Communal protective factors are strong peer support, meaningful relationships with friends, schools with a strong academic record and attentive and caring teachers who take personal interest in students, the availability of role models and mentors, safe and cohesive neighborhoods, accessible housing, employment, health and social services, spiritual and recreational opportunities offered by social and religious organizations, as well as cultural traditions (Garmezy & Rutter, 1983; Ungar, 2013; van Hook, 2008). Two recent doctorate dissertations (Carrion, 2010; Rassiger, 2011) provide evidence on the importance of such environmental factors in academic success of Latino middle school students.

A later conceptual development by Luthar, Cicchetti & Becker (2000) offers a more refined terminology that differentiates between: *general* protective factors with direct ameliorating effects; *protective-stabilizing* factors, which are interactive or moderating processes that create stability in competence despite increasing risk; *protective enhancing* factors that allow individuals' competence to be augmented with increasing risks; and *protective but reactive* factors whose protective power decreases when risk increases.

Protective factors can work in different ways. They may reduce exposure to risk, interrupt the connection between the risk-carrying event and negative outcomes, or moderate or buffer negative effects of such exposure, i.e. decrease the likelihood of undesirable outcomes, although exposure to the event or its related manifestations cannot be prevented. It is helpful to think about this as similar to primary, secondary, and tertiary prevention, i.e. precluding the development of a bad condition, avoiding negative effects of an occurrence that cannot be prevented, or reducing the negative impact, which cannot be prevented. Protective factors can also be viewed as having inoculating effects, i.e. similar to vaccination: exposure to manageable doses of risk may prepare for coping with adversity by strengthening the ability to mobilize adaptive reactions.

There seems to be agreement that, like risk factors, protective factors may evolve. They have a cumulative effect such that the more protective factors are present the higher the likelihood for resilience. Because the factors that constitute both risk and resilience combine universal with culture-specific dimensions, several scholars have addressed the role that culture plays in resilience.

For example, Clauss-Ehlers (2008) discussed the influence of cultural background, traditions, legacies, and values on the negotiation of stress by individuals. Research showed that protective factors transcend ethnic, social, geographical, and historical boundaries. Both risk and protective factors are dynamic and can change at any point during one's life; furthermore, the same factor may play a protective role at one point and become a risk factor at a different phase of an individual's life or as circumstances change. Some (e.g. Kent, Davis & Reich, 2014) criticize the failure of the concepts of risk and protective factors to enhance the study of resilience; however, a systematic review of the literature (Windle, 2010) supports the centrality of these concepts in the field, though the mechanisms involved are complex and contextually and culturally dependent (Ungar, 2013).

Resilience

The concepts of resiliency and resilience have been used inconsistently and often interchangeably. Sometimes, resilience is viewed as capacity and resiliency as assets associated with it. Furthermore, there is an unresolved debate as to whether resilience is a personal trait, a dynamic process, a capacity, or an outcome of successfully bouncing back from adversity. Different theoretical perspectives, specifically ecological and constructionist, have been used to understand resilience. Nevertheless, there has been considerable consistency across multiple studies, risk factors, and methodologies used regarding the multidimensionality of resilience and many of its correlates. That resilience is multidimensional is evident from the fact that people who have encountered adversity may demonstrate resilience in some areas but not in others, in relation to some environmental hazards but not others, and with respect to some outcomes but not all (Rutter, 2007). For example, a child from a poor minority abusive family may be academically successful (educational resilience) but manifest poor social skills (absence of social resilience).

Resilience is the product of the interaction between personal and social environment factors. Predictors of resilience include gender (males have been documented as more resilient than women in some but not all studies), age (older people show more resilience than younger ones), education (educated people showed higher resilience), and personality traits (flexibility, coping, and agency are associated with more resilience). Furthermore, recent studies have identified several genes as determining predisposition to resilience (Kim-Cohen & Turkewitz, 2012; Luthar & Brown, 2007; Rutter, 2007). Environmental factors that enhance the probability of resilience include mostly social resources such as effective parenting and social support.

Several theoretical models have been developed on the human potential to cope successfully (e.g. Kobasa, 1979; Werner & Smith, 1992; Fraser, Richman & Galinsky, 1999). One of the most recent and comprehensive models of resilience was developed in the mid 1990s by Tedeschi and Calhoun (1996), who coined the term *posttraumatic growth* (PTG) based on their experience with adults who had become physically handicapped and with older women who had lost their spouses. PTG refers to perceived positive changes following the encounter and struggle with highly stressful events, i.e. the promotion of gaining new meaning, developing new perspectives and directions, and a sense of learning valuable lessons after the initial distress (Calhoun & Tedeschi, 2006).

The model (Figure 3.1) focuses on cognitive-emotional processing of challenges triggered by exposure to a stressor event and denotes an individual's perception of significant positive changes resulting from the struggle with the event. To trigger PTG, the event must be of a magnitude that disturbs the status quo and threatens one's assumptive world. The challenges created by the exposure may include intense emotional distress, threats to beliefs and goals,

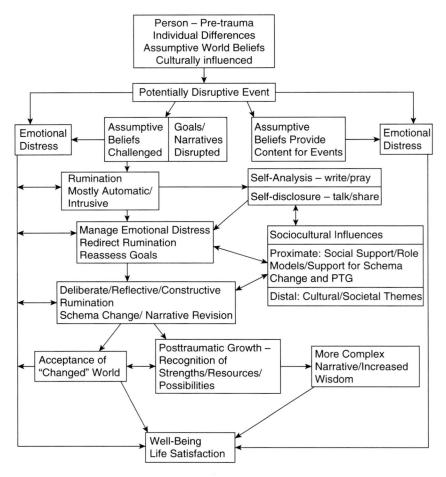

Figure 3.1 The PTG Model

Source: Reprinted with permission from Calhoun, Cann & Tedeschi (2010).

and interruption in the life narrative. According to this model, challenges depend on pre-trauma characteristics of those exposed and on the nature of the stressor event. In response to the challenges, people engage in both automatic and deliberate rumination, i.e. a process of trying to make sense of the event, for example, by writing and talking about trauma-related content. Two types of rumination have been conceptualized: reflective rumination, which focuses on coping with the difficulty, and brooding rumination, which involves constantly revisiting the traumatic event in detail, attempting to counter its reality by imagining another scenario, which might have prevented or changed it (if I had chosen a different route, the accident would not have happened). Reflective rumination is anticipated to enhance the likelihood of PTG more than brooding rumination (Tedeschi & Calhoun, 1996). Rumination leads to changes in cognitive schemas, reconstruction of a new narrative and reorganization of global beliefs, and culminates in PTG, which has been viewed as both a process and an outcome (Zöllner & Maercker, 2006). Two aspects of the socio-cultural context affect the process. Proximal factors include micro/mezzo aspects of the environment including family, friends, peers, and organizational affiliation. Distal macro level factors are social values and discourse.

PTG is a multidimensional construct. Originally, Tedeschi and Calhoun (1996) identified theoretically three dimensions of PTG: perception of self, experience of relationships with others, and a philosophy of life. Later literature showed the universality of PTG as well as its culture-specific nature, such that particular aspects and manifestations may vary in different cultural contexts as do related conditions. However, across cultures, core components of interpersonal relationships, values, beliefs, and view of self persist in various combinations and variations (Weiss & Berger, 2010).

Because of its subjective nature, concerns have been raised about the validity of the concept of PTG. Questions have been asked as to whether it is a self-deceptive distortion, a self-protective, ego-enhancing process, or a *real*, lasting, noticeable change (Frazier et al., 2009). Critiques have claimed that reports of PTG show wishful thinking or positive illusion of those exposed to a highly stressful event rather than a genuine change, and are thus non-adaptive. People may report PTG as a defensive effort to avoid recognizing the threats posited by a traumatic experience and its possible frightening outcomes. Thus people actively seek to see gains as a way to self-reassure that the experience was not exclusively awful, and to help cope with the challenging realities (Davis et al., 2000; Maercker & Zoellner, 2004). Furthermore, some authors have called for action-focused growth, suggesting that to demonstrate a real, positive change following the struggle with stressful events people need to also be involved in relevant activities rather than just their perception of such changes (Hobfoll et al., 2007a).

A team of researchers from Minnesota, Connecticut and Colorado (Frazier et al., 2009) tried to address these concerns by comparing scores on the most commonly used measure of PTG – the PTGI (Tedeschi & Calhoun, 1996) – with scores on five reliable and valid scales that assess each of the domains of

PTG individually, such as the quality of relationships with others, meaning of life, and religiosity. Their findings failed to offer strong support for the idea of growth related to traumatic experience whereas other studies found some support for the authenticity of the concept (e.g. Weinrib et al., 2006). Another approach to the critique was by Zöllner and Maercker (2006), who claimed that the PTG literature has been one-sided. They developed the Janus-face model and postulated that PTG includes both an illusory, maladaptive, self-deceptive side, and a constructive, functional aspect. The former is a distorted positive illusion used to help people to counterbalance emotional distress mostly short term, whereas the latter appears later in the process and its adaptive effects are evident in the long run.

> In successful coping with trauma, the constructive, self-transforming component of PTG is assumed to grow over time while the illusory component is assumed to decrease over time. The two-component model might explain why longitudinal studies usually show positive relationships between PTG and psychological adjustment, whereas cross-sectional studies tend to be inconclusive.
>
> (Wagner & Maercker, 2010, p. 81)

Finally, Calhoun and Tedeschi (2006) addressed this issue and concluded that although on some occasions perceived growth is illusory, this is not the case in most reports. They based their conclusions on the fact that reports of growth have been corroborated by others (Park, Cohen & Murch, 1996; Weiss, 2002), growth has been correlated with levels of distress and severity of exposure, and research failed to find associations between reported PTG and social desirability. Clearly, more research is necessary to gain clarity as to whether PTG indeed exists, its nature and adaptive value, what enhances its likelihood of occuring, and what part emotions play in it (Helgeson, Reynolds & Tomich, 2006).

Life is full of reports of PTG. Dr. Kimberly Allison, a breast cancer specialist and mother to two young children from Seattle, was diagnosed with a particularly large and aggressive growth in her early thirties. In an interview three years later she stated that the experience helped her find inner strength, taught her "not to sweat the little things, reconnected her to many people she rarely saw" (Brody, 2011). The Israeli holistic therapist Rona Ramon personifies the power of dedication to a mission to gain post trauma growth. The widow of the Colombia fallen astronaut Ilan Ramon lost her brother to leukemia three months after the death of her husband and her son Asaf, an air force pilot, was killed in a training accident seven years later. Specializing in personal exploration and transformation following the struggle with crisis, she made her own numerous personal tragedies a crane for understanding other people's losses and enhancing their ability to experience growth and transformation in association with the struggle, a process which she herself reports going through. Lance Armstrong returned to sport after battling with testicular cancer with metastases in his brain and lungs and went on to win the Tour de France seven consecutive times. He used his fame and money to promote awareness and research of the disease and became a PTG inspirational icon. Carolyn McCarthy, a nurse from Long Island, whose husband was killed and her son severely wounded in a 1993 shooting on a crowded train, became an activist and a NYS congresswoman fighting for gun control.

Contemporary Innovative Biopsychological Theories

Scholars have increasingly focused on the role of biology, especially genetic and neural components, in trauma and the effects of traumatic exposure on brain structures, neurological pathways, and neuroendocrine systems of exposed individuals (Masten & Narayan, 2012). Many of these approaches follow Boston-based psychiatrist Bessel van der Kolk (1994, 2003), who developed a conceptual framework for understanding trauma which incorporates developmental, biological, psychodynamic, and interpersonal aspects. Focusing on the psychobiology of trauma, he posited that when an individual experiences a highly stressful event, the body enters an alert state, which produces changes in activity of the brain in preparation for a defensive reaction and the central nervous system begins to develop neurochemical pathways and physiological reactions to adapt to the situation. Exposure to traumatic events affects negatively parts of the brain (hippocampus, left cerebral cortex, and cerebellar vermis), and is associated with changes in hormone secretion leading to changes in the capacity to integrate sensory input, i.e. the way in which people process what they see, hear, touch, smell, and taste. Also, problems develop in the maturation of specific brain structures, physiological and neuroendocrinological responses, and the ability to coordinate cognitions and regulate emotions and behavior. Following the exposure, the memory of the traumatic event tends to be dissociated from consciousness and becomes stored as sensory fragments with little or no narrative attached to them. Traumatic memories become "biologically fixated" with no flexibility for revisiting or re-evaluating them in a realistic manner and changing in an adaptive way, thus shutting the individual down from new experiences that might provide resolution. When a person recalls such memories or experiences during a later situation that reminds them of the original event, they are as vivid as if they were reliving the event. Effects of isolated incidents differ from those of chronic exposure to stress. The former tend to produce discrete behavioral and biological reactions, which are reactivated whenever the individual encounters a situation or a person that reminds him or her of the original trauma, whereas the latter have pervasive effects on neurobiological development.

Van der Kolk (2003) posited that stress reactions embedded in the brain may impact three of its developmental aspects as well as cortical and subcortical responses. First, stress may affect the maturation of specific brain structures; second, physiological and neuroendocrinological responses may be impacted; third, the capacity to coordinate cognition, emotion regulation, and behavior may be compromised. These potential effects are interrelated and may exacerbate each other. Negative effects of trauma on the brain are espe-cially critical at times of intensive development such as early childhood and adolescence, leading to the inability of children to meet developmental tasks appropriate for their age. Furthermore, young children who are consistently exposed to stressors are deprived of the opportunity to learn how to process and integrate information, cope with stressors and regulate their own reaction effectively (Ford, 2009). Consequently, traumatized individuals fail to integrate the traumatic event into their whole experience and continue to be prisoners of their past. This idea has its roots in the ideas of Janet (1889), who discovered that when memories of traumatic exposure are too painful to be integrated into one's experience, they are split from the rest of one's experience.

Research indeed shows that early exposure to trauma may negatively affect the secretion of norepinephrine and amino acid, the structure and develop-ment of the neuroendocrine system, especially the hippocampus, amygdala, and prefrontal cortex (Tomoda et al., 2009). Recent evidence is mounting that MRI and PET scans can trace permanent and irreversible changes in distinct brain structures of children who endured severe trauma, leading to problem-atic functioning throughout life. Furthermore, research has shown that infants begin to store memories from a very young age as somatosensory experiences. Consequently, the ability to recall life events and remember relevant details, distinguish threatening from non-threatening stimuli, and process stress and respond to it effectively both in terms of problem solving and emotionally may be compromised and the resulting dysfunctions in impulse control, aggression, and processing of emotions may be long lasting (Penza, Heim & Nemeroff, 2003).

Recent studies based mostly on adoptees and twins point to the possibil-ity that genetic and biological influences moderate sensitivity to environmen-tal forces thereby creating differential susceptibility. Research has provided increasing support for the idea that certain individuals are genetically more susceptible to the effects of trauma than others and that traumatic experiences may affect the biological mechanisms that control reactions to trauma and compromise their effectiveness. Thus, studies have found that risk for PTSD is associated with heritable genetic vulnerability. Specifically, severe childhood or adolescence trauma may interfere with normal development of the logical system by narrowing the networks and pathways that interconnect neurons, leading the brain to move from a mode of learning to a defensive mode of survival and stress reactivity. The focus becomes avoiding harm rather than curiosity and openness to perceiving and processing new experiences; flexibil-ity of assessing the environment and responding to it is compromised and the immune system is weakened (Ford, 2009). It has been found that secretion of cortisol, which affects a coordinated response to stress of multiple physiological systems, is influenced by environmental stressors such as child abuse, domestic violence, the Holocaust, rape, and other types of trauma, leading to a decrease in the level of cortisol (the attenuation hypothesis) and consequently to reduced ability to cope effectively. Early psychosocial interventions have the potential to reverse these effects and prevent the disruption (Trickett et al., 2010). Consistent with these findings, studies have shown that the structure and function of the brain of individuals diagnosed with PTSD is altered, leading to behavioral, cognitive, and emotional manifestations.

A different biologically informed theory of stress focuses on psychosensory aspects. The relevance of understanding psychosensory symptoms (i.e. experiencing non-existing noises, smells, touch, and sights) to stress-related experiences has been analyzed (e.g. Roca & Freeman, 2002) and traumatization has been conceptualized as the lifelong distress caused by encoding of enduring memories, emotions, and sensations in the human body and mind. Ruden (2011), a New York-based physician, developed the idea of a psychosensory approach to trauma, focusing on the role that senses play in the development of disorders following an encounter with a potentially stressful event. Why an encounter with a highly stressful event leads to the development of trauma in some individuals but not in others is explained by the perception of an available escape in the face of a traumatic experience. Sensory input such as touch, smell or sight triggers a process that permanently encodes a link among emotional, cognitive, and somatosensory components that are present when the encounter with the stressful event occurs. If the event is perceived as inescapable, it is encoded in the part of the brain called the amygdala as traumatic whereas if a perceived escape exists, the event is encoded as just an unpleasant memory. Furthermore, if an event is encoded as a traumatic memory but upon recall and retrieval of the emotional component related to it, the individual experiences safety, the link between the event and the experience of trauma can be disrupted.

Additional Theories

Beside the aforementioned leading theories, additional conceptual frameworks have been developed that share combinations of components and ideas with those discussed above. For example, Silver and Wortman (1980) identified four variables that impact on the individual coping process: the presence of perceived social support, an opportunity to ventilate feelings, the ability to find meaning in the outcome of the stressful situation, and prior experience with other stressors. Janoff-Bulman (1992) identified three aspects of finding benefits: discovering strengths through the process of suffering, coping by making changes in one's worldview to be better prepared for future adversities, and existential revaluation, i.e. gaining fuller awareness of one's position in the world. Based on previous theoretical conceptualizations and empirical research mostly of breast cancer, cardiac patients, and rape victims, Taylor (1995) proposed a theory of cognitive adaptation to threatening events, which incorporates concepts recognized by the scholars discussed earlier in this chapter, as important in determining the outcomes of exposure to a stressful event. She viewed individuals as active agents in restoring psychological equilibrium after an encounter with a potentially traumatic event and identified two types of mechanisms that people use to this end: cognitive reinterpretation and selective focus. She claimed that because traumatic life events challenge people's sense of meaning, mastery, and self-esteem, efforts to adapt to the encounter and regain or exceed their previous level of psychological functioning focus on three elements: a search for meaning in the experience by finding a causal explanation for the event and its implications, an attempt to regain control of the situation in particular and mastery over life in general, and an effort to restore and enhance self-esteem by producing self-enhancing cognitions and focusing on life domains where regaining control, mastery, and self-esteem are achievable. Taylor further argues that the cognitions upon which meaning, mastery, and self-enhancement are based, are in a large part illusions – i.e. people's positive beliefs about themselves and their situation rather than factual evidence – and that these beliefs are helpful in creating psychological adaptation. This idea resonates with the concepts of appraisal and perception discussed relative to other theories (e.g. Lazarus, 1966; McCubbin, Thompson & McCubbin, 1996). Gidron and Nyklicek (2009) provide empirical support to Taylor's framework based on an experiment with Dutch students; however, because their research was conducted under laboratory artificial conditions and used imaginary rather than actual stress situations, the applicability of the conclusions to real life is unknown.

Tyhurst (1951), who studied reactions to floods and fires, developed the *Natural History of Individual Reaction to Disaster*, which emphasized the duration of the stressor and the perspective of the individual relative to the stressor. Three phases of response were identified: the impact phase, when the most direct effects of the stressor are felt; the recoil phase, which is the immediate period after the stressor; and the posttrauma phase. The model was criticized as limited in its applicability only to disasters.

Family Theories

Family stress refers to the exposure of the family to a stressor event that upsets the steady state of the family system and the process that follows. It is more complex than individual stress because it combines the concurrent journey through a stressful situation of different individuals as well as the system as a whole. Family stress theories focus on the role that experiencing stressful events plays in the development and functioning of the family system. Because individual family members experience the stressor event in unique ways and respond to it differently, the same event may create different types and degrees of stress for different family members. For example, a mother's diagnosis of cancer may cause extreme stress for some of the children but not their siblings, irrespective of age or gender; for the woman the stress will most probably be around her mortality and concerns regarding the impact on her husband and children, while for the husband the stress may be related to the family's finances, taking care of his sick wife, helping the children, and the threat of loss of his partner. Furthermore, while an event itself may not cause stress in one family member, the reactions of other members or even their ways of coping, may become a stressor. Thus, the news about a man being fired may cause his wife little stress as she is confident that he will soon find employment; however, the husband's alarmed reaction rather than the news itself may become stressful for her.

While individual stress models view the family mostly as the context, which may be a source of stress and/or support in coping, family stress theories emphasize the systemic experience and reaction, i.e. rather than the mere accumulation of individual perspectives and responses, the perception of a stressor event and coping with it are viewed as a phenomenon of the dyad or the family as a unit. Thus, the concept of relationship-focused coping was added to denote cognitive and behavioral efforts of family members to attend to each other's needs while maintaining the integrity of the relationship. The main theories of family stress, trauma, and coping are discussed in the next section. While this list is not exhaustive, it does present the development of central ideas in the field.

Angell, Cavan, and Ranck

Two studies of families following the Great Depression in the US are considered the cornerstones of family stress theory. Robert Angell (1936), a sociologist from the University of Michigan, studied the experience of 50 families in the US in the 1930s and developed the earliest published scholarly work about families coping with stress. Based on reports from students about their own families, he sought to identify family characteristics, which determine how the family as a unit reacts to and copes with a crisis. He conceptualized *integration* and *adaptability* as the major determinants of the family's ability to combat challenging conditions and using these parameters developed a typology of families' patterns of coping with stress. Family integration was defined as the bonds of coherence and unity and its main components were identified as common interests, mutual affection, and a sense of economic interdependence. Adaptability or flexibility, which Angell viewed as more critical in determining the family's ability to cope with stressor events, was defined as a combination of the philosophy of life (i.e. the value a family attributes to materialistic versus non materialistic assets), family mores (which indicate whether the family is traditional or non-traditional and the level of responsibility), and willingness to change family roles, behaviors and attitudes as a unit rather than in relation to individual family members' characteristics. Based on the combination of these dimensions, Angell developed a typology of families and distinguished three degrees of integration and adaptability, the combination of which produced nine family types. Plastic families were more integrated and flexible, non-materialistic, non-traditional and responsible, and were viewed as better adapted and more successful in managing stress. Several components of Angell's model impacted later theories. Thus, the same core characteristics of integration and adaptability as well as a similar typology of families were the backbone of Olson's Circumplex model (Olson, Sprenkle & Russell, 1979; Olson, Russell & Sprenkle, 1983), which is discussed later. Similarly, spousal, parental, and sibling relationships, the importance of which were emphasized in Angell's model, were building blocks in the structural theory of families developed in the 1970s by the South American psychiatrist Salvador Minuchin (1974).

Shortly after Angell, Ruth Cavan and Katherine Ranck (1938), a sociologist and a psychiatric social worker from the University of Chicago, developed a conceptual model of familial processes of addressing the adversities of the Depression era. They applied group theories to families and classified families as organized if members shared responsibilities such as caring for children, collaborated, were committed to common goals, and manifested positive and affectionate relationships with each other and with their environment. In disorganized families, members failed to meet these criteria. While all families experienced a process of disorganization and reorganization following an encounter with adversity, families tended to continue their previous modus operandi, with well organized families coping with their difficulties better. As is the case with Angell's theory, many of the aspects of Cavan and Ranck's ideas also resonate in later conceptual frameworks of family stress.

Koos' Profile of Trouble and Roller Coaster

Koos (1946) focused on low income immigrant families in New York City and conceptualized the Profile of Trouble, which was later developed into the Roller Coaster Model (Figure 3.2) to address developmental aspects of the family's experience of and ways of coping with stress. This model emphasized the time dimension in the process of the family's experience of and ways of coping with stress, which he called "trouble". Koos differentiated three main phases: pre-stressor, crisis, and post crisis. In each phase, the family's level of functioning was determined by four criteria: how individual family members saw their roles, how much they worked to achieve systemic goals, their satisfaction with the family, and the degree to which the family had a sense of direction and was moving in that direction. During the pre-stressor phase, the family has a typical mode of functioning though it may fluctuate slightly in response to normal changes in

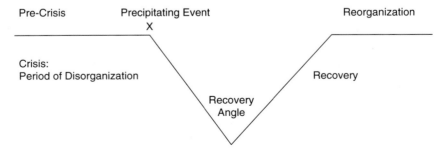

Figure 3.2 Koos' Roller Coaster Model

Source: Adapted from Koos (1946).

daily life such as a family member's sickness. The stressor event represents input from the environment, which triggers a transition to the second phase – the crisis, a period characterized by disorganization, when the family's previous ways of doing things lose their relevance and new ways have not yet developed. Koos posited that stressors may vary in the amount of disorganization they cause. This phase is followed by a transition to the recovery period, which starts after the family reaches the lowest point in the crisis. The pace at which the family moves is manifested by the angle of recovery such that some families can move swiftly (a narrow angle of recovery) whereas for others the process is slower (wide angle of recovery). In addition, families may move from phase to phase differently because of different stressors or where they are in their life cycle. During the recovery period, families use various coping strategies in an effort to rectify the situation and transition to a regained organized mode, which may be similar, lower, or higher than the pre-stressor level. Sometimes, before a family is able to recover, it is hit by additional stressors, creating an ongoing cycle of stressor-crises-recovery effort-partial recovery-stressor. Not surprisingly, Koos found that families that were functioning better before the stressor recovered faster.

Reuben Hill (1949, 1958) tested Koos' model, relabeled it as the Truncated Roller Coaster Model, and renamed the phases. Family organization became family adaptability, integration, and marital satisfaction (concepts he later integrated into his own model). He identified in the process the following phases: pre-crisis family level of organization, anticipatory reaction and preparation for first stressor, first disorganization in reaction to first stressor, adjustment leading to post-crisis level of organization, anticipatory reactions to subsequent stressor, second disorganization in reaction to the second stressor, readjustment process and new level of reorganization.

While the model has been commonly adhered to in the field of family stress for several decades, it was critiqued for two reasons. First, the model was criticized as offering a simplistic view of family stress, crisis, and coping with traumatic exposure as if it were a stand-alone linear process (e.g. Reiss, 1981). In reality, families may encounter several difficulties simultaneously and even a seemingly single stressor event such as an accident that leaves a child hospitalized translates into several stressors such as the need to find childcare arrangements for other children while the parents take care of the injured child, and additional medical expenses, which may strain the family's finances. Second, the universality of the model was unsupported and the failure of some families to recover ignored (Burr & Klein, 1994). Consequently, more sophisticated models started to emerge in an effort to capture the complexity of families' reactions to stress as well as the diversity of the ways in which various families respond to different adversities at different points in their lives.

Reuben Hill's ABCX

Informed by his extensive observation of Iowa families who lived in extreme poverty during the Great Depression and his service as a consultant to the US

army during the Second World War in issues related to post-war reunification of veterans' families, Hill (1949, 1958) developed the ABCX model for
understanding families under stress. The model dominated the field of family
stress and trauma for over half a century, earning Hill the status of the father
of family stress theory, and some variation of its core ideas informs many of
the theories and models of family stress, crisis, and trauma that followed. The
model was built on four assumptions. First, that unanticipated or unplanned
events, for which the family had no prior preparation, are perceived as stressful; second, internal events such as serious illness are perceived as more stressful
than those originating from outside the family, such as war or natural disaster; third, families that lack previous experience with stress tend to perceive
events as stressful more than families with a history of stressful encounters;
finally, ambiguous stressors produce more stress than non-ambiguous situations. According to Hill, families' adjustments to stress swing between a normal
state of homeostasis and a disorganized state created by the encounter with a
stressor event, leading the family to struggle to resolve the problem and regain
the lost homeostasis.

The ABCX model (Figure 3.3) includes four elements. A represents a life event
with enough magnitude to become a crisis-precipitating stressor and the hardships attached to it. The activating event can originate from within the family, such as marital affairs, a severe sickness of a family member, or intimate
partner violence, or from an external source, such as war, natural disaster, or
economic crisis. B refers to physical, financial, emotional, personal, and social
resources available to the family for coping with the event and preventing a
crisis, e.g. family structure, attachment, bonds, effective communication, integration, role allocation, flexibility, adaptability, cohesiveness, social support,
and previous experience with stressful events. Later versions emphasize that
the fit between resources and demands is more important than the availability
of resources per se. Thus, two families may encounter similar demands and
have access to similar resources; however, the family for whom the fit between
the two is better will fare better (Hobfoll & Vaux, 1993). C describes the way
in which family members and the family as a whole view both the event and
its resources. The meaning a family assigns to the event reflects its values, priorities, and beliefs. This concept of meaning-making was developed in later
models to reflect perception and interpretation of circumstances and contexts

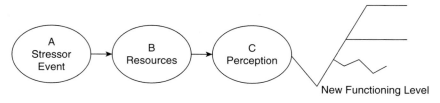

Figure 3.3 The ABCX Model

Source: Adapted from Hill (1949).

beyond the particular stressor event. X is the crisis or the outcome, i.e. the severity of the stress experienced by the family and its coping with the situation; in other words, X refers to the result of the exposure, such as the degree to which the family was able to restore balance in its functioning.

According to the model, the interaction between the event characteristics, available resources, and the family's perception of the event and resources (i.e. A, B, and C) determines the family's reaction such that if a family was well organized before the stressor event, has a history of successful coping with stress, and sees an event as one it can handle, a crisis will be lessened or prevented and the family can gain a level of functioning similar to the pre-stress or even higher, whereas if the family was disorganized, failed to address successfully previous stressors, and the event is viewed as insurmountable, or the family views itself as lacking the resources necessary to cope with it, a crisis may occur or become more severe and the family's ability to function may dwindle.

For example, a young father was severely injured in the Iraq war. This required his wife to care for him in addition to the couple's two young children. Consequently, she had to quit her job, shrinking the family's income. This combination of circumstances constitutes the A. However, the wife is very well organized and the husband's extended family, including parents and siblings, made themselves available for services such as driving the man to treatments and medical tests, and offered financial and emotional support. This expanded the family resources. Furthermore, the family took the attitude of "These are difficult times but we are hopeful and trust that the hardship is resolvable and temporary" (i.e. the family's perception of the situation, C, is as a transient adversity rather than a chronic disaster). The interactions between the A, B, and C determine whether the family experiences a crisis as well as its severity.

When a situation is perceived as a crisis, a family may go through a period of disorganization, from which it eventually may emerge but never regain the pre-crisis level of functioning. On the other hand, it may recover a to pre-stress level of functioning or better, i.e. developing what later models describe as posttraumatic growth. Hill predicted that if high-quality resources are available to the family, the likelihood of stressor events being perceived as a crisis is much lower, and the recovery from those that are is faster. Families with few resources are likely to be in crisis more often, experience longer periods of disorganization, and recover to a lower level of functioning and at a slower pace. In a later version of his model, Hill (1958) posited that some families are more "crisis prone" than others, i.e. their characteristics make them more susceptible to stressor events, more likely to fail to address stressors effectively primarily due to fewer resources (the B factor) and negative perception of the situation (the C factor), and potentially at higher risk of crisis following an encounter with a stressful situation. This may create a status of chronic stress. Thus, of two families with similar resources that face a similar stressor event, one may be more vulnerable than the other because it defines the situation as insoluble.

The model has been critiqued for four major issues (Burr & Klein, 1994; Perlman & Warren, 1977). First, stressor events are multi-dimensional and addressing them as a single discrete unit ignores their complexity and intricacies, and their cumulative effects. For example, when hurricane Katrina hit the city of New Orleans, Louisiana, in 2005, a family whose house had been destroyed was facing numerous stressful events including the loss of a place to live, clothes, books, valuable and emotionally important possessions such as family albums and mementos, the death of friends and neighbors, and the loss of social support because their community was destroyed. Second, the model was criticized as reflecting the assumption that the normal status of families is homeostatic and so the constant changes that they face is ignored; also, although slow attrition and building up of daily experiences does not involve one major event, it may become a source of ongoing stress for families. Thus, the model fails to take into account as stressful the fluidity of family life and the changes that occur as the family progresses through its life span. Third, families do not react to stressful event in unison and while members may share the perception of an event and its meaning, individual family members may view the same event differently. Thus, a father may perceive losing substantial amounts of the family assets as a disaster, whereas the mother may see it as difficult but manageable by adopting certain strategies to decrease non-essential costs. Finally, the linearity of the model and the positivistic assumptions on which it is based fail to capture the circular nature of experiencing stress, such that the attempt to cope with a stressor event may become a stressor in itself.

Burr's Family Ecosystemic Model

In a model that built on Koos' model, yet was considerably different from most of the previous positivistic models, Wesley Burr proposed using general ecosystemic theory, which emphasizes the discovery of processes within the family to explain its behavior under stress. He focused on families' vulnerability and regenerative power as predictors of the likelihood that a family will experience a crisis following an encounter with a highly stressful event, and considered the emotional climate of the family system as the dimension at highest risk (Burr & Klein, 1994). With a team of researchers, Burr studied 50 families that experienced diverse stressors including bankruptcy, chronically ill or institutionalized handicapped children, or struggles with infertility. Based on in-depth interviews, they focused on possible alterations in family paradigms, i.e. beliefs, values, unspoken ground rules, and the core identity of a family system, and conceptualized a typology of families' reactions to stress. They identified three types of family stress based on the degree of change that the situation required from minor changes in rules, behaviors, role expectations, and coping strategies (Level I), to changes in meta-rules and other fundamental aspects of family structure and processes, such as communication patterns (changing the way family members relate and speak to each other), degree of cooperation and collaboration (Level II), or major changes in values, philosophy, and beliefs such as discontinuing belief in god following the death of loved ones (Level III).

Olson's Circumplex

David Olson and colleagues (1979, 1983) developed one of the most extensively used models of marital and family functioning and the FACES instrument, which measures families' reactions to stressful situations. Originally, two main dimensions crucial for understanding family functioning were identified: *family adaptability* and *family cohesion*. *Family adaptability* is the position of the family on a continuum from flexibility to rigidity of power structure, role relationships and allocation, the quality and expression of leadership, and family rules; it describes the degree of the family's capacity to change in response to stressors and shifting demands that they inflict on the family. *Family cohesion* describes the family's position on the continuum of emotional bonding, from connectedness to separateness among family members (Olson, 2011). However, what is considered cohesion varies by culture. Thus, Middle Eastern and Latin cultures are very familistic and encourage high levels of mutual involvement among family members such that behaviors typical to an Italian, Puerto Rican or Israeli family may be viewed as enmeshment from an Anglo-Saxon perspective.

Five possible positions have been identified in each of these dimensions. On the adaptability continuum, the family can be rigid/inflexible with very low ability for change, somewhat flexible, (limited ability to change), flexible, very flexible (mid to high ability for change), or chaotic (i.e. very high ability to change). The dimension of cohesion includes the positions of disengagement/disconnectedness, i.e. very low bonding among family members, somewhat connected, connectedness, very connected, and enmeshment. The combination of the family's position on both dimensions yields three groups of possible family types: balanced, midrange or extreme, of which the first is viewed as functional and the latter as the most dysfunctional.

In a later version of the model, a third dimension, *family communication*, was added (Olson, 1991), referring to the ability of the couple or family to exchange information that is emotionally relevant (e.g. empathy, encouragement) and content-appropriate, to facilitate families in negotiating and changing their levels of cohesion and adaptability (Olson, 2011). The instrument that measures the location of the family has been consistently revised (currently version VI is available), translated into many languages, validated in diverse cultural contexts (e.g. Teichman et al., 1987), and used extensively. The main assumption is that functional families manifest balanced levels of adaptability, cohesion, and communication whereas unbalanced levels (i.e. very low or very high levels) are likely to be manifested by problematic family functioning.

Since the development of the original model, numerous studies have been informed by it, used various versions of the instrument that went with it, and documented its high validity, i.e. its ability to accurately reflect families' levels of cohesion, adaptability, and communication as well as clearly identify well-functioning versus dysfunctional families (Thomas & Lewis, 1999). Research provided ample support to the importance of adaptability and cohesion in enhancing family coping with potentially stressful situations such as marital conflict and divorce, alcoholism and chemical dependency, developmental issues, health, and mental health (Kouneski, 2000; Olson & Gorall, 2003; Traupman et al., 2011).

McCubbin and Patterson's Resiliency Model of Family Stress, Adjustment, and Adaptation

The ABCX model was a springboard for the development of increasingly more complex variations. Recognizing some shortcomings of Hill's ABCX model and based on a longitudinal study of families where fathers/husbands were prisoners of war or missing in action during the Vietnam war, the nurse Marylin McCubbin and the sociologists Hamilton McCubbin and Patterson (McCubbin & Patterson, 1983; McCubbin & McCubbin, 1988), who also worked in collaboration with Cauble (McCubbin, Cauble & Patterson, 1982), built on a family systems approach and earlier family stress theorists such as Angell, Hill, Lazarus, and Folkman to expand Hill's ABCX model. The expanded Double ABCX model of stress and adaptation (Figure 3.4), and eventually the ecologically based Resiliency Model of Family Stress, Adjustment and Adaptation (FAAR) that grew out of it, further developed and elaborated on the components of the original model and added several important aspects. These revisions contribute to generating more nuanced analysis of how various families operate under stress. First, a process perspective was offered by identifying steps through which some families successfully adapt to

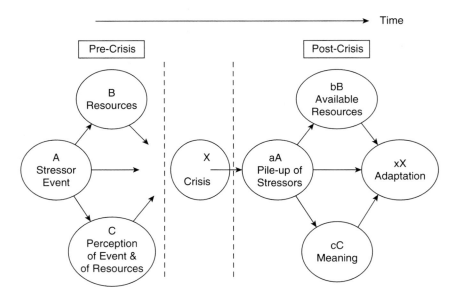

Figure 3.4 The Double ABCX Model

Source: Adapted from McCubbin, Cauble & Patterson (1982).

and recover from stressful circumstances whereas other families under similar conditions fail to progress towards functioning, remain vulnerable or deteriorate and disintegrate (McCubbin, Thompson & McCubbin, 1996). Second, a more realistic view of the nature of adversities was adopted by addressing multiple simultaneous or sequential stressors that lead to pile-up of stress. Third, family type was included as a salient factor that interacts with the interpretation of the event and perception of resources to determine the level of a family's adaptation to a stressor (McCubbin & McCubbin, 1988). To the *balanced* families, which are cohesive and flexible, as identified by Olson, two additional types of families were added. *Regenerative* families emphasize coherence (meaningfulness, involvement in activities, and commitment to learn and explore) and hardiness (internal strengths and durability) as main strategies in managing problems, and *rhythmic families* use time as a means for coping by carefully planning activities and implementing predictable routines.

In the double ABCX model, *a* represents initial multiple external and internal, normative and non-normative stressors, and the demands they place on the family; *b* refers to existing and expanding internal (cohesion, flexibility, interpersonal relationships, and open communication among family members) and external (social support from family, friends, and service providers) resources available to the family for addressing its needs; *c* reflects the family's appraisal, i.e. the meaning it assigns to stressors. The C factor in the double ABCX model was expanded from the original concept by introducing the idea of family schema, i.e. shared values, priorities, expectations, goals, beliefs, and general worldview that shape the family's collective interpretation of its reality. The family as a whole constructs and shares meanings assigned to stressful situations, its own identity, and life and the world in general, creating the family paradigm (Reiss, 1981). aA represents the post-crisis pile-up of stressors including the original stressor, chronic hardships that emerged from it, and the consequences of the family's coping efforts. bB is the combination of pre-crisis resources and those developed for coping with the crisis, and cC is the family's perception of the crisis, the pile-up and the combination of pre- and post-crisis resources. xX is the family's functioning during and following the stressful encounter.

The FAAR model was based on longitudinal observations of families whose husband/father was missing or in captivity during the Vietnam War and includes components that help explain cultural aspects of family stress and crisis. According to this model, families engage in active processes to balance *demands* (i.e. normative and non-normative stressors) with *capabilities* (available resources and established patterns of functioning) that interact with *family meanings* to reach the level of *family adaptation*. Family meaning refers to a particular situation, its seriousness and controllability, and an abstract global meaning of life in general, which evolves slowly, is the hardest to change, creates the context for family identity and perception of more concrete and labile events, and is reflected in the family's basic set of beliefs and use of strategies for solving problems (Patterson & Garwick, 1994). The meaning a family attributes to a specific situation, its sense of itself (family identity) as manifested by its routines and rituals, and its global worldview and assumptions is collectively constructed in a shared process, and is distinct from the sum of individual members' perceptions or consensus among them (Reiss, 1981). While family members may disagree about the meaning of a specific situation, when action is needed, the family must develop a cohesive systemic interpretation of the situation. For example, adult siblings must reach agreement as to whether an elderly widowed parent in a vegetative condition who did not designate one of them to make health decisions should be disconnected from life support.

The basic assumption of the FAAR model is that facing hardships is a natural aspect of family life, and that when confronting them, families attempt to regain balance and harmony by coping (i.e. cognitive and behavioral attempts of individual family members, and the family as a whole), developing and using their competencies to address challenges related to the situation that created the stress to help the system recover from crisis. The community and relationship systems of the family play a major role in these efforts (McCubbin, Thompson & McCubbin 1996). The nature of family coping is a predictor of adaptation, i.e. the outcome of the struggle with the stressor.

Family coping is a non-linear process, which consists of two phases: *adjustment* and *adaptation*. In the adjustment phase the family has established patterns of interaction, roles, and rules that govern everyday life, and strikes a balance between demands and capabilities by making minor modifications in the existing patterns. In the adaptation phase, the family changes roles, rules, patterns of interaction, and perceptions after confronting a real or perceived threat to family functioning in an effort to regain balance. The new balance can be achieved between individual members and the family unit, and between the family unit and the community. Both adjustment and adaptation are on a continuum from optimal *bonadaptation* – i.e. a satisfactory balance between the demands on the family and its capabilities such that needs of the family as a whole and of individual members can be addressed successfully – to *maladaptation* – i.e. the failure to address the family's needs because of a discrepancy between the demands on the family and its capabilities; this failure may lead to the family becoming dysfunctional and more vulnerable to future stresses. The Resiliency Model predicts that families manage more effectively and adapt better to stressful situations when they have better capacities and a larger repertoire of resources accessible to them, such as cohesiveness, flexibility, instrumental and emotional communication, interpersonal relationships, well-being and spirituality, family income, parents' education, and a supportive community milieu. A later version added to the model the component of family type (vulnerable, durable, secure, or regenerative) based on Olson's (1979, 1983) model, and the adjustment and adaptation components from the FAAR to create the seldom used complex Typology Model of Family Adjustment and Adaptation, which posits that a family's perception of and reaction to stressors is shaped by its characteristics.

The most recent development of the model was offered by Nelson Goff et al. (2007), who developed the Couple Adaptation to Traumatic Stress (CATS)

Model on the basis of experience with military personnel on couple relationships (Nelson Goff & Smith, 2005). According to their empirically informed model, individual levels of functioning, predisposing factors, and resources of the primary trauma survivor and the secondary partner, as well as couple functioning, interact to determine a couple's adaptation to stress. The mechanism is such that the direct survivor's reaction sets in motion a systemic response with the potential for secondary traumatic stress symptoms in the other spouse, which in turn may intensify symptoms of the direct survivor, creating an ongoing circular process of mutual exacerbation of both partners' trauma reactions.

The Resiliency Model of Family Stress informed the development of several inventories to measure various aspects related to it in diverse population groups. An elaborate discussion of these measurements and their psychometric characteristics can be found in McCubbin, Thompson, and McCubbin (1996). Using these and additional instruments, the model has received strong support in numerous studies. For example, Lavee, McCubbin and Patterson (1985) found that pile-up of demands significantly influenced post-crisis strain and that the resources and social support accessible to the family facilitated the adaptation process directly, as well as buffering the effects on the outcome by reducing post-crisis strain. Similarly, Saloviita, Itälinna and Leinonen (2003) studied the stress of parents of children with disability and in agreement with previous studies (Lustig & Akey, 1999; Manning, Wainwright & Bennett, 2011; Nachshen & Minnes, 2005), found that parents' view of their child and the meaning that they assigned to the situation, i.e. their perception and interpretation of the stressor event (the Aa component in the model), determined their level of stress. Parents who viewed their child's condition as a catastrophe and a burden reported higher levels of stress. In a study of 20 families where husbands/fathers were missing in action during the Vietnam war, Campbell and Demi (2000) found that the families that were able to work together to solve problems felt in control of outcomes of life events (though not of the events themselves), used an active approach to manage stress, and tended to achieve bonadaptation.

Specifically, research has shown that availability of social support as a resource is critical in determining the outcomes for families of exposure to stressful events. As early as the 1980s it had been reported that parents who express satisfaction with support received from spouses, members of the extended family (such as grandparents), friends, and people in the community, also report less negative outcomes of encountering stressful situations (e.g. Dunst, Trivette & Cross, 1986). That social support predicts adaptation has been reported in diverse situations, such as in families of children diagnosed with autism, cerebral palsy or a severe heart attack (Bristol, 1987; Senol-Durak & Ayvasik, 2010; Shu-Li, 2000). This was true for both informal and formal support. For example, Bristol, Gallagher, and Schopler (1988) documented how critical was spousal support, especially the feeling of being loved, understood, and valued to marital adjustment, the absence of psychological distress, and parenting in families with a disabled child. However, such reports were not without opposing voices of researchers who failed to find evidence of social support as a protective factor (e.g. Mulia et al., 2008). Furthermore, such empirical support has not been consistent across cultures. For example, Shin and Crittenden (2003) found that the model applied to American but not to Korean families with children with disabilities.

Pauline Boss' Contextual Model

With the creation of more sophisticated, valid, reliable, and culturally sensitive family measurements, more nuanced understanding of differential reactions to, coping with, and outcomes of the struggle with various kinds of stress in diverse types of families and cultural contexts has developed. This has allowed practitioners to broaden the menu of effective intervention strategies used to help families handle stresses.

Pauline Boss, from the University of Minnesota, introduced the ecosystemic Contextual Model of Family Stress (1980, 2002, 2007). This model, informed by symbolic interactionism and family systems theory and built on the ABCX model, underscores the importance of understanding and addressing family stress in the contexts in which it occurs as context affects all aspects of the experience, i.e. the stressor event, family resources, perception, and outcome. Family context refers to the larger environment in which the family exists, and its smaller internal contexts. Boss identified external and internal contexts that may influence how a family's stress process plays out over time. External contexts are those over which the family has no control, such as culture, including societal and cultural rules and expectations, history, economy, ethnicity, religion, the developmental phase of the family, and heredity. Internal contexts include structural (boundaries, role allocation, rules), psychological (cognitive and emotional processes), and philosophical (values, beliefs, and assumptions) aspects and can be changed by the family.

A major contribution of Boss' model is the concept of ambiguity and the role it plays in understanding family stress. Specifically, she focused on ambiguity of loss and boundaries. *Ambiguous loss* refers to a stressor situation (i.e. it is located within the domain of the A factor) due to the absence of clarity on where a loved one is and in what condition. Not knowing whether an individual is indeed lost and who is performing which roles and tasks in the family system is viewed by Boss as a major source of family stress. Examples of ambiguous loss are when bodies of soldiers missing in action, fire, flood, or terrorist attack have not been recovered and buried. Ambiguous loss may also occur when a person is absent-present (i.e. there physically but not mentally and emotionally) and not functioning as part of the family, such as a family member who suffers from Alzheimer's disease or other types of dementia, is in a vegetative state, or suffers from severe post trauma effects (Dekel & Monson, 2010). *Ambiguity of boundaries* is a perceptual response (and thus part of the C factor) to the degree of clarity (or lack thereof) about who is included in the family and who is performing which roles within it. Boundary ambiguity contributes to shaping the outcomes of exposure to the stressor – more ambiguous boundaries tend to produce more negative outcomes.

Ambiguity may paralyze or freeze a family's ability to process the situation and make decisions, prohibiting it from achieving closure and moving on to adapt to the situation. The family becomes stuck, immobilized, unable to reorganize and construct a new reality appropriate to the changed conditions, eventually becoming dysfunctional. Because ambiguity blocks the family's regenerative power, it must be resolved for the family to be able to reorganize and move on toward new functioning. Ambiguous loss is viewed as traumatizing to most individuals and families and may be associated with unresolved anger, self-doubt, and guilt (e.g. "Have I done all that I could to find or save the person?"), interfere with the mourning process, and complicate and prolong grief, preventing the family from moving on. A couple was referred to me 20 years after their son disappeared in a sunken military submarine, from which remains could not be recovered. When the company that employed the husband relocated, the family refused to move because they were thinking, "What if by some miracle he comes back, cannot find us, and does not know where to look for us?" Consequently the husband lost his job and the family experienced extreme financial difficulties that exacerbated the stress in the marital relationship.

Conservation of Resources

Hobfoll (1989) developed the conservation of resources (COR) theory, which is applicable to both systems and individuals. Like Boss, he viewed stress as embedded in social context, specifically the availability of actual resources, defined as things that people value. Rather than subjective appraisal, this model emphasizes objective reality of stressors. This focus may be viewed as an elaboration of the B factor (resources) in Hill's ABCX model. Although what people value varies, shaped by socio-cultural context and changes along the life cycle, Hobfoll posited that universal resources exist. Parallel to Holmes and Rahe's (1967) list of stressors, a list of 74 resources clustered in four types was identified based on the judgment of multiple groups. *Object resources* include shelter, clothing, medical treatment, and transportation. *Condition resources* are environmental circumstances that foster, protect, and enrich or impoverish and obstruct people's resource reservoir, such as well-being, emotional support, assistance from friends and family, good marital relationships, secure employment, socio-economic status, and neighborhood and community safety; many such conditions have been conceptualized as caravan passageways because they travel together, sustaining their aggregation such that if one is available, the probability for others is higher, and are transferred within one's family or social circle via inheritance, gifts or mutual favors. *Personal resources* are skills and capacities, specifically for mastery and control, self-efficacy, and self-esteem. *Energy resources* may include access to money, information, time, knowledge, and assets.

These resources are salient in gaining new resources and in enhancing well-being as those with access to more resources are less vulnerable to the demands placed on them and better equipped to successfully cope with these demands whereas those with access to fewer resources are more vulnerable and at a higher risk of experiencing escalating loss, because once they encounter an initial stressor they are more likely to consequently face a series of additional losses. For example, if a father is deployed for overseas military services, a family where the mother and older children can shoulder tasks usually performed by the father, such as managing accounts and taking care of younger siblings, will fare better than a family where role allocation is rigid.

When a stressor event occurs, people mobilize accessible personal and environmental resources while trying to avoid depletion of these resources. Because of their importance in addressing stress, individuals on their own or within systems strive to maximize the resources that they obtain, protect, and retain. Stressor events may lead to actual or potential loss of resources. A basic assumption of the COR theory is that those with higher levels of resources adapt better to traumatic events and are anticipated to have more positive outcomes whereas those with fewer resources use more maladaptive coping, which predicts poorer outcomes. The main mechanism driving adaptation to stressor events is change in resources. The loss of, threat of loss of, or failure to regain resources leads to the development of distress. Just like stressors may pile up, so can the loss of resources; thus the deficit in one resource may begin a downward escalating cumulative loss of additional resources. For example, in the early 2000s worldwide economic crisis depleted financial resources and often led to house foreclosure, which sent families into homelessness or inappropriate living conditions, which in turn may have compromised children's school attendance or performance, leading to stress in parent–child relationships.

Hobfoll's theory has been criticized as too mechanistic in focusing on the objective availability and accessibility of resources rather than the fit between needs and resources and the subjective meaning that individuals or families attribute to their situations. Further, the assumption that change per se does not overtax people, is not necessarily stressful, and may become a stressor only when it is negative is incompatible with claims by other scholars and practitioners that change can lead to stress whether it is negative or positive (e.g. Boss, 2007). One issue is that the judgement of changes as negative or positive is in the eyes of the beholder and what some see as positive, others may view as negative. Nevertheless, the theory has been supported by research to some degree (Heath et al., 2012).

Family Resilience, and Posttraumatic Growth

Theoretical conceptualizations about family resilience and posttraumatic growth are much less developed than those about individuals. Building on the paradigmatic shift from looking at families through a deficit-based lens to a strength-based perspective, the concept of resilience in its familial version refers to characteristics, dimensions, properties, patterns, and competencies that family units manifest in their trajectory following encounters with stressful situations, buffering the impact of the stressful event and allowing the family to maintain its integrity and the well-being of its members (Lietz, 2006). What enables some families to flourish in spite of a stressful challenge and potentially grow from the experience whereas other families succumb? One may wonder whether the family as a system can be resilient beyond the additive collective resilience of its individual members. While measuring it would be challenging theoretically, the constructs of hardiness and resilience of the family unit are reasonable, where the whole (family resilience) is more than the sum of its parts (cumulative individual members' resilience). Patterson (2002a) emphasized that a crisis is often a turning point for a family, leading to major structural and dynamic modifications that could represent improvement in the level of functioning, and that parallel to individual resilience, families as social systems can be considered resilient. She advocated calling *family resiliency* "the capacity of a family system to successfully manage their life circumstances" and *family resilience* "the processes by which families are able to adapt and function competently following exposure to significant adversity or crisis" (p. 352).

Family hardiness refers to the resources, especially internal strength and a feeling of control over life events and difficulties (similar to some aspects of Antonovsky's SOC), that a family has access to for resistance to stress and adapting to it such that the effects of stressors can be buffered or mitigated, and the family can function effectively (Kobasa, 1979; McCubbin, Thompson & McCubbin, 1996). Three aspects of family hardiness have been identified: (1) co-oriented commitment, i.e. family members' collaboration in efforts to address stressor events and their effects; (2) perception of hardships as opportunities for growth and improvement; (3) the family's active rather than passive approach to challenges, and the belief that a family has in its ability to control the outcomes of life's adversities. Family hardiness changes along its life cycle from its lowest level at the pre-children couple stage and peaks when children are very young (McCubbin, Thompson & McCubbin, 1996). Research has reported hardiness in families among diverse population groups, such as families with members suffering from chronic diseases and disabilities, and of diverse ethnic/racial backgrounds and socio-economic statuses (McCubbin, Thompson & McCubbin, 1996).

Similarly to individual resilience, the evolving and limited literature on family resilience is divided regarding the question of whether family resilience is a static characteristic (i.e. the ability of a family to bounce back and maintain its level of functioning in the face of stressful and potentially traumatic experiences) or a developmental pathway a family follows in response to stressor events (Hawley, 2000). However, there seems to be consensus on three points. First, that family resilience is a continuum rather than a dichotomy such that one should think about a degree of resilience rather than yes or no. Second, that resilience is not an all-encompassing characteristic, and a family can be resilient under some circumstances or in some aspects but not in others. Third, that family resilience is built on complex interactions between risk and protective factors operating at individual, family, and community levels (e.g. Benzies & Mychasiuk, 2009).

Adopting a developmental approach, Lietz (2007) suggested five phases in the process of achieving family resilience: (1) survival refers to keeping the family going in spite of the stress; (2) adaptation includes making changes to allow the incorporation of the new situation into familial life; (3) acceptance, i.e. learning to live with the changed situation as part of the family identity; (4) growing stronger and learning to see positive changes in the family as a result of the traumatic experience; (5) using what the family has learned to offer support to others, especially families facing similar challenges. For example, when a child with a disability is born, the family first needs to find solutions from day to day, such as nursing a baby who is frail and responding to unpleasant reactions from the environment. Next, the family must adopt strategies for continuing to function in the face of challenges created by the needs of the child, such as recruitment of specialized childcare. Later, the family develops ways of living with being a family with a child with special needs, such as figuring out effective ways of dealing with the child in public places and coordination of various treatments and medical appointments, while attending to other family members' needs. Next, the family may begin to see what they benefit from the struggle with the situation, such as becoming closer to each other. Finally, family members may become active in organizations and self-help groups for families with children with special needs, share what they have learned and advocate for better services.

Drummond and colleagues (2002) developed the Family Adaptation Model on the basis of resilience theory and research conducted at the University of Alberta, Canada. Their model looks at the interaction between family vulnerability and protective factors and posits that family adaptation is the product of ongoing development and successful use of familial protective processes. Building on various theories of family stress and conceptualizing family adaptation as an ongoing process, this model theorizes that families use appraisal of the situation and available support to cope with and adapt to the demands of the situations by developing and maintaining protective processes. These processes include commitment to flexibility, e.g. willingness to change and fluid role allocation, development of support such as recruiting help from relatives and the environment, responsibility outside the home such as employment and community involvement, stability that can be manifested in family rules and minimizing conflict, and effective parenting, which involves warmth and providing of secure attachment.

Family resilience can be enhanced by structural and dynamic characteristics of the family system and the social milieu. Familial characteristics that contribute to family resilience include cohesion, warmth, adaptability, commitment, clear and congruent communication with permission to express and ability to respect incompatible feelings, effective collaborative problem-solving and decision making, rituals and celebrations, which have a stabilizing effect at times of crisis, a strong belief in their ability to control life, sense of self-determination and responsibility, a belief system that allows making meaning of stressful events and maintaining optimism, a positive outlook, a strong and stable organizational structure, access to economic and social resources, clear age-appropriate rules, an effective parenting style, strategies to address the needs of all family members, and spirituality (Benzies & Mychasiuk, 2009; Black & Lobo, 2008; Coyle et al., 2009; Howard, Dryden & Johnson, 1999; Walsh, 2003). Contextual factors of the social milieu that support family resilience, minimize their distress, and contribute to their ability to recover from the encounter with highly stressful events include community-based social support, which can serve as a buffer against family crisis, and cultural values such as a collectivistic emphasis (McCubbin, Thompson & McCubbin, 1996).

Berger and Weiss (2008) expanded Calhoun and Tedeschi's (2006) model of posttraumatic growth (PTG) to the family system level. Whereas in the original model the family was viewed as the context for individual growth, the family can also become the unit that grows. The family PTG model, like the individual model, includes six main aspects: (1) pre-trauma family characteristics such as shared power, leadership, role flexibility, collaborative problem solving, parental alliance, clear boundaries, and family resource; (2) event characteristics; (3) challenges that develop following the exposure to the event, e.g. family pain, interruption of family narrative, dysfunctional communication, and impaired intimacy; (4) processing of the experience, shared meaning-making and problem solving, family reminiscing; (5) proximate (extended family, neighbors, friends) and distal (community) social contexts; and (6) posttraumatic growth – the family's new legacy, priorities and relationships.

Pre-Trauma Family Characteristics: Predisposing Factors

The challenges that a family faces and the likelihood that it will engage in the processes that lead to PTG are shaped by family structure, resources, and patterns. Relevant structural characteristics are organization and power distribution, including parental alliance, cohesion, and clarity of boundaries; resources involve finances, the family belief system, and members' educational and employment levels; important patterns are coping, communication and problem-solving strategies, adaptability (flexibility) and family history of successful management of normative stressor events (Beavers & Hampson, 2000; Olson, Sprenkle & Russell, 1979; Nadeau, 2001; Patterson, 2002a, 2002b; Rolland, 2003; Walsh, 2003).

Characteristics of the Stressor Event

Direct or indirect exposure of an individual member, a sub-system, or the whole family to an internal or external stressor puts pressure on the whole system and pushes it beyond its regular mode of coping, potentially impairing its ability to function adequately and efficiently (Boss, 2002). Typically, routines are temporarily or permanently disrupted and the view of the system (our family is . . .), as well as the sense of safety, are compromised (Boss, 2002; Schuman, Vranceanu & Hobfoll, 2004; Wells, 2006).

Challenges

Exposure to a highly stressful event may create challenges for the whole system or specific sub-systems within it, such as the spouses, parent–child, siblings, and extended family. These challenges may include a threat to basic beliefs, ways of being and goals, interruption of the system's narrative, interference in intimacy, impaired ability for attachment, as well as structural and communication problems (Boss, 2002). Such challenges have been documented in families of traumatized children and those of second-generation Holocaust survivors (Nelson Goff & Smith, 2005; Rowland-Klein, 2004; Weingarten, 2004).

Rumination

Questions were raised whether cognitive processes of making meaning and challenging prior beliefs and values can apply to systems. Scholars and clinicians have concluded that indeed the unit as a whole develops a collective meaning-making of reality, which is a unique systemic entity different from a sum of individuals' meanings or an agreement among them. The system mutually co-constructs and shares "family perception" or "family response" (Boss, 2002; Patterson & Garwick, 1994; Garwick, Detzner & Boss, 1994). Such family reflection may include the recognition that existing rules no longer fit the new situation. Based on this recognition, family members may work together to solve problems, and create changes. These changes can be situational and concern a specific event, they may be focused on the family identity and the view of its patterns, or they may be global and address core beliefs and worldview (e.g. moving from being devoted Christians to becoming non-believers). Families ruminate by exchanging stories about the family legacy, sharing dreams and memories, discussing expectations, echoing, finishing each other's sentences, elaborating, and questioning as strategies for rumination (Nadeau, 2001).

Social context

Social context has been increasingly recognized as affecting the process of rumination. Like individuals, families' processing of the stressor event is a transactional interaction between the family and its immediate (proximate) and broad (distal) social environments. Based on a review of the literature, Berger and Weiss (2008) conceptualized the effects of social environment on the family dynamics of processing the stressor event and eventually growth. The family's definition and interpretation of an event and its view of acceptable ways and sources for seeking help are shaped by socio-cultural beliefs and norms in their community, which also provides formal and informal support. The time and place in which the family lives and its transactions with the community affect the family's effort to reconstruct a new worldview (Boss, 2002; Patterson, 2002a, 2002b). For example, the global economic crisis that started in 2008, characterized by numerous foreclosures, bankruptcies, a high unemployment rate, political turbulence, and a fatalistic social climate, has affected how families combat stress. A conflict between the norms of the dominant society and the family's ethnic-racial norms may lead to a secondary stress and exacerbate the original event.

Posttraumatic growth

Posttraumatic growth in families includes three dimensions, parallel to those conceptualized in the original model (see Chapter 4): (1) Positive changes that the family perceives in itself. For example, members of a family from New Jersey who lost their house and many of their belongings in the 2012 Hurricane Sandy stated in a family meeting: "This experience made us realize how much stronger we are than we would have ever believed before this." (2) Improved relationships among family members and with extended family, friends, and neighbors. For example, the husband and adolescent children of a survivor of breast cancer reported that struggling with the fear of losing the wife/mother and the additional chores they had to share both in running the household and caring for her brought them closer together ("we are a team") and they were able to let go of past conflicts. (3) Changed belief system and priorities.

While the theory on family resilience has been evolving, research is still limited. The last decade witnessed a modest yet growing number of studies that attempted to document resilience as a familial trait under challenging conditions such as life threatening or psychiatric disease of a family member, immigration, war, military deployment, or a community disaster. However, many of these studies have not measured resilience directly; rather, they have focused on aspects of family functioning such as cohesion, family belief systems, coping strategies, and effective communication, which are associated with successful adaptation following an encounter with highly stressful events.

Additional Models

In addition to the models that conceptualize family stress in general, specific models relating to particular types of stressors have been developed; however, they generated a limited amount of support from research. Conger and Donnellan (2007), from the Center for Family Research in Rural Mental Health at the Institute for Social and Behavioral Research in Iowa, developed a model of family stress focusing on the effects of economic pressure on family processes. They posited that economic hardships lead parents to feel pressure, become preoccupied with their own frustration, distress, and anger in reaction to the situation, and therefore develop a low level of mutual tolerance, and are not attentive to the needs of their partner or available to offer empathy. This amplifies negative and conflictual events within the family, affects negatively marital stability and quality (as manifested in diminished warmth and increased hostility), leading to marital distress, and compromises parenting practices, leading eventually to deterioration in the quality of interactions among family members, and damaging the development of children and adolescents. Consistent with other stress theories, this model identifies mutual social support between spouses as a mediating variable. In couples where spouses can mutually soothe, reassure and listen to each other's concerns in the face of hardship, individual and marital distress are buffered. This model has received extensive empirical support in diverse cultural contexts including African American, Latino, Chinese, Finnish, and Korean families (Benner & Su Yeong, 2010; Conger et al., 2002; Formoso et al., 2007; Hee-Kyung et al., 2003).

Miller (1980) developed the *Model of Coping Model* (MCM), which explains differences in coping with stress as determined by the individual dispositional preference to cope with stress-related situations by employing vigilance, i.e. trying to reduce the uncertainty and ambiguity of a situation or using cognitive avoidance by disregarding aversive aspects of a situation. Based on families' tendencies to use different combinations of avoidant and vigilant strategies, four types of coping were identified: sensitizing (high vigilance, low avoidance), repression (high avoidance, low vigilance), non-defensive (low vigilance, low avoidance), and high anxiety (high vigilance, high avoidance). The theoretical hypothesis was that those susceptible to the emotional arousal involved in stressful situations tend to use avoidance, whereas those who are affected by the uncertainty embedded in stressful situations opt to use vigilant coping.

Two models emphasize the role of external stressors in the life of couples and families. Because coping with adverse conditions requires time and energy, as do the activities that maintain relationships, mounting stressful external demands may make it harder to invest the efforts necessary for maintaining the spousal bond. Karney and Bradbury (1995) developed the vulnerability-stress-adaptation model of relationships, which posits that the stability and quality of marital relationships are influenced by three major factors: first, enduring vulnerabilities (i.e. personality traits, familial background, and characteristics of spouses such as low educational and income levels, a troubled family of origin, and current living in a resource-poor neighborhood), all of which impact on susceptibility to stressful life events, and the availability of resources to address them effectively; second, stressful events such as unemployment; and third, adaptive processes, i.e. patterns of interpersonal interaction such as conflict resolution strategies. These factors interact to affect marital stability and quality such that enduring vulnerabilities influence the perception, interpretation, and response to the stressful events, which consume spouses' resources that might otherwise be spent on relationship maintenance; eventually, an adaptive process is shaped that determines the couple's relationships. For example, couples with limited financial resources experience more stressful events and are more vulnerable to their negative effects. When one spouse is diagnosed with a severe disease and the couple has difficulties obtaining the proper medical attention and lacks resources to help care for that spouse, the amount of stress the situation creates increases, tension between the partners rises, and the other spouse may feel exhausted, overburdened and resentful, eventually wanting to get away from the situation because, as often heard in practice with such couples, "I just cannot take it any longer."

Guy Bodenmann (Bodenmann, 1995; Bodenmann & Randall, 2012), a professor of psychology at the University of Zürich in Switzerland, developed the systemic-transactional model. Focusing on acute or chronic daily stressors, specifically those that are minor, normal, and originate out of the family, the model depicts these stressors as affecting internal stresses. The external stressors put demands on spouses that pile up, leading to an overload of individual and dyadic resources, resulting in less time spent together and thus less shared experiences, weakening the sense of togetherness. Communication becomes more tense and less supportive, dyadic coping becomes poorer, partners go their separate ways, potentially becoming mutually alienated, and gradually marital stability decreases. Dyadic coping, which is a dynamic and transactional process of stress management, emphasizes mutual understanding and support of each other, showing empathy and concern, expressing solidarity, and working as a team to develop a coordinated effort for addressing the stressful situation. This type of coping alleviates the negative impact of stress on the marriage and strengthens mutual trust and intimacy, thus leading to higher marital quality and better well-being.

Part II

Pathogenic and Salutogenic Outcomes of Exposure to Stress in Individuals, Families, and Communities

Traditional trauma literature has been criticized for accentuating negative effects and minimizing positive aspects of exposure to adversity. Research and clinical experience have shown that such exposure may have both negative and positive effects. Both will be reviewed in this part of the book. Chapter 4 discusses effects of stress on individuals, Chapter 5 reviews effects on couples and families, and Chapter 6 addresses effects on communities.

4 Effects of Stress on Individuals

Many if not most people will have some negative reactions to an encounter with highly stressful events. When such an event occurs, the very foundation of one's being and the assumptions that have built up over one's whole life regarding how the world operates – specifically that life is predictable, safe, and secure – are shattered (Janoff-Bulman, 1992). This has potentially both universal and specific impacts.

While each individual's experience is unique and subjective, there are some universal common reactions. Researchers and clinicians have reported emotional, cognitive, physiological, interpersonal, and behavioral reactions to the exposure to a highly stressful event. Emotionally, people may manifest diverse reactions including grief, anxiety, confusion, shame, guilt ("What have I done to provoke it?" "Why do I deserve it?" "What could I have done to save others?" "Have I tried hard enough?"), anger, and depression. Cognitive reactions may include difficulty in concentration and in making decisions, confusion and disorientation, self doubt, and loss of a sense of competency (Hobfoll et al., 2007b). Possible physical reactions are somatic symptoms such as insomnia, tension, aches, fatigue, nausea, and loss of appetite. Typical interpersonal effects are distrust, compromised ability for attachment and intimacy, increased involvement in conflicts, or withdrawal. Behavioral problems may include the inability to perform daily living tasks effectively.

These reactions tend to be short-lived. Although it may take time, most people resume their functioning and well-being. Only a small percentage of individuals experience long-term negative effects of exposure to highly stressful events and even in those severely affected, many recover at some point. This recovery is achieved by both deliberate and automatic reactions activated to decrease stress reactions. A group of researchers in Australia who recently conducted the first study that examined PTSD over the lifetime in the general population (Chapman et al., 2012) found that most of those diagnosed with PTSD eventually remit. However, the process is very long and may last for decades. Prospects for remission were lower following some stressor events (specifically interpersonal violence, or childhood trauma), when individuals suffered also from anxiety or affective disorders, and when PTSD symptoms were more severe. Generally, those exposed react, at least initially, with sadness, anger, anguish, and sorrow, which may inhibit the ability to see a bright future. Most are able to come to terms with the event, frame it as a past occurrence, and move on with their life, whereas others continue to live the trauma and perceive the danger as imminent even if it happened in the remote past. Some become more spiritual or religious, or change to another religion or spiritual belief system, whereas others lose their faith because the traumatic exposure shakes their belief and they feel deserted by God (Falsetti, Resick & Davis, 2003). For example, the Nobel Prize winner Elie Wiesel described in his book *Night* (1960) how his religious belief died after he was forced at age 15 in the Nazi death camp in Auschwitz to witness the cruel and slow death of a young child who was hanged but was not heavy enough for the weight of his body to break his neck and heard someone ask: Where is God now? "And I heard a voice within me answer him . . . Here He is – He is hanging here on this gallows" (p. 62).

However, it has been long recognized that the struggle with highly stressful events may also yield benefits, growth, and transformation. Bonanno and Mancini (2008) divided possible reactions to exposure to a potentially traumatic event into four categories: chronic dysfunction, delayed reactions, recovery, and resilience. Masten and Obradovic (2008) identified eight outcome trajectories along the continuum of maladaptive reactions to recovery and positive transformation.

Research is still evolving relative to what determines how individuals react to and are affected by traumatic exposure, how they cope, and what the outcomes are of different ways of coping, as well as why some people succumb, others tolerate and cope, and yet others are able to thrive. Evidence has been emerging that coping style, personality characteristics such as dispositional optimism, a higher level of differentiation of self (i.e. the ability to engage and be intimate with others while maintaining a sense of individuality and autonomy), as well as the nature of the event, and previous experience with stress play a role in determining short- and long-term effects of traumatic exposure (Hooper & DePuy, 2010). This chapter will review short- and long-term negative and positive effects on individuals of a traumatic exposure.

Negative Effects

Trauma creates pain that is sometimes intolerable ("I wanted to crawl out of my skin"). People who have been traumatized may develop a broad range of psychopathological and neurological reactions, which, prior to the recognition of PTSD as a distinct syndrome, often led to misdiagnosis as various disorders. Negative reactions may include depression, substance abuse (sometimes as an effort to self medicate against the unbearable pain), obsessive compulsive and antisocial and borderline personality disorders, as well as damage to the structure and functioning of the brain. Traumatized individuals may develop such disorders in addition to classical trauma reactions or without a co-occurring traumatic reaction (Samardzic, 2012). The most recent edition of the DSM-V (2013) identified five disorders directly related to exposure to a stressful event: reactive attachment disorder, disinhibited social engagement disorder, acute stress disorder, posttraumatic stress disorder (PTSD), and adjustment disorders. Because both of the first disorders result from absence of adequate care during childhood, they are discussed in Chapter 7, which focuses on developmental aspects of the exposure to stressful and traumatic events. The other three outcomes are discussed here, as is complicated posttraumatic stress disorder (C-PTSD), which, although not included in DSM-V as a trauma-related disorder, is critical to understand.

Acute Stress Disorders

ASD has been introduced in the DSM-IV (APA, 1994) and revised in DSM-V (APA, 2013) as a brief, time-limited reaction to exposure to a highly stressful event that involved threat or actual accidental or violent death, or after learning that such an event occurred to a close family member or friend, or after direct (rather than via media) exposure to repeated or extreme aversive details of the traumatic event. Symptoms may include an initial state of being in a daze and disoriented, flashbacks, distressing memories and dreams related to the event, numbing, inability to experience positive feelings, derealization, emotional detachment, inability to remember important aspects of the event and efforts to avoid distressing memories, thoughts and feelings, people, places, objects and situations associated with the event, difficulty sleeping or concentrating, irritability, exaggerated startle response, and aggressive behavior. Consequently, the person cannot function well at work and in social relationships. This diagnosis typically refers to reactions that occur within one month following the exposure and last for at least three days but no longer than four weeks. The diagnosis is often predictive of the development of PTSD at a later stage (Marmar et al., 1994). Studies suggest rates of ASD in 13–21 percent of survivors of road accidents, typhoons, industrial disasters, and violent assaults (Gibson, 2007).

Only a few studies examine who is at risk for ASD. In these studies, those who were closer to the event, exposed to previous traumatic situations, younger, or female, or who had a previous mental health diagnosis, extended exposure to stressful exposure, or lacked an effective system of social support were more likely to develop ASD and to do so in a more severe form. The work group preparing revisions in the ICD (Maercker et al., 2013) regarded the reactions of acute stress as non-pathological and falling within the normal range, yet deserving assistance.

PTSD

The most well-known stress-related negative mental health outcome is PTSD, which is associated with impairment across various psychosocial domains and extensive psychiatric comorbidity (especially with depression, drug abuse, suicidality, anxiety, and dissociative and personality disorders), and involves huge cost in unemployment and service utilization. Clinical literature reflects ongoing controversies over the validity of the diagnosis, specifically the very existence of it as a syndrome and criteria for its usage relative to any particular individual (North et al., 2009). Also debated are the extent to which human suffering should be medicalized, overuse of the diagnosis, and its employment while people are actively exposed to extreme stressors. These questions challenge the ability to differentiate between PTSD, adaptive fear reactions, and grief (Maercker et al., 2013).

History

Posttraumatic stress disorder's historical roots are in treatment of male war combatants. It was originally conceptualized as a combat-related reaction and called "soldier's heart" in the American Civil War, "shell-shock", "war neurosis", or "war hysteria" in the First World War, and "combat fatigue" or "battle fatigue" in the Second World War. The psychoanalytic name "combat neurosis" reflected Freud's idea that a severe traumatic exposure is suppressed and later manifested indirectly by symptoms. Because until 1980 there was no single diagnostic category for people who exhibited stress reactions, those suffering from what today is known as PTSD received different diagnoses, such as depression and anxiety disorder. However, a precursor of the diagnosis was offered by Kardiner and Spiegel (1947), who described war veterans' "traumatic neurosis" characterized by fixation on the trauma, irritability, explosive aggression, and compromised general functioning, all of which are very similar to what today encompasses PTSD.

The syndrome was first presented as a psychiatric condition in DSM-III (APA, 1980) and has since gone through several revisions, where criteria have been modified and added. For example, in 1987 the criteria that the stressor event be out of the ordinary and have a specific time frame were added and in 2000, in the DSM-IV-R, the criteria were expanded to include the individual's perception of the event (APA, 2000); however, this addition was reversed in the 2013 edition as it was deemed immeasurable. The most recent version, reflected in the 2013 DSM-V (APA, 2013) and the forthcoming 2015 ICD-11, recognizes disorders associated with stress as separate from other anxiety-related mental health conditions. The development of the diagnosis led to ongoing discussions relative to what constitutes trauma, what are the etiology and process of the disorder, what determines how it affects those exposed to potentially traumatic events, and what are the most effective ways to address such effects. The women's liberation movement raised awareness that PTSD did not discriminate by gender, although coping differs in men and women, and rape, sexual assault, and incest became recognized as potentially traumatizing experiences (Herman, 1992a). Studies and practice guides mushroomed with sometimes inconsistent and confusing recommendations. Furthermore, an unresolved debate exists as to whether PTSD is indeed one solid diagnosis or an umbrella under which a spectrum of trauma-related mental health conditions reside. Specifically heated was a recent and unresolved debate over whether complex PTSD should be formally recognized as a separate diagnosis.

Diagnostic Criteria

To meet the current diagnostic criteria for PTSD, an individual must have at least one gateway criterion (i.e. have been exposed to actual or threatened death, serious injury, or sexual violation) and symptoms must have begun or worsened after the exposure. The exposure can be by being the direct victim, witnessing the event, learning about exposure of a significant other to a violent or accidental traumatic event, or repeated or extreme indirect (rather than via media) exposure to aversive details of the event, such as experienced by disaster workers (Friedman et al., 2011). The diagnosis is not given before a month after the stressor event because most of those experiencing such stress exposure recover after a short period of acute stress and never develop PTSD.

Those diagnosed with PTSD may develop 20 symptoms clustered in four groups. The first cluster includes intrusive involuntary distressing thoughts, memories, distressing dreams, flashbacks, or nightmares related to the event, a sensation of re-experiencing it, as well as physiological reactions to reminders of the event (APA, 2013). One survivor of rape described the experience in the following way: "I see the movie of what he did to me again and again and I cannot turn off the projector." What appears to others as minute may trigger extreme reactions in those who are traumatized; for example, for Holocaust survivors, people in uniform or a smell of something burning may bring back the memories of the camp adversity and related anxiety, helplessness, and hopelessness.

The second cluster includes persistent avoidance of thoughts, feelings, or acts related to the traumatic event, as well as reminders of it such as associated people, places, and activities. Individuals may consume drugs and alcohol, cut themselves, or keep extremely busy as a means to forget. Becoming numb and lacking motivation, emotional energy, and hope may block seeking and utilizing help, thus creating a catch-22 – the more help they need, the less they are able to seek it. In therapy, they may skip sessions or change the topic.

The third cluster involves negative alterations in cognition and mood such as persistent inability to remember important aspects of the traumatic experience, including what exactly happened, who was there, and the sequence of events, persistent exaggerated negative expectations about self, others, or the world, distorted self-blame for causing the event, pervasive negative emotions of fear, horror, anger, guilt, or shame, feeling detached or estranged from others, emotionally numb, or disconnected, difficulty in relating to others, and inability to experience positive feelings. Third-cluster symptoms may be manifested in lack of interest, motivation, hope, or desire to participate in diverse activities, including those that were previously enjoyed, just going through the motions without genuine involvement sometimes causing the person to appear depressed. Also evident are statements such as "I am no good/ruined/bad" and "Nobody can be trusted/the world is totally dangerous/there is no hope."

The fourth cluster includes hyperarousal and reactivity, increased irritability, hypervigilance, and agitation. This may be manifested in difficulties concentrating, sleeping, learning, or remembering, being easily startled, frightened and angered, exhibiting aggressive, reckless or self-destructive behavior, being constantly over-aware of surroundings and on alert as if the danger may return at any minute. Because they are always watchful and restless, traumatized individuals may experience difficulty falling and staying asleep. Warning signals lose their effectiveness as everything evokes an excessive reaction, without differentiation between real danger and normal conditions, as if the filter for degree of threat has been lost and even the minutest stimulus triggers an explosive response. All these symptoms lead to difficulties in functioning for those diagnosed with PTSD. They can also easily get into conflicts and thus be unable to adequately maintain a relationship with their spouse.

In addition to these symptoms, the DSM-V includes a dissociative subtype of PTSD with symptoms of depersonalization (feeling not real) and derealization (feeling like the world is unreal) to escape from an unbearable external environment or internal distress. Individuals may vacillate back and forth between diverse clusters of symptoms, which makes diagnosis challenging, and a full assessment of trauma history and current stressors is of utmost importance. Furthermore, Monson and colleagues (2011b) emphasize the importance of collecting information for assessment from significant others (spouses, parents) as traumatized individuals may underreport symptoms because of shame or lack of awareness.

In some cases, the manifestation of PTSD symptoms is delayed and begins to appear, increase, or worsen over time rather than immediately following the event. For example, Berntsen and colleagues (2012), who studied PTSD in combat soldiers before, during, and after deployment to Afghanistan, found diverse trajectories in the development of PTSD: some developed symptoms during (or immediately after) deployment and others manifested a gradual increase later. There is an unresolved debate as to whether partial or subthreshold PTSD also exists, i.e. having some but not all symptoms as well as some impairment in work and social interaction although less so than those with full-blown PTSD (Breslau, Lucia & Davis, 2004; Friedman et al., 2011).

The disorder may create a permanent change in one's personality, often described by family members as: "I feel that I live with a different person." PTSD often occurs together with other mental health issues such as depression, anxiety, and substance abuse, which is sometimes used by survivors as an attempt to self-medicate against symptoms, e.g. drinking in an effort to mitigate pain and calm the nerves. Simon, 28, was a typical example. He came from a working-class family, was married with two young children, and worked as a butcher, when he was drafted as a reservist to serve in the 1973 Yom Kippur war between Egypt and Israel. Most of his small unit was killed when an Egyptian bomb fell on their bunker. He was saved because he went out to attend to nature's call. He and his wife reported that he was restless, agitated, snapping, and impatient with his family, refused to see friends, could not sleep, lost his appetite, and could not work because the blood and meat of the animals reminded him of the sight of his killed friends. When he was exhausted enough to fall asleep for short periods, he woke up screaming from nightmares full of ghosts and the angel of death. During our sessions, he jumped from topic to topic, could not sit, paced the room nervously, and almost jumped out of his skin whenever a loud or sudden noise (such as a car braking) occurred.

Prevalence

PTSD is associated with diverse, myriad experiences, including natural catastrophes such as earthquakes (Nasar Sayeed Khan et al., 2007) and hurricanes (Caldera et al., 2001), accidents, assault, rape, robbery, killing while in combat (Maguen et al., 2010), and bomb attack (Jehel et al., 2003; Verger et al., 2004). Epidemiological studies found that a quarter to a third of those exposed reported symptoms within months after the experience. However, lifetime prevalence for PTSD is estimated in 5–15 percent (Bonanno & Mancini, 2008; Kessler et al., 1995; Litz et al., 2002; Verger et al., 2004) and an additional 5–15 percent experience sub-clinical forms of the disorder (Kessler et al., 1995). Variations in estimates result from differences in definitions of the condition, ways of measuring it, and population groups studied. These numbers fluctuate depending on political, social, and economic conditions, such as an increase in veterans returning from the Iraq and Afghanistan wars. In spite of the range of estimates as to what percentage of those exposed to highly stressful events develop the disorder, the overall consistent finding is that it will be a relatively small percentage. Studies of community samples have shown that while almost 90 percent of adults have experienced at least one lifetime traumatic event, only a few develop PTSD (Adams & Boscarino, 2006). Most people are able to bounce back and recover but those who get stuck on the traumatic experience and fail to discontinue living it, feeling it, and thinking about it are at high risk of developing PTSD. It is important to remember that while a relatively small number of those exposed develop PTSD, some develop a partial syndrome and others develop other disorders, such as depression and addictions, making the psychosocial toll higher than what the figures relating to those who meet criteria for PTSD suggest. Because most people who encounter a potentially traumatic event do not develop PTSD, researchers have invested efforts in identifying characteristics that predict who is at risk for developing the disorder and more likely to suffer long-term problems. Such knowledge would enable the development of prevention and intervention to target those at highest risk. Nuanced knowledge of the disorder, the mechanisms involved in creating it, and its complicated and multi-faceted nature is at an early stage (Litz et al., 2002).

Correlates

Characteristics of the event, those experiencing it, and the environment affect the probability of PTSD and the shape it takes. Numerous studies have shown that *event* characteristics, which shape the likelihood of developing the disorder, include the severity, especially its subjective appraisal, type, magnitude, frequency, duration, and controllability of exposure, the nature and number of concurrent losses, and the degree of physical injury and immediate risk for life (Friedman et al., 2011; Gabert-Quillen, Fallon & Delahanty, 2011). In most studies, proximity to the event was a predictor of PTSD symptoms. It was consistently found that those closer to the event, although not directly exposed, were affected the most (Brewin, Andrews & Valentine, 2000; Neria, Nandi & Galea, 2008). Thus, research has shown that after the terrorist attacks of 9/11, people who lived close to the World Trade Center were twice as likely to report PTSD symptoms as those who lived in other parts of New York City or those who experienced it vicariously through the media (Galea et al., 2002). One study (Schlenger et al., 2002) found that traumatic reactions were significantly more prevalent in the New York City metropolitan area (11.2 percent) than in Washington, DC (2.7 percent), other major metropolitan areas (3.6 percent), and the rest of the US (4.0 percent). The highest prevalence of PTSD was found among survivors and first responders. Furthermore, while the prevalence of PTSD declines over time, the effects on these groups tend to endure (Neria, Nandi & Galea, 2008). However, there are exceptions. For example, Shalev and others (2006) failed to find a significant difference in PTSD symptoms among residents of a Jerusalem neighborhood that was experiencing continuous direct exposure to terrorist attacks and a neighborhood indirectly exposed. The researchers concluded that continuous terror created similar distress in proximal and remote communities. Findings about the higher likelihood for PTSD in those who suffered physical injury as a result of a traumatic event were consistent across studies. For example, in a study of survivors of an earthquake in Pakistan, Nasar Sayeed Khan and his colleagues (2007) found that survivors who suffered physical injuries were more susceptible to PTSD than those who did not. This finding echoed in numerous studies in different parts of the world following diverse stressor events. However, the exact nature of the relationships between the severity of the stressor event and its impact as well as possible factors that moderate and mediate this connection are not yet clear, and have been the subject of diverse theoretical interpretations and inconsistencies of research findings.

The recognition of personal correlates as shaping the outcomes of stress exposure grew gradually. Originally PTSD was conceptualized as a normal response to an overwhelming trauma (Brewin, Andrews & Valentine, 2000); however, progressively the idea started to evolve that individual vulnerability factors play a role in predicting PTSD. Personal risk factors include three groups of characteristics: personality traits, life history, and socio-demographic attributes. In addition, there has recently been growing support to the role genetic risk factors and their interaction with environmental factors play in the development of trauma reactions such that some genetic variants predispose individuals to developing PTSD symptoms whereas other variants offer protection. For example, a team at Emory University in Atlanta, Georgia (Jovanovic & Ressler, 2010) found that some changes in the structure and activity of the neural and limbic systems (e.g. the process responsible for communication between the reasoning circuitry in the cortex and the emotional circuitry of the limbic system) may contribute to the probability of those exposed to highly stressor events developing long-term severe stress reaction. Therefore, it may be that PTSD has bio-markers, i.e. biological characteristics that may predict who is more susceptible to developing PTSD following traumatic exposure. This research is still in its infancy; therefore, the discussion below will focus on aspects about which we have more established knowledge.

Personality traits associated with the likelihood of developing PTSD are coping style, level of sense of control and mastery, sense of self, and optimism or pessimism (Lechner, Antoni & Carver, 2006). For example, three major types of coping style have been identified: *active coping*, which is problem-focused; *acceptance* and *positive reinterpretation*, which involve focusing on the perception of the stressor as unavoidable and on positive aspects of the situation; and *avoidance coping*, which involves using emotion-focused coping to deny the situation or withdraw from it. An active coping style may be most adaptive in controllable and modifiable situations; acceptance and positive reinterpretation are more prevalent in situations that are not controllable by direct action; and an avoidant coping style may reduce short-term distress but is less adaptive and can ultimately lead to negative outcomes. People with positive expectations about themselves and the world (dispositional optimism) are less likely to develop severe long-term negative reactions to adverse experiences than those with negative expectations. Negative affectivity and a pervasive dispositional negative mood marked by anxiety, depression, and hostility are also pre-existing vulnerabilities that are risk factors for negative stress reaction (Updegraff & Taylor, 2000). People who repeatedly respond to stressful situations with an extreme flood of emotions, which is considered a maladaptive strategy for regulating affect, and who maintain this response as a long-term mechanism to cope with stress, are more likely than others to eventually develop mental health problems of anxiety or depression (Wei et al., 2005).

In most studies, *life history* predictive of the development of PTSD includes the preliminary reaction to the traumatic exposure, previous experience of trauma or abuse, and mental health issues, specifically acute stress disorder (Cohen Silver et el, 2002; Jehel et al., 2003), as well as concurrent additional stressors such as divorce, job loss or physical injuries (Nasar Sayeed Khan et al., 2007; Verger et al., 2004). Many studies of diverse populations and stressful exposures found that those who experience acute stress disorder are at a very high risk for developing chronic PTSD. For example, Koren, Arnon and Klein (1999) showed that in victims of road accidents, existence of posttraumatic symptoms immediately after the accident was a better predictor of later PTSD than were accident or injury severity. Similarly, abundant evidence shows that a previous encounter with a highly stressful event is a major factor in shaping the development of stress disorder (e.g. Cukor et al., 2011). For example, Michultka, Blanchard and Kalous (1998) and Blanchard and colleagues (1996a) found that higher numbers of war experiences predicted the severity of PTSD. In particular, a history of exposure to interpersonal violence in childhood or adulthood may shape the reactions to later traumatic exposure. Nishith, Mechanic and Resick (2000) found that a history of child sexual abuse contributed to increased vulnerability to adult sexual and physical victimization and PTSD symptoms. Furthermore, a history of being raped or of being a victim to physical abuse in childhood increased the likelihood that PTSD symptoms become chronic in some women (Cougle, Resnick & Kilpatrick, 2011).

While these findings were quite consistent across different population groups (Brewin, Andrews & Valentine, 2000), some reports showed that individuals in war zones who had a history of psychiatric and psychological problems sometimes manifested improvement in the aftermath of a potentially traumatic event (Curran, 1988). One explanation for this paradoxical outcome was that individuals benefited from the increased social cohesion that often occurs under such situation. Similarly, Rubin and his team (2005), who studied the impact of the 2005 bombings in London on the stress levels of the population, reported that having previous experience of terrorism was associated with reduced rather than elevated levels of stress.

Two different explanations have been suggested for the mechanism that connects earlier traumatic exposure to negative reactions to a later exposure. Some, like Dougall et al. (2000), think that the earlier traumatic exposure sensitizes individuals to trauma, increasing vulnerability to subsequent exposure and consequently its negative effects. Others, such as Meichenbaum (1985), posited that individuals who dealt effectively with moderate-level stressors may have acquired successful coping strategies and confidence in their ability to address threats and are thus inoculated or immunized to potentially pathogenic effects of subsequent stressful events. One idea has been that the relationship between previous trauma and the effects of subsequent exposure are non-linear or U-shaped, such that a moderate amount of previous adversity, especially if the person was successful in coping with it, may prepare for effective coping with later traumatic events whereas no exposure or expansive exposure do not (Rutter, 2007; Seery, Holman & Silver, 2010). Only limited methodologically sound evidence exists relative to this question (Bonanno et al., 2010; Masten & Narayan, 2012). Clear understanding of the role of previous trauma exposure on the reactions to later threats is yet to be developed.

Socio-demographic attributes that have been identified as associated with the prospect of developing PTSD are being female (Cohen Silver et al., 2002; Jehel et al., 2003; Kessler et al., 1995; Verger et al. 2004), younger age, especially school age (Adams & Boscarino, 2006; Norris et al., 2002), and being of disadvantaged or minority ethnic origin (Caldera et al., 2001). However, differences related to gender and age were found in some studies but not in others. For example, Blanchard et al. (1996b) and Breslau et al. (1991) reported that women were more likely to develop PTSD after a major traumatic event, Bowler et al. (2010) found significantly higher prevalence of probable PTSD for female police responders 2–3 years following exposure, and Solomon, Gelkopf and Bleich (2005) found that vulnerability for women was six times higher than for men. By contrast, Palinkas et al. (1993) failed to find gender-based differences. Stuber, Resnick & Galea (2006) did not find significant difference between men and women in the prevalence of PTSD related to 9/11 but found differences in types of symptoms, such that women were more likely to report re-experiencing and hyperarousal. Ehlers, Mayou and Bryant (1998) found short- but not long-term gender-related difference. Indeed, a meta-analysis conducted by Brewin, Andrews and Valentine (2000) showed that the effects of gender, age at the time of the trauma, and race are inconsistent across studies and could predict PTSD in some population groups but not in others. Therefore, we do not know for sure whether women are at a higher risk than men and if younger people are at a higher risk than older ones or which particular subgroups among these populations are more susceptible for developing PTSD. The absence of such knowledge may compromise the ability of professionals to properly triage and target intervention for those most vulnerable.

Furthermore, although understanding the trajectory of the disorder is challenging because it requires expensive and logistically complicated studies for years, Orcutt, Erickson and Wolfe (2004) were able to follow up a large group of military and National Guard veterans of the first Gulf War and test them for PTSD three times: in 1991 immediately following their return from service, two years later (1993–1994), and finally in 1997–1998. The findings showed that women, minorities, the less educated, and those exposed most were not only more vulnerable to developing PTSD, but their symptoms were more likely to increase over time, whereas symptoms in other population groups tended to decrease. However, risk factors change as time from the exposure elapses. In a study of communities in New York, Adams and Boscarino (2006) found that, a year after the 9/11 terrorist attack, young age, gender, and access to social support were associated with PTSD but that this was no longer the case a year later (i.e. two years after the original exposure), and that being Latino and 30–64 years old rather being young, a woman and with limited resources, became predictors of the disorder. At this time, we do not know why such changes occur and why certain groups are more susceptible at different times following the original stressor event. Nevertheless, although we do not understand the dynamics of the effects of various conditions, we know that we need to keep an eye on groups that were found to be sensitive to adverse reactions at different points in time.

Even when differences in prevalence among diverse groups are documented, the interpretation of what contributes to them is challenging. For example, the higher prevalence of PTSD in minority populations has been attributed to their increased risk for exposure to stressful events rather than the difference of ethnicity itself. Because no studies exist that controlled for this potentially "contaminating" effect, we have no accurate knowledge as to whether ethnicity impacts on the outcomes of experiencing highly stressful events (DiMaggio & Galea, 2006; Norris et al., 2002).

Environmental characteristics of the communities where people live that are associated with the prospect of developing PTSD include both objective aspects (e.g. crime rates, population density, poverty, prevalence of deviance, and drug use), and perceived aspects (e.g. feeling of safety versus dangerousness) – specifically, the degree of social conflict, disruption of existing ways of living and neighborhood disorder, the need for resources, which may put extensive demands on public services, social disconnectedness, and community cohesion (i.e. community members mutually relating to and providing support for one another). For example, Palinkas and colleagues (1993) studied the effects of the 1989 Exxon Valdez oil spill into the Prince William Sound on people living in 13 Alaskan communities. While not life-threatening, this disaster created a major change in the lives of the residents in the small rural communities around the area where the spill occurred. People lost their jobs because fisheries were closed, economic opportunities became unequal as clean-up jobs and renting boats and equipment owned by local residents paid a lot of money to some but not to others, and an influx of outsiders who came to seek work in the clean-up altered the communities' traditional way of life and strained community services. One year after the disaster, those living in communities most affected by the spill and the consequent clean-up efforts reported more symptoms of depression, PTSD and anxiety compared with residents of less affected communities. Critical in coping with PTSD is the availability of social support in the environment. For example, Brewin, Andrews and Valentine (2000) found that social support was a strong predictor of adjustment and PTSD symptomatology in various civilian and military samples.

Cultural Aspects

The diagnosis has been criticized as a limited construct that lacks cultural sensitivity in understanding culture-specific factors in the expression of symptoms and expectations of treatment. Until recently, most professional literature about diagnosing and treating trauma took a western-centric perspective because the definitions and descriptions of mental conditions are informed by western values of individuality, autonomy, personal happiness, and relativity (Joyce & Berger, 2007; Canive & Castillo, 1997; Kulka et al., 1990). Typical manifestations of traumatic reactions acceptable in some cultures but different than the norm in western cultures (e.g. somatic symptoms) may be viewed as pathological or neglected and ignored.

Consequently, trauma and its effects have been underdiagnosed, overdiagnosed, and mis-diagnosed, especially in minorities groups, depriving them of appropriate treatment (Joyce & Berger, 2007). For example, the National Vietnam Veterans Readjustment Study reported significantly higher rates of PTSD among Latinos and Blacks than among whites (Kulka et al., 1990). Similarly, a study of children and adults in New York after 9/11 found among Latinos a disproportionately higher percentage of psychological problems than in any other ethnic group (Schuster et al., 2001).

PTSD in Indirect Victims

Individuals indirectly exposed to a trauma, such as family members of direct victims, may develop traumatic reactions (Galovski & Lyons, 2004; Rosenheck & Nathan, 1985), conceptualized as Secondary Traumatic Stress Disorder (STSD). These individuals experience the blurring of boundaries between themselves and the direct victim and have described a feeling that stress disorder is "contagious" (Dekel et al., 2005). When the direct survivor is present physically but not available emotionally or socially, a situation that Boss (2007) called "ambiguous loss" develops, which creates additional secondary traumatization. The social withdrawal of the vicariously traumatized can decrease the amount of social support available to them, thus creating a vicious circle further exacerbating the situation and decreasing the likelihood of successfully coping with the adversity. Such vicarious traumatization has been documented in numerous circumstances and diverse cultural contexts including in Israel, Croatia, and the US. A specifically rich literature exists about vicarious traumatization relative to warfare (Ben Arzi, Solomon & Dekel, 2000; Francisković et al., 2007). For example, families of soldiers wounded in combat or prisoners of war have been documented as manifesting somatic, emotional, cognitive, and behavioral symptoms that mirror those of the direct victim (Dekel & Monson, 2010).

A particular issue related to the effects of traumatic events on those who are not directly exposed is the question of sequential traumatization, i.e. the transmission of trauma. Knowledge about this aspect of trauma is inconsistent. For example, scholars have posited that children of Holocaust survivors manifest symptoms of second-generation (Danieli, 1985; Yehuda et al., 1998), and others found that trauma may be transmitted from former child soldiers in Burundi to their offspring (Song, Tol & de Jong, 2014). Furthermore, some evidence is emerging relative to possible effects of maternal stress response on fetuses and newborns (Masten & Narayan, 2012). However, a recent meta-analytical study of 32 samples involving 4,418 participants (van IJzendoorn, Bakermans-Kranenburg & Sagi-Schwartz, 2003) found no evidence for the influence of the parents' traumatic experiences on their children in a non-clinical sample of offspring of Holocaust survivors. A recent review of literature on intergenerational transmission of PTSD from fathers to sons in families of war veterans concluded that findings are mixed and highlighted that the paucity of knowledge does not allow for the development of a more nuanced understanding of the consequences of parental traumatic experiences for offspring or the identification of familial aspects that contribute to intergenerational transmission of PTSD (Dekel & Goldblatt, 2008). Possibly, the symptoms of PTSD in those directly experiencing the trauma rather than the traumatic experience itself lead to secondary traumatization (Dekel & Goldblatt, 2008; Galovski & Lyons, 2004). Thus, if the direct victim manifests numbing, arousal or aggressive behavior, these reactions may cause troubled family relationships and secondary traumatization in family members. Another explanation is that traumatized parents respond by dissociation, which compromises their ability to identify future threats to both themselves and their children, and thus they become repeated victims as well as exposing their children to traumatizing encounters.

Specific groups at risk from vicarious traumatization are those whose work requires extensive and prolonged interaction with trauma survivors. Social workers and other mental health professionals who treat military personnel and their families, victims of domestic violence and childhood abuse, survivors of other traumatic experiences, first responders, disaster workers such as Red Cross personnel, and journalists covering war are at risk of experiencing both short- and long-term symptoms of trauma reactions (Armagan et al., 2006; Batten & Orsillo, 2002; Cornille & Woodard Meyers, 1999; Culver, McKinney & Paradise, 2011; Cunningham, 1999; Harrison & Westwood, 2009; Hesse, 2002; Meldrum, King & Spooner, 2002; Linnerooth, Mrdjenovich & Moore, 2011; Shamai & Ron, 2009). To cite just a few of the numerous available examples, such reactions have been found in social workers who served survivors of Hurricane Katrina in New Orleans and the 9/11 terrorist attacks in New York (Adams, Boscarino & Figley, 2009; Batten & Orsillo, 2002; Eidelson, D'Alessio & Eidelson, 2003), nurses and social workers during the second Lebanon War in Israel (Lev-Wiesel et al., 2008), and rescue teams after the 1995 Tokyo subway attack (Ohtani et al., 2004), earthquakes in Turkey (Kiliç & Ulusoy, 2003), Mexico's 1999 flood (Norris et al., 2004), and the Oklahoma City bombing (North et al., 2002).

Estimates of the frequency of vicarious traumatization vary. Cukor and her colleagues (2011) found that almost 9 percent of non-rescue disaster workers deployed to the NYC World Trade Center site following the 9/11 terrorist attacks suffered from severe disaster-related pathology four and six years later. Another study of relief teams diagnosed PTSD in a quarter and almost two thirds had at least one symptom and reported negative effects on social life (Armagan et al., 2006). In a study of 282 social workers in southern USA, Bride (2007) found that about 70.2 percent of his sample reported at least one symptom of secondary traumatic stress and a significant minority (15.2 percent) met the criteria for PTSD. Campbell and McCrystal (2005) described the negative impact on the mental health of practitioners who worked within the violent political conflict in Ireland, and Lindsay (2007) reported similar findings in Palestinian social workers and psychosocial personnel in situations of acute political conflict. In their study of Israeli hospital-based emergency room social workers who were repeatedly exposed to the aftermath of terrorist attacks, Somer et al. (2004) found overwhelming emotional distress among some but not all participants. A study of mental health effects of the Chernobyl nuclear power plant disaster concluded that first responders and clean-up workers' levels of depression and PTSD remained elevated two decades later (Bromet, Havenaar & Guey, 2011). However, other studies identified secondary traumatization in a lower frequency than in the general population (e.g. Adams & Boscarino, 2006; Adams, Boscarino & Figley, 2009; Dekel et al., 2007; Shamai & Ron, 2009).

Symptoms of vicarious traumatization in service providers, like in other victims of secondary traumatization, may be physical, cognitive, emotional, or relational and affect their ability to perform professionally. Reported reactions include sadness, powerlessness, detachment, decreased professional functioning, chronic physical and emotional exhaustion, headaches, weight loss, depersonalization, irritability, difficulties in interpersonal relationships, feelings of loss, fear, pain, grief, despair and helplessness, nightmares, intrusive thoughts, flashbacks, anxiety, loneliness, hostility, decreased optimism, changes in memory and in views of self and the world, distress, self-doubt, guilt, and anger (Cohen & Collens, 2013; Galovski & Lyons, 2004; Mikulincer, Florian & Solomon, 1995). In addition, professionals may begin to question their personal and professional identity, lose their sense of agency, develop self-blame ("Why can't I help? Did I do everything possible to prevent this?"), fear for their own safety, experience guilt and shame for being oriented to their own needs rather than those of their clients, feel vulnerable and helpless and at the same time responsible for the protection of their clients, or become dissatisfied with life in general and particularly with work. These reactions may increase consumption of alcohol and lead to overeating, overspending, overworking, and decreased professional competence and performance (Culver, McKinney & Paradise, 2011; McCann and Pearlman, 1999; Tehrani, 2007).

The effects of vicarious traumatization depend on the nature, duration, and intensity of the exposure to direct victims (it is different to provide immediate short-term help following a flood than to carry a long-term caseload of clients with persistent PTSD or to hear repeated horrible graphic accounts from many clients) and the degree of helpers' similarity to them. It may become more complex in situations of past or present shared traumatic exposure (often called shared reality), where clients' experiences resonate within professionals who either had similar experiences in the past (for example, a victim of child abuse who works in child welfare) or live and practice in the same communities as their clients (e.g. a war zone) and thus are exposed to or personally threatened by the same stressful events as those whom they serve. Thus, they are simultaneously service providers and co-survivors, and may be traumatized both directly by exposure to a stressful event and indirectly by treating those who have been were exposed to one (Dekel & Baum, 2010; Shamai & Ron, 2009). This often happens in community disasters and was the focus of attention especially in the public and professional discourse that followed the 9/11 terrorist attacks. Consequently, practitioners may be caught in the struggle to fulfill professional responsibilities of providing help to clients while negotiating their own reactions and personal needs, and encounter a conflict between their loyalty to their own families and to their clients. This was manifested by a hospital social worker whom I supervised. Required by a hospital that received causalities from a major disaster to work long hours and be absent from home for days, she was torn between her ethical obligation to stay at work and serve victims and her need to take care of her own children, who were frightened and alone, and her elderly and sick parents. The shared traumatic experience of service recipients and providers may lead to the blurring of traditional boundaries and bring to professional relationships more intimacy and greater empathy, which may become actual identification with the client and lead to difficulty maintaining the emotional distance commonly considered necessary for the delivery of effective services.

Effects of vicarious traumatization vary. Perrin and colleagues (2007) compared the prevalence of PTSD across occupations involved in rescue and recovery work at the World Trade Center site 2–3 years after the 9/11 attack. They found that the risk was higher for construction, engineering, and sanitation workers, who do not routinely encounter disaster, than for policemen, who commonly deal with trauma-related tasks. Shamai (forthcoming) posits that political orientation and sense of belonging affect traumatic experiences among helpers such that supporters of the government tend to relate collective traumatic events to chance whereas opponents often blame ineffective policies. Most but not all studies found that at the highest risk for developing vicarious traumatization are those who work mostly or exclusively with trauma survivors and those with past personal experience of trauma for whom a client's story may resurrect unresolved issues related to their own experience. Novices with less professional experience are at higher risk, though prolonged exposure through lengthy service also contributes to negative effects (Arvay, 2001; Ellwood et al., 2011; Guo et al., 2004). However, Fullerton, Ursano and Wang (2004) failed to find an association among vicarious traumatization symptoms and gender, age, previous experience of traumatic events, and tenure.

The development of secondary traumatic stress is also influenced by the levels of empathic engagement practiced by a professional and the sense of compassion satisfaction, i.e. contentment derived from helping others (Bride & Figley, 2009; Pearlman & Caringi, 2009). A practitioner who enters the world of the client and experiences their stress and pain may become highly emotionally involved with the client's experience and develop distress as if being actually exposed. While the ability to have intimate access to and tune into the client's experience is important in a therapeutic relationship with clients, whose trust in people has been severely damaged by the traumatic experience, it also puts the practitioner at risk for secondary traumatization.

Typically, effects on rescuers and professionals are short-lived and in most studies the secondary traumatization tends to be temporary. For example, Israeli social workers who provided help to direct and indirect victims of national terror attacks experienced symptoms similar to those of secondary traumatic stress disorder (STSD) for a few days, whereas in the long-term they reported that the experience led to personal and professional growth (Shamai & Ron, 2009).

Adjustment Disorder, and Complicated Grief (CG)

A trauma-related adjustment disorder includes emotional or behavioral symptoms (such as distress) disproportional to the stressor event, with intensity, quality, or persistence exceeding what normally may be expected within the cultural, religious and social norms, and which interferes with the ability to function at work, in social relationships, and other life domains but disappear after the stressor event discontinues. A specific bereavement-related reaction is called complicated grief and is also referred to as traumatic grief, prolonged grief disorder, and bereavement-related disorder. In the DSM-V (APA, 2013) it is called a persistent complex bereavement disorder and is part of "other specified trauma and stressor related disorders" because to make it a distinct category more research is needed. This is a debilitating syndrome of persistent bereavement reaction to the death of a loved one, which involves considerable limitations of the ability to function as usual, and interferes with adaptation and re-engagement in life. For example, I treated a woman who, ten years after the death of her son, kept his toothbrush, toiletries, and unwashed shirts in a plastic bag, to maintain his smell, and continued to set a place for him at the family dinner table. Whereas most people are able to return gradually to pre-loss levels of functioning within several months to a year, an estimated 9–15 percent continue to suffer for as long as several years from chronic and disabling grief that fails to get better by interpersonal psychotherapy. In bereaved parents, African Americans who lost a loved one to homicide, and members of poor families the prevalence was higher and did not decrease with the passage of time (Prigerson et al., 2009).

While some manifestations of complicated grief resemble those of uncomplicated grief and depression, the cluster of symptoms is similar to PTSD, including intrusive thoughts and preoccupation with the deceased, the circumstances of the death and images related to the event, strong continued yearnings for the person who died, numbness, difficulty acknowledging the death and accepting it, feelings of emptiness, anger and bitterness related to the death, extreme loneliness and detachment from others, frequent crying and unrealistic self-blame for the loss, avoidance of reminders (for example, making detours to avoid going by the hospital where the death occurred), a pervasive sense that life is meaningless and a desire to die to reunite with the deceased, difficulty trusting others, and disbelief in one's own ability to function without the deceased ("I will never be able to balance the checks/bring the car to the annual test . . ."). These symptoms tend to be chronic and cause significant cognitive, social, and interpersonal impairment (Boelen & van den Bout, 2008). According to the National Institute of Mental Health (2002), complicated grief often occurs when the death was caused by war, suicide, homicide, or other traumatic circumstances.

As is the case relative to complex PTSD, debates as to whether complicated grief is a distinct psychiatric syndrome exist. A team of international experts in grief and trauma (Prigerson et al., 2009) conducted a study and concluded that, indeed, the disorder is different from other diagnoses and has unique characteristics and impairments which current diagnoses fail to capture. However, at this time, a resolution is yet to be achieved.

Complex Posttraumatic Stress Disorder (C-PTSD)

The most pervasive trauma-related negative outcome is complex PTSD, which consumes the individual's whole life, determines their global worldview, and causes impairments in social, cognitive and emotional functioning. The manifestations of this outcome of trauma exposure are abundant in number and severe in nature. They include grave problems in perception, inability to focus, concentrate and process information, mood swings and difficulty regulating emotions, especially anger, rage, defeat and horror, self-destructive, impulsive, erratic and risky behaviors, which may perpetuate revictimization, self-injury, suicidal thoughts and attempts, dissociative episodes, extreme resignation and avoidance responses, a sense of being permanently damaged and empty, a general negative worldview, inability to develop trust in others, chronic pain, despair and hopelessness, a loss of a coherent sense of self, shame, guilt, self-blame, and inability to self-soothe, with potential use of addictive and compulsive measures in an effort to reduce stress (Ford & Courtois, 2009; Taylor, Asmundson & Carleton, 2006). These individuals see themselves as worthless nobodies and the world as totally hostile; thus the principle that guides their decisions and behavior is anticipating dangers always and everywhere with no ability to assess situations rationally and differentiate among various conditions and their possible meanings.

The idea that complex PTSD is a separate distinctive entity has been developed because the current PTSD diagnosis sometimes fails to capture the severe psychological harm that occurs with prolonged, repeated interpersonal trauma. The disorder was first introduced by Judith Herman (1992a, 1992b) who, on the basis of her clinical observations, suggested the concept to describe the pervasive psychosocial injury to psychological development and identity formation that damages sense of self and interpersonal relationships. Rather than a single episode even of an extremely high magnitude, this serious disorder develops after prolonged chronic repetitive multiple exposures to interpersonal traumatic events that occur typically at developmentally critical times such as early childhood or adolescence and are disempowering, stigmatizing and often highly invasive, without an escape route or the ability to control the situation (Cloitre et al., 2012). The disorder typically develops in survivors of childhood abuse, torture, ethnic cleansing, genocide and concentration camps, hostages, and prisoners of war, rather than following injury in an accident or combat activity, diagnosis of a life threatening disease, or suffering a major loss. The cumulative nature of the exposure may lead to severe effects on broad aspects of the individual's personality and functioning. It is not surprising that a person in a vulnerable position who has been abused by another with no protection loses trust in others and in self and experiences the world as a dangerous and threatening place, where one must protect oneself at all cost.

The need for a distinct diagnosis evolved because traditional definitions of PTSD were based on the prototypes of survivors of circumscribed traumatic events such as combat, disaster, and rape, consequently failing to capture the possible damage by a consistent and wide-ranging experience of stress. However, debates are burgeoning as to whether this condition is indeed a separate disorder. It has been conceptualized as a disorder of extreme stress not otherwise specified (DESNOS), personality change after a catastrophic event, developmental trauma disorder, and posttraumatic personality disorder (Resick et al., 2012). Some have suggested reconceptualizing borderline personality disorder as a complex trauma spectrum disorder because of the overlapping of symptoms in the two conditions (Lewis & Grenyer, 2009). In recent years, during the revisions of the DSM and the *International Classification of Diseases*, controversies relative to the validity of complex PTSD as a separate diagnosis have intensified (Weiss, 2012), and the *Journal of Traumatic Stress* dedicated its June 2011 issue to the dispute.

Proponents of recognizing C-PTSD as a distinct disorder posit that neglecting to do so compromises the possibility of understanding and helping these extremely injured individuals who have traditionally been diagnosed as suffering from PTSD and co-morbid conditions, as if they occur independently of the traumatic reaction, rather than viewing the additional issues (e.g. depression, anxiety, phobias) as part of the big picture of trauma-related problems. Consequently, their mental health issues have often been misunderstood and mistreated. Furthermore, because such diagnoses typically preclude them from participation in studies (many researchers have as excluding criteria co-morbid conditions to maintain the purity of the study), development of knowledge about those who suffer from extreme traumatic exposure has been hindered. Indeed, studies conducted by van der Kolk and colleagues (van der Kolk et al., 2005; D'Andrea et al., 2012) showed that prolonged interpersonal trauma, which first occurs at an early age, can have significant effects on psychological functioning above and beyond PTSD. However, Resick and her colleagues (2012) conducted a systematic review of the available literature about complex PTSD and concluded that a clear conceptual distinction from other diagnoses, more reliable and valid assessment measures, and more empirical evidence are needed to justify viewing complex PTSD as a different and categorical construct. Specifically, they claimed that because most symptoms, except changes from previous personality and loss of previously sustaining beliefs, are so similar to those of other disorders, such as PTSD and borderline personality disorder, evidence is necessary that complex PTSD has unique causes and/or process rather than being a more severe form of PTSD. Their review ignited a dialogue between proponents and opponents of viewing complex PTSD as a separate diagnostic category and at the time that this book went to press, a separate diagnosis was not named in the DSM-V but is still being considered and expected to be adopted for the ICD-11. However, a dissociative subtype of PTSD has been recognized. It includes symptoms of depersonalization (feeling not real) and derealization (feeling the world is unreal) to escape an unbearable external environment or internal distress. It appears in those who have been traumatized repeatedly and early on and is often accompanied by other psychiatric disorders, inability to function, and suicidal thoughts, plans and attempts.

Positive Effects

In addition to negative effects, the struggle with stressful life experiences can lead to good outcomes and be an impetus for personal growth. An increasing body of research has lent ample credibility to this idea. Estimates are that a considerable percentage of those exposed to adversity demonstrate resilience (Bonanno & Mancini, 2008). Such resilience can be achieved by deliberate controlled processes as well as by automatic activation of positive emotions and varies by types of exposure and populations. Positive effects reported most often are sense of coherence (SOC) and posttraumatic growth.

Sense of Coherence (SOC)

Studies generally supported Antonovsky's (1998) ideas, discussed in Chapter 3, and found that a SOC is a protective factor in different cultural contexts (Israel, Japan, China and the US) and in different populations including adolescents, parents to children with developmental problems, older adults after a flood, those who have experienced life-threatening accidents or illnesses, and therapist who suffered vicarious traumatization. Individuals with a higher SOC also reported lower levels of stress, anxiety, and distress following exposure to work-related, community, and familial stressors (e.g. having a child with a disability or taking care of a sick spouse), and better physical and mental health outcomes. They manifested fewer symptoms, better psychological adjustment, general well-being and life satisfaction, and better professional functioning (e.g. Brock-house et al., 2011; Evans, Marsh & Weigel, 2010; Flensborg-Madsen, Vente-godt & Merrick, 2005; Pisula & Kossakowska, 2010; Tuohy & Stephens, 2012).

Amirkhan and Greaves (2003) studied a combined sample of college students and community residents who endured a chronic stressor, and concluded that the mechanism by which SOC leads to better outcomes involves both a perceptual aspect – i.e. the way people view stressful events (similar to Lazarus and Folkman's [1984] idea of primary appraisal) – and a behavioral process of clarifying the nature of the stressor, selecting resources appropriate for the specific situation, being open to feedback that allows modification of behavior, and employing more problem-solving and less avoidant coping strategies.

Factors that enhance the SOC of individuals include personality traits such as optimism and environmental characteristics such as cultural context and the nature of family climate, particularly for children. Thus, children in rigid and non-cohesive families manifest a lower SOC than children in more flexible families with strong interpersonal bonding among members (Sharabi, Levi & Margalit, 2012). Findings relative to social and community factors that affect SOC vary. Some studies found that individuals who live in stable religious societies have a higher SOC whereas findings regarding the impact of minority status are inconsistent (Braun-Lewensohn & Sagy, 2011).

Posttraumatic Growth

Between 30 and 70 percent of participants in various studies reported perceiving benefits from struggling with a highly stressful event (Weiss & Berger, 2010). Such benefits included changes in self-perception, including greater self-trust, self-efficacy, self-worth, and self-reliance, modification of interpersonal relationships, transformation in the general approach to life, spirituality and religiosity, heightened awareness of new possibilities, and a greater appreciation of life. Growth was reported following traumatic bereavement, war, human-made and natural disasters, accidents, rape, sexual assault, infertility, parenting infants hospitalized in neonatal care units, chronic and life-threatening disease such as severe heart attack, HIV/AIDS, bone marrow transplant, and breast and pediatric cancer, abuse, immigration, and the birth of a seriously ill child (Affleck et al., 1987; Barakat, Alderfer & Kazak, 2006; Barr, 2011; Belizzi & Blank, 2006; Berger & Weiss, 2006; Davis, Nolen-Hoeksema & Larson, 1998; Linley & Joseph, 2004; McMillen, Smith & Fisher, 1997; Moore et al., 2011; Senol-Durak & Ayvasik, 2010). There is mounting evidence that individuals across the globe report perceived benefits from their struggle with traumatic events or life crises in diverse cultural contexts including the Middle East (e.g. Israelis, Palestinians), Europe (e.g. Germany, the Netherlands, Spain), the Balkans (e.g. Kosovo, Turkey), Asia (e.g. China, Japan), the US, and Australia (Powell et al., 2003; Weiss & Berger, 2010). Furthermore, parallel to vicarious trauma, vicarious PTG, i.e. the process of positively redefining self and worldviews following exposure to vicarious traumatic distress, was also reported. Vicarious growth has been documented across samples, stressor events, and circumstances. McCormack, Hagger and Joseph (2011) and Dekel (2007) documented personal and relational transformation that included finding new meaning, and increased humility, love, gratitude and empathy in wives of veterans diagnosed with PTSD. Practitioners who serve trauma survivors reported being changed in positive ways to become more inspired, altering their priorities and behaviors and becoming more ready to cope with stressors in their own life (Calhoun & Tedeschi, 2013). For example, practitioners who treat survivors of war, abuse and losses can become more grateful for what they have, change their priorities and relationships with others, and improve their strategies for addressing challenges. However, Hobfoll and colleagues (2007a), who conducted longitudinal studies with large prospective samples, raised questions about PTG and its correlates and suggested that for there to be a marker of positive adaptation, reported cognitive changes must be accompanied by actual changes in behavior.

Cultures and subcultures vary in the level of reported PTG, its manifestations and meanings. Non-whites have reported greater spirituality and greater PTG than whites (Milam, 2004, 2006; Milam, Ritt-Olson & Unger, 2004). In some Anglo-Saxon cultures (Australia, US) the manifestations of PTG were different than in more traditional and familistic or collectivistic societies such as Latino, Palestinian, Israeli, Spanish, and Chinese societies. For example, in some western cultures part of what people conceived as PTG was feeling more pride, whereas in cultures which glorify modesty (e.g. Japan), PTG was conceptualized as increased self-awareness of one's weaknesses and limitations and loss of desire for possessions. However, these differences may reflect cultural permission to express growth rather than differences in the experience itself. In addition to differences in the amount of reported PTG, culture appears to influence aspects where change is reported. Thus, reports of changes in religiosity and spirituality were lower in highly atheistic societies such as East Germany, the Netherlands, and Australia (Weiss & Berger, 2010).

Correlates of PTG

Correlates of PTG include event-related, personal, socio-demographic, and environmental characteristics. Event-related aspects include the degree of stressfulness of the triggering situation and its perceived severity, the amount of initial distress, and the type of coping strategy used. For example, problem-related active coping has been documented as helpful in developing PTG as has sharing of feelings with family members, friends and professionals, a stronger sense of connectedness to the community, and the availability of models (Antoni et al., 2001). The availability and use of social support are important factors in facilitating better short- and long-term outcomes following an encounter with distress. Getting instrumental, emotional, financial, and other types of support from friends and family following the exposure to a potentially traumatic event can help those affected to grow from the stressful experience. A significant other or co-workers may provide support to help coping and lessen the stress because people know that they have sources of help. For example, Schroevers and her colleagues (2010) found that the more support survivors of breast cancer received shortly after the diagnosis, the more they reported having received benefits up to eight years later. Of course, it is possible that those who have a positive attitude to begin with are more likely to reach out for support and get it as well as to report growth; thus we cannot be sure what the actual role of support is in the achievement of benefits from a stressful encounter.

Personal aspects associated with PTG are self-esteem, extroversion and optimism (Helgeson, Reynolds & Tomich, 2006; Hobfoll et al., 2007a; Moore et al., 2011), cognitive processing, combining the perceived growth with action, and spirituality or religiosity (Calhoun et al., 2000; Shaw, Joseph & Linley, 2005; Updegraff et al., 2002; Weiss & Berger, 2010). Religiosity and spirituality have been conceptualized as a multi-dimensional construct, which may include both world-oriented spirituality (i.e. focusing on the relationship with ecology and nature) and humanitarian/people-centered spirituality, which stresses human achievement and potential, and can be expressed through various channels

(Spilka, 1993). Because research has shown that spiritual behaviors are generally correlated with well-being scores, it is not surprising that spirituality plays an influential role in how an individual deals with a trauma (Shaw, Joseph & Linley, 2005). Thus, religious individuals tend to report more growth than do those who do not observe any religion (Kleim & Ehlers, 2009); however, the specific routes to spiritual change are still unclear.

Socio-demographic features connected with PTG are ethnicity, marital status, employment status, gender, education, and income (Belizzi & Blank, 2006; Cordova et al., 2001; Frazier, Conlon & Glaser, 2001; Polatinsky & Esprey, 2000; Wortman, 2004). Thus, African Americans and other non-Caucasians who survived sexual assault as well as those struggling with HIV reported greater PTG than their white counterparts (Kennedy, Davis & Taylor, 1998; Kleim & Ehlers, 2009; Milam, 2004). Just like they report more PTSD than men, women also tend to report more PTG (Bates, Trajstman & Jackson, 2004; Kleim & Ehlers, 2009; Updegraff & Taylor, 2000; Wortman, 2004), although such gender differences were not always significant (e.g. Polatinsky & Esprey, 2000). Findings regarding the association between income and PTG were inconsistent. For example, Cordova and her colleagues (2001) found that higher income was associated with higher probability for some aspects of PTG, whereas Tomich and Helgeson (2004) failed to find such an association. Clearly, more knowledge than we currently have is needed to clarify the nuanced ways in which one's financial resources may or may not be related to the potential for growth. Specific attention has been devoted to the question of PTG and age. Because their cognitive ability is not yet fully developed and PTG requires a certain level of cognitive sophistication and maturity for rumination and processing of the highly stressful event, the question arises as to whether PTG is possible in children. This question will be examined in the chapter dedicated to developmental aspects of trauma (Chapter 7).

Environmental correlates of PTG are the attitudes of the immediate reference groups and the broader society towards the possibility of getting benefits from the struggle with adversity, and the availability of people who have experienced PTG. For example, Cobb et al. (2006) found that individuals who experienced domestic violence and knew somebody who reported PTG following a similar experience described higher levels of growth than those who did not.

Secondary Positive Effects

Parallel to the aforementioned secondary negative effects, practitioners serving those affected by trauma may also experience secondary or vicarious resilience and vicarious posttraumatic growth (Arnold et al., 2005; Hernandez, Gangsei & Engstrom, 2007). Human service providers may develop changed perceptions of themselves, their relationships, or their environment, and may get inspiration and strength from working with survivors of extreme traumatic conditions such as political violence or kidnapping. Secondary benefits may include increased general understanding of the therapeutic process and of stress reactions, a transformed perception of their own problems, and a greater sense of efficacy. Thus, practitioners in the US and Israel who have served survivors of diverse traumatizing events reported better empathic ability, a renewed sense of professional commitment, increased altruism and positive feeling about their work, personal growth, and satisfaction (Eidelson, D'Alessio & Eidelson, 2003; Batten & Orsillo, 2002; Shamai & Ron, 2009).

The Relationship Between Negative and Positive Outcomes of Exposure to Stress

Two questions can be raised regarding the relationships between negative and positive effects of trauma exposure. First, are these two sides of the same phenomenon or are these two separate and distinctive processes? Second, if indeed the two are different, what is the nature of the relationships between them?

While there is some debate as to whether PTSD and PTG are entirely separate constructs or opposite ends of the same spectrum (e.g. Westphal & Bonanno, 2007), there is evidence that people can have in response to the exposure to a highly stressful event a mixed reaction of suffering from PTSD and experiencing PTG (Zöllner & Maercker, 2006). Numerous studies have shown that these two types of reaction to stress can co-occur and are not mutually exclusive; rather, they are two separate processes that can be seen as a double track. This co-existence of stress responses and PTG is evident in clients as well as in the practitioners who help them. Combined positive and negative effects of direct and vicarious trauma were found in children, families of children with disability, wives of veterans and prisoners of war, and young adults following diverse life-threatening situations (Alisic et al., 2008; Dekel, 2007; Hastings & Taunt, 2002; McCormack et al., 2011; Schuettler & Boals, 2011). However, some studies have challenged the idea of two separate processes. Johnson et al. (2007) found that people with higher levels of PTSD reported less PTG, supporting the idea that there is a negative relationship between the two.

The sequencing of negative and positive post-trauma reaction is quite clear such that distress precedes growth and the greater the level of PTSD symptoms, the higher the posttraumatic growth; however, the precise nature of the relationship between them is not clear (Kleim & Ehlers, 2009) and findings relating to the relationship between growth outcomes and symptom severity have been mixed (Grubaugh & Resick, 2007). Some studies have shown an association between higher levels of PTG and better mental health outcomes, including less depression, anxiety and distress, higher self-esteem, and better functioning (Carver & Antoni, 2004; Frazier, Conlon & Glaser, 2001; McMillen, Smith & Fisher, 1997; Park & Fenster, 2004). One explanation was offered by Linley and Joseph (2004). Focusing on the finding meaning component of PTG, they posited that people search through cognitive processing for meaning of the event and its aftermath. When such meaning is found, assumptions about the self and the world, which were shattered following the exposure, are reconstructed, disruption and confusion decrease, and eventually symptoms of

PTSD diminish. Other studies found that higher levels of growth were associated with more distress, more trauma symptoms, and poorer quality of life (Butler et al., 2005; Tomich & Helgeson, 2004). Yet other studies failed to find any relationship between the levels of negative and positive outcomes of the struggle with highly stressful events of intimate partner violence and earthquakes (Cobb et al., 2006; Cordova et al., 2001; Grubaugh & Resick, 2007; Sattler et al., 2006).

It has been suggested both in individual studies (e.g. Lechner, Antoni & Carver, 2006) and in a meta-analysis (Helgeson, Reynolds & Tomich, 2006) that, similar to the relationships between exposure to potentially traumatic events and levels of negative effects, the relationship between growth and psychopathology is also complicated and possibly curvilinear. For example, Lechner, Antoni and Carver (2006) found in survivors of breast cancer significant long-term curvilinear relations among reports of finding benefits and indicators of psychosocial adjustment such as perceived quality of life, positive and negative affect, social disruption, and intrusive thoughts. Those who reported high benefits also scored higher on optimism and use of positive reframing. Similarly, in two studies of the relationship between PTG and psychopathology in survivors of an assault, Kleim and Ehlers (2009) found a curvilinear association of PTG with the existence and symptom severity of PTSD and depression: those with severe symptoms reported moderate growth whereas those with less PTSD and depressive symptoms reported either high or low levels of PTG. If indeed this relationship is curvilinear, it may explain the inconsistency in the findings of different studies. Another explanation for the inconsistency, offered by Linley, Joseph and Goodfellow (2008), is the time frame of the study and the changing nature of the relationship between negative and positive outcomes along the journey of cognitive processing of the event.

5 Effects of Stress on Couples and Families

Because families are systems of interconnected and interrelated individuals, what happens to one family member impacts others. Thus, traumatic exposure always affects couples and families, irrespective of who was directly exposed. For example, whether the whole family lives in disaster or war zone, or one or some family members were involved in a road accident, all members are affected by association (secondary traumatization). Effects on individual family members who were not directly exposed to the traumatic event but are experiencing it second hand were discussed in Chapter 4. This chapter focuses on the impact on relational systems, specifically the couple and the family as a whole.

Traumatic exposure may erode family structures and processes, disrupt family routines, dynamics and ability to function adequately, compromise role allocation (e.g. a father returning from deployment who fails to provide as before), coping and communication (such as members sharing their trauma narratives), and impair family relationships and the family atmosphere. Such changes may be accompanied by intense emotional reactions including feelings of isolation, depression, and incompetence in individual family members, and beget domestic violence and child abuse. For example, when a mother is diagnosed with cancer, the husband, older children and possibly in-laws and other relatives must shoulder both part of her chores as well as additional tasks that her illness demands (e.g. accompanying her to treatments). Such changes may create added stress, conflicts, and anger, as evident from the heightened prevalence of separation, divorce, marital dissatisfaction, and other relational issues in families encountering highly stressful events. For example, negative effects on family adjustment and on relationships with spouses and partners have been documented in families of soldiers returning from deployment in Iraq and Afghanistan (Sayers et al., 2009).

Some of these effects may linger across generations. Thus, Holocaust survivors may have developed overprotective parenting practices and suffered from trauma-related depression, nightmares and irritation. Consequently, their children may become parentified, feeling responsible for making it up to their parents while refraining from developing their own autonomy and fulfilling their own goals. This may cause negative reactions, which have been called second generation syndrome, and which in turn could negatively affect the next generation of children.

While the impact of trauma exposure on individuals has been studied extensively, there is much less knowledge about the impact it can have on couples and families. However, the existing knowledge suggests that, as with individuals, couples and families may be affected both negatively and positively by exposure to highly stressful events.

Negative Effects

An encounter with a highly stressful event strains the fabric of even the strongest, most resilient couples and families. A crisis brings some families closer together to the degree of enmeshment while others are torn apart. It may intensify relationship issues that have been successfully dealt with during non-crisis times and lead to the manifestation of tensions, competition, resentment and splits that were under the rug when conditions were normal. For example, immigration in many families leads to changes in roles, such as women who were home makers becoming the main breadwinners and adolescents becoming cultural translators for their parents; consequently changes occur in the power structure in the family, which may lead to heightened tension and increased prevalence of domestic violence.

Negative Effects on Couples

Trauma may be detrimental to all aspects of couple relationships including mutual trust, friendship, communication, decision making, problem solving, marital satisfaction, sexual life, and child rearing. Data emerging from studies in the last two decades suggest that even satisfied couples with adequate coping skills may have difficulty functioning effectively under conditions of relatively high demands posed by stressful circumstances. This is specifically true when couples live in environments that pose severe challenges and offer diminished resources and support. Under stress, spouses may have more pressing problems and a diminished ability to exercise the skills that they normally possess for coping (Karney & Bradbury, 1995).

Because dyadic conceptualizations of stress are relatively recent and no comprehensive models of couple stress have been developed (Randall & Bodenmann, 2009), research on negative effects of encountering highly stressful events on couples are scarce, and findings are inconsistent. Some studies have shown that wars, unemployment, economic hardships, and natural disasters are associated with an increase in marital solidarity whereas other studies found lower marital adjustment and an increase in divorce rate following such experiences (Cohan, Cole & Schoen, 2009). Nevertheless, while there is more clarity about the effects of some types of stressor events than others, overall, quite solid evidence exists that stress may strain couple relationships, threaten their stability and functioning, and generate mental health and relational problems that can disrupt the marriage. It also may shake spouses and motivate them to reflect about their life and future. This self-examination and psychological stock taking may lead to the conclusion that "this is not the person with whom I wish to live the rest of my life." In my practice in Israel, I have encountered men who have come back from military service with the realization of the fragility of human life and who have decided to divorce, seek new opportunities, and fundamentally change their lives.

Couples may be affected by trauma when both spouses are exposed together to a highly stressful event or when the exposure is direct for one and indirect for the other with individual stress reactions spilling over to the dyadic relationships. Negative effects on couple relationships can result from diverse stressors such as an illness in the family, the birth of a child with a disability, unemployment, or the struggle with economic hardships (e.g. Conger & Donnellan, 2007). Shamai (2012) compared Israeli couples who resided in communities along the border with Gaza and experienced together direct consistent threat of rocket attacks and terror with couples whose exposure was limited in scope or indirect through the media. Couples who experienced together a high dose of threat reported significant effects on their marital life. For some the impact was negative – such as heightened tension and anxiety, and compromised intimacy – whereas others said that the experience brought them closer and strengthened their bond, and they learned to collaborate better in coping. Couples with less or indirect exposure tended to state that it had no effect on their relationships. Similarly, Farhood (2004) found in a study of families who lived in Beirut during the 1975–1991 Lebanon war that the closer the family lived to the war zone, the greater were the negative effects on the marital relationship.

Relative to the spillover effect, Dekel and her colleagues (2005, 2007) studied couples where the husbands were diagnosed with PTSD or were prisoners of war and found damaging effects on the relationship and the ability of the couple to function together. Sometimes, the direct victim needs to share and process the experience as a way to try to come to terms with it whereas the spouse cannot tolerate such discussion, leading the former to feel lonely and the latter to feel guilty, eventually creating tension in the couple relationships. A recent meta-analysis (Lambert et al., 2012) confirmed that PTSD symptoms have detrimental outcomes for intimate partners as it affects negatively the quality of relationships and increases spouses' distress, especially for female spouses of males diagnosed with PTSD. Effects on partners' distress but not on the quality of relationships were stronger where the traumatic event occurred in the more distant past.

Negative effects vary and include lower satisfaction with relationships, less sharing of emotions, more distanced and aggressive interactions, and diminished and troubled sexual intimacy. Often, the stressful situation begets negative personal reactions such as loss of patience, anger, anxiety, tension, frustration, distress, and depression, which diminish the ability of spouses to relate to each other in a supportive and amicable way and communicate in a pleasant and collaborative manner to the degree that they do not want to spend time together and start to distance from and blame each other, resulting in increased marital conflict, distress, and deterioration of the marital bond.

These negative effects on a marriage may be mitigated by dyadic properties. Mutual support and the ability to collaboratively solve problems and resolve conflicts may protect couple relationships and decrease spouses' negative emotional reaction to highly stressful events. Couples who are able to soothe, nurture and sensitively assist one another at times of stress and are competent at effectively assessing and addressing predicaments together are better able to maintain their relationships intact and to become less distressed (Bradbury, Fincham & Beach, 2000). Findings as to how compatibility (coping congruence) or complementarity between spouses' modes of coping affects the outcomes have been mixed (Revenson & DeLongis, 2011). Some studies have suggested that spouses' use of similar strategies for problem-focused coping and diverse and complementary coping strategies for emotional coping enhances adaptability.

Negative Effects on Families

Stressful situations may exacerbate previously existing problems and create new ones. Stress exposure may include erosion of financial, emotional and social resources, and cause damage to the adaptation of family members and their relationships (Farhood, 2004). Figley (1989) identified four types of negative effects of traumatic events on families: simultaneous, vicarious, chiasmal, and intrafamilial. *Simultaneous* effects occur when the family unit is directly exposed to the event together; for example, the whole family is involved in a car accident or lives in a war zone. *Vicarious* effects occur when one or several family members are directly exposed and others are affected by the constant interaction with the direct victims and their reaction, i.e. the direct victim's reactions are the traumatizing trigger for other family members. *Intrafamilial* effects develop when the family is the source of the trauma and thus both the cause and the effects are within the family system as in cases of abuse and domestic violence. *Chiasmal* effects strike when the traumatic stress of a direct victim infects the entire system. Typical vehicles for the infection are *transmission* of trauma symptoms to non-directly exposed family members and *caregiver burden*, i.e. distress caused by the need to care for a spouse, parent, child or other relative or loved one who struggles with the aftermath of direct exposure (Ben Arzi, Solomon & Dekel, 2000; Dekel & Monson, 2010; Fromm, 2012). Symptoms of PTSD in a family member can make daily life difficult. Avoidance reaction of a trauma survivor, who refuses to attend children's graduations, holiday parties, visit friends, or shop in a crowded mall can frustrate, disappoint, and anger their spouse and children. Hyperarousal symptoms may cause others to maintain a distance or walk on egg shells for fear of igniting anger. Thus, an irritable reaction to an adolescent listening to loud music or a spouse laughing watching TV may trigger fights, hostility, and violence. Children and adolescents may prefer to spend time at friends' houses or on the street and refrain from inviting friends for fear of an embarrassing emotional explosion of the traumatized parent, requiring the non-traumatized parent to take a side or act as a mediator, consequently expanding distance among family members and intensifying tensions.

When several family members experience a traumatic exposure together, their respective symptoms may exacerbate each other. A traumatized child may need maximum support at the time that the traumatized parent is least capable of providing it. Conflicts may arise among family members whose pace of recovery differs. For instance, a father who is further along in processing his grief over a deceased son may be impatient with his wife who is still in earlier phases of mourning. A recent study of Israeli families living under ongoing missile attacks from the Gaza strip (Neutman-Schwartz, personal communication, October 2012) documented the effects on parents and children in concert, and the development of anxiety and partial or full-blown post-trauma reaction.

As with individuals, the nature of the event is an important factor in determining the effects of a traumatic experience on families. For example, families where one member committed suicide are often engulfed by guilt-focused questions such as: Why? How did we not notice? What could we have done to prevent it? Important family characteristics which predict how they react to stress are role allocation, degree of stress in the family atmosphere, the nature of the relationships among family members, the family's developmental stage (e.g. exposure to a stressor when the family is coping with the challenges of raising an adolescent may have different effects than experiencing a similar event at an earlier or later phase of the family lifespan), and the type of coping used. As the focus on systemic reactions to stress has emerged, additional types of coping have been identified, such as relationships-focused, congruent, and dyadic coping. For example, in a study of Israeli families during the 1991 Gulf war, four types of families were identified: anxious families, cautious families, confident families, and indifferent families (Ben-David & Lavee, 1992).

Positive Effects

Parallel to positive effects on the individual, exposure to highly stressful events may carry for couples and families in addition to negative effects possibilities for negotiating successfully challenging life situations, bouncing back, regaining the ability to function effectively, and thriving. Because studying systems, including couples and families, is more challenging than studying individuals, significantly less research has been done on the positive effects of stress-exposure on couples and families. However, some conceptual discussion and a handful of studies do exist. McCubbin, Thompson and McCubbin (1996) presented a comprehensive volume on empirical knowledge regarding families' resiliency, coping, and adaptation. Since its inception in the mid 1970s, the project focused on developing research instruments to study families' reaction to stress and crisis, understanding what allows some families to endure and even thrive following adversity whereas other families encountering similar circumstances deteriorate and disintegrate, and evaluating intervention programs in diverse cultural contexts. Many approaches to the positive effects of struggling with highly stressful events in individuals that were discussed in Chapter 4 were expanded to couples and families, and others unique to families have been developed.

Almost no studies exist on the positive effects of stress on marriage and couples and research on such effects on families is scarce. Nevertheless, in clinical practice it is not unusual to meet couples and families who report how encountering a highly stressful experience tore their relationship apart, sometimes to the point of separation, divorce and estrangement, whereas others felt that it brought them closer, increased their confidence that they can depend on each other and jointly address future challenges, and solidified their relationships. Ruth and Max are a case in point. The couple had their first baby, Tom, after lengthy, emotionally taxing, and financially draining infertility treatment, which challenged their marriage and particularly their intimate relationships. Shortly after birth, Tom was diagnosed with Down Syndrome, a chromosomal condition which puts the baby at risk for a wide range of digestive, heart, hearing, sight, thyroid, respiratory and skeletal illnesses, and mild to severe cognitive and developmental delays. The first few years were very challenging. Because of the need to take Tom to numerous medical and educational services, Ruth took a job that required fewer hours and paid much less, adding to the family's existing financial strain, caused by the mounting expenses for Tom's services. At one point, Max left the home because he could not tolerate the pressure and constant arguments about managing Tom's condition. Several years later, with Tom at preschool, attending a program for children with special needs, and Ruth and Max back together and again fully employed, they reported that while the road had been bumpy, depressing, and challenging, in retrospect they felt that the struggle had strengthened their mutual bond, their ability to strategize and problem-solve as a team, and their love for each other. As with individuals, couple and familial benefits from struggling with highly stressful events have been conceptualized as sense of coherence, resilience, and post-traumatic growth (PTG).

Sense of Coherence

The family sense of coherence (Antonovsky & Sourani, 1988) combines individual cognitive representations and a collective map or worldview of the whole system including members' (1) global belief that the environment is comprehensible, predictable, manageable, meaningful, and explicable, (2) perception of demands of stressor events as challenges, and (3) conviction that the family has the resources to meet them.

The question arises as to whether there is a mutually constructed shared family perception or a collective dispositional orientation of the unit as a whole that goes beyond the sum of individual appraisals. Can a system perceive and have a worldview? There seems to be consensus among scholars that the answer is yes and that family-level collective construction of reality and meaning making is a unique, distinct systemic entity, which is a product of shared interactive processes, and while a family collective characterization is not independent of that of individual family members, it is different from the sum of their individual perceptions (Berger & Weiss, 2008; Boss, 2002; Patterson & Garwick, 1994; Sagy & Antonovsky, 1992).

The concept of familial SOC has received support from research in different cultures and ethnic groups, following types of stressful conditions including families struggling with members' medical issues (e.g. cystic fibrosis), children with disabilities, divorce, and occupation-related stresses. Findings suggest that a family's SOC is associated with its adaptation, well-being, ability to manage acute stress, and quality of life (Anderson, 1994; Lavee, McCubbin & Olson, 1987; Olson, Russell & Sprenkle, 1983; Patterson et al., 1993).

Resilience

Much of the debate about individual resilience, such as lack of conceptual clarity, whether it is a trait or a process, and the conditions required to identify one as resilient apply to families. Patterson (2002a) posited that to qualify as resilient, a family should have encountered a risk and due to protective mechanisms manifested a systemic level of doing well in the face of the adversarial condition with limited poor outcomes. Families may be resilient in some but not all aspects of their life and at some but not other times.

PTG

The applicability of the PTG model to families has been advocated (Berger & Weiss, 2008) but hardly researched. Despite recognition that human systems of any size may grow in the process of addressing stressful events (Calhoun & Tedeschi, 2006), most knowledge to date has referred to families as an enabling or constraining *context* for individual growth (Harvey, Barnett & Rupe, 2006) rather than the family itself as transformed following the struggle with a stressor event. In one of the handful of studies that examined PTG in couples, Weiss (2004) examined PTG in breast cancer survivors and their husbands and found that they shared not only the pain but also the potential for gaining benefits from the trauma, such that in the context of a supportive marriage with a deep sense of commitment and the spirit of facing the cancer together, the likelihood of PTG was higher, regardless of how much conflict the marriage endured. Other studies found that correlates of PTG included whether the event met criteria for traumatic stressor, if the direct victim reported PTG, time since the traumatic event, how the original stressor was processed cognitively and emotionally, depth of commitment to the relationships with the direct survivor, and social and marital support (Manne et al., 2004; Weiss, 2004).

6 Effects of Stress on Communities

Recent years have seen a growing interest in community trauma exposure. Wars, ethnic cleansing such as the Holocaust, the Turkish genocide of Armenians and the slaughter of the Tutsi minority by the Hutu majority in Rwanda during the 1990s, tsunamis, school violence, terrorist attacks, hurricanes such as hurricane Sandy, which devastated the Caribbean and the US east coast, and technical disasters such as the failures of atomic nuclear power plants in Chernobyl in the Ukraine (1986) and in Fukushima, Japan (2011) are a few of the highly stressful events that affect whole communities. Such exposure involves multiple people who simultaneously experience emergencies and crises.

What comes to be viewed as a community trauma as well as the meaning of such an event for the collective depends on who the victims are, what their social status is, and how powerful or vulnerable, stigmatized, or marginalized they are both from their own perspective and as viewed by others including helpers, journalists, researchers, and society at large (Shamai, forthcoming). Victims' age, gender, social position, racial/ethnic background, sexual orientation, and immigration status shape the social construction of a stressor event as a community trauma, the attention it receives, and the type of help provided to victims. For example, the HIV/AIDS epidemic became recognized as a community trauma when it began to affect newborns and blood transfusion recipients, challenging the original view that it was exclusively "a gay man's disease" (Herek, Capitanio & Widman, 2002). A more recent example is the October 2012 hurricane Sandy. Deaths, destruction, and consequent homelessness in Cuba, Haiti, the Bahamas, the Dominican Republic, Jamaica, and Puerto Rico went relatively unmentioned while the spotlight focused on the devastation in the US. Furthermore, as with individuals, the cultural context of the event, the construction of such an event within the particular social values, attitudes toward the victimized collective, and acceptable discourse about stress and reactions to it in the affected community affect what is defined as traumatic.

One mechanism that often creates an immediate construction of and responses to a collectivistic traumatic event is the spreading of horror stories, which can generate a communal pressure cooker as descriptions are inflated and disseminated. Such rumors tend to include exaggerated reports about numbers of victims and seriousness of events, driving up anxiety and panic.

While rumors exist in all community traumas, they tend to be more present when real time accurate information is missing, as frequently happens when communication networks collapse, and an information vacuum is formed providing fertile soil for the development and spreading of misinformation. For example, in the fall of 2011, a newspaper published an article about a pedophile gang operating in an Ultra Orthodox enclave in Jerusalem, Israel. The rumors that tens of children had become victims of sexual abuse by over two dozen adults spread like wildfire; scared parents provided horrendous reports, the police were blamed for failing to investigate vigorously, disregarding children's testimony and making inappropriate arrests, and parents were blamed for contaminating evidence by coaching their children. Eventually, there was no evidence that such mass child abuse ever occurred.

When a catastrophic stressor event of severe magnitude such as a natural disaster hits or an external pressure persists (e.g. slavery or anti-Semitism), it compromises the structure and culture of communities, which may become overwhelmed and their ability to cope impaired. These effects change the life of the community as a whole and consequently of individuals and families within the affected population. Research on the effects of trauma on communities is relatively limited, because conducting such studies is complicated. Commonly used strategies for this task include epidemiological surveys, data about hospital admissions and referrals, psychotropic drug usage, suicide and attempted suicide rates, and assessment of actual victims. Curran (1988) used these measures to assess the impact of rioting, shootings, bombings and other acts of violence by terrorist organizations in Northern Ireland on community mental health during two decades of what is called The Troubles, and Somasundaram (2004) used similar procedures to assess psychological and social effects on the population of two decades of ethnic war in Sri Lanka. An additional challenge is the existence of multiple and sometimes conflicting perspectives among different sub-groups within the community and among outsiders such as researchers, policy makers, and the public at large.

Following traumatic community events such as the 9/11 terrorist attacks and hurricane Katrina, which resonated in trauma studies, understanding of the effects of community trauma began to develop. Irrespective of the nature of the event and the affected community, like with individuals and families, community traumatic events may have both negative and positive effects.

Negative Effects

Task forces such as the Inter-Agency Standing Committee (2007), designed by governments and international bodies to develop knowledge about mass trauma, seem to agree that it erodes normally protective supports and increases the risks of family separation and disruption of social networks and community structures, as well as amplifying pre-existing social injustice, inequality, poverty, discrimination, marginalization, human rights violation, and political oppression. For example, following the economic collapse of Greece in the summer of 2012, which led to massive unemployment, violent attacks on immigrants, especially those who were Muslim, increased significantly.

When a large number of people is exposed to a collective trauma, individual losses become a collective loss and evoke collective pain, uncertainty, anger, anxiety, depression, and guilt (Possick, Sadeh & Shamai, 2008). The combination of such emotions with the collapse of social institutions responsible for law and order may lead to immediate chaos, looting, and violence, especially towards women, children, and minority groups. Thus, following 9/11, numerous incidents of vandalism, arson, assault, shootings, harassment, and threats were reported, and after hurricane Sandy in October 2012, over a dozen people were arrested for looting in the most devastated areas. Dimaggio and Galea (2006) demonstrated the exponential possible effects of a traumatic event on a community using the following example. In the 9/11 terrorist attacks on the World Trade Center, 2,795 were killed and 7,467 were injured. They had 17,642 family members and 17,859 individuals were involved in rescue activities. In addition, 32,361 employees in the area and their 87,383 family members were exposed, bringing the number of the immediate community victims to 164,710; thus, for every individual killed, an additional 59 were affected. Going one step further and including residents of neighboring communities brings the number up to about five million people. In addition to direct effects, a community traumatic exposure often triggers processes that exacerbate poverty, crime, and homelessness, as well as pandemics of drug abuse and mental illness (Landau, Mittal & Wieling, 2008).

A collective traumatic experience may lead to the dissolution of even highly cohesive communities and beget fundamental negative changes in their social fabric. It can destroy support systems, fragment and weaken relationships among groups, create an in-group versus out-groups (those who share the experience and can be trusted and those who do not), damage social structures, disrupt normal social activities and challenge their integrity, as well as lead to violation of norms and yield unacceptable behaviors (Adger, 2000; Kimhi & Shamai, 2004; Landau, Mittal & Wieling, 2008; Norris et al., 2008; Paton & Johnston, 2001). Kaniasty and Norris (2004) highlighted the complex nature of social support in communities affected by mass trauma. While initially post-disaster social support is mobilized and people become closer, it is soon followed by a decline, erosion of a sense of companionship, and deterioration in traumatized communities due to overuse of resources and different pace in people's recovery, typically leaving behind weaker groups.

Ethnically, racially, religiously and otherwise heterogeneous communities that manage to co-exist in normal times tend to experience heightened polarization, growing distrust, and xenophobia while tolerance diminishes when they encounter highly stressful situations (Berger, 2010b). Previous friends, neighbors, and colleagues may turn on each other, betray, and blab, as happened in multi-ethnic societies such as Rwanda, the former Yugoslavia, Darfur, and other countries inflicted by racial, ethnic, religious, and social conflicts. This is especially true when community resources that can promote resilience are themselves victims to the stressor, damaging the ability of the community to address the challenges caused by the exposure. These effects frequently endure for years. For example, although estimates varied among studies, it has been consistently documented that civilian communities have been devastated by heightened prevalence of mental health issues, creating a severe public health problem, especially in resource-poor communities, years after living in a warfare zone, such as in Lebanon, Algeria, Cambodia, Ethiopia, Rwanda, the Balkans, and Timor-Leste (Priebe et al., 2010).

A traumatic experience may affect the exposed community in four major ways: it may affect the collective identity by enduring in the collective memory as part of the community narrative and creating a cultural legacy (Pastor, 2004; Shamai, forthcoming); change the community's values, beliefs, and legacies; create a cultural trauma; and increase moralizing.

The *collective identity*, particularly the self-sense as cohesive, and the individual identity of those who belong to the collective may be severely damaged following a community trauma and the wounds may remain for generations, both conscious and visible, and becoming less discernible as time passes. Thus, following hurricane Katrina, poor neighborhoods, which tended to be located below the water level (the lower nine), suffered a slow pace of restoration and years later numerous houses remained boarded up and waiting to be demolished. People dispersed to alternative housing and this relocation of many families led to the disintegration of the strong sense of community that previously characterized these neighborhoods. Similarly, the war in the former Yugoslavia damaged the national identity of the various collectives involved – Serbs, Kosovars and Croatians; the Holocaust, when six million Jews were systematically massacred by the Nazis, shattered the national Jewish identity of survivors; and slavery wounded African Americans' collective identity. A damaged collective identity may be manifested both individually and collectively. Individual manifestations may include depression, self-destructive behavior, suicidal thoughts and attempts, anxiety, low self-esteem, anger, difficulty recognizing and expressing emotion, and drug abuse in an effort to ameliorate the pain associated with the trauma. On the collective level, negative stereotypes of one's own community, norms and traditions may develop (Yellow Horse Brave Heart, 2003), and in escalating cyclic processes further exacerbate the collective trauma. A narrative of splitting may also be used, painting the others as bad and threatening, leading to the legitimizing of diverse measures for self-protection (Geron, Malkinson & Shamai, 2005). Furthermore, a community's encounter with a traumatic experience may create the self perception of badness, i.e. feeling that the trauma represents a punishment for negative characteristic or actions of one's community, which reflects on individuals and makes them part of the collective badness. Such self-perception may beget efforts of reparation such as manifested by German youth coming to provide services in Israel to atone for the genocide of Eastern European Jews by their parents and grandparents. However, such reparative activities do not always relieve the feelings of guilt (Shamai, forthcoming).

Change or modification of *values, meanings, legacies,* and *beliefs* may follow a collective trauma, accelerating or inhibiting the pace and direction of enduring social changes (Pastor, 2004). For example, the ethnic war in Sri Lanka led to deterioration in the Tamil community of social values relating to sexual mores, violent crime, and work ethics (Somasundaram, 2004). In the Caucasus, which has been involved in recurrent wars, the totalitarian dictatorial Soviet regime enforced the eradication of the history and cultural, ethnic, and linguistic diversity of various regions, leading to omission of memories from the collective narrative and distortion of the history with many periods and events modified, repressed, and undocumented. Consequently, past traumas remained unaddressed and this resulted in the compromised ability of the community to process later traumatic experiences (Makhashvili, Tsiskarishvili & Droždek, 2010). However, when the occurrence of the traumatic event is consistent with existing beliefs and norms, such changes may not occur.

A *cultural trauma,* i.e. a shock to the cultural tissue of a society, may emerge in the aftermath of a community stressful exposure. Sztompka (2000), a leader in understanding cultural trauma and its effects, analyzed how a whole community may experience adverse, dysfunctional changes following the exposure to a highly stressful event. Conceptualized as a cultural disorientation, such changes may involve "split, ambivalence, clash within the culture emerging suddenly, rapidly and unexpectedly and embracing core areas of cultural competence, such as basic values, central beliefs, and common norms" (p. 453). When a cultural trauma occurs, the regular and known context of social life loses its stability, coherence, symbols and norms, and beliefs lose their meaning. Thus, after the ethnic war in Sri Lanka, fishing villages lost their way of life and culture (Somasundaram, 2004). Consequently, trust and leadership collapse and people may lose their confidence in the commitment and ability of regional and national institutes to provide protection and services, as was demonstrated following the catastrophic outcomes of hurricane Katrina with numerous deaths, injuries, and loss of property. The combination of a cultural trauma with anger and despair experienced by the hurt society, and the destruction of social institutions responsible for law and order, creates fertile ground for violent behavior.

Finally, *moralizing,* i.e. excessive use of judgmental language (e.g. good and bad, right and wrong) and of moral reasoning, may increase in an effort to cope with the shattered societal beliefs about the safety and protection of the collective (Janoff-Bulman & Sheikh, 2006). For example, some people interpreted the terrorist attacks of 9/11 as an assault on the United States and its way of life, endangering America's presumed greatness and invincibility. Like survivors of individual trauma, survivors of national trauma struggle to rebuild a sense of safety and protection in a world that suddenly becomes threatening and harbors the potential for stressor events at any given moment. Janoff-Bulman and Sheikh (2006) posited that moralization has been over-used in efforts to explain the attacks as a punishment for bad behaviors and to advocate for behaviors that are deemed moral to prevent further traumatic events.

Positive Outcomes

In addition to negative effects, community trauma has the potential to yield also positive outcomes (Adger, 2000; Breton, 2001; Paton & Johnston, 2001). These may include a more adaptive cultural system (Sztompka, 2000), emergence of grass roots organizations, especially those promoting activities and initiatives related to the traumatic event, destruction of dysfunctional social structures and strengthening feelings of social cohesion, solidarity, and altruism. For example, following the 9/11 terrorist attacks, numerous non-profit organizations developed initiatives to support those who suffered physical and psychological damages (Steinberg & Rooney, 2005), and in Sri Lanka, the highly hierarchical caste system and liberation of women from their traditionally suppressed status declined following the war and the displacement of Tamils (Somasundaram, 2004). However, it is important to remember that an increase in cohesiveness may be characterized by homogeneity and monolithic thinking, and thus limit openness to external output and the legitimacy of differences or conflicts (Lahad & Ben Nesher, 2008; Shamai, forthcoming).

Community resilience, community hardiness, community competence, community efficacy, and communal mastery are concepts that, with varying nuances, have been used to describe the ability of a community to employ its social capital, physical infrastructure, and cultural patterns to withstand, recover and thrive despite adversarial circumstances and external stresses caused by social, political, and environmental change (Adger, 2000; Ungar, 2011; Norris et al., 2008; Zautra, Hall & Murray, 2008). Models depicting resilient communities vary; however, they view similar dimensions as crucial for the community to be resilient. For example, Bruneau and colleagues (2003) identified four characteristics (the four Rs) of community resilience: robustness, redundancy, rapidity, and resourcefulness. *Robustness* is somewhat similar to hardiness and refers to having resources and the ability to withstand exposure to highly stressful situations without negative effects. *Redundancy* describes a community's access to a wide and diverse range of resources that can mutually substitute each other, such that if one resource fails, others are available to address similar needs. *Rapidity* refers to the pace and timeliness at which the community can use its resources to address damages and recover. *Resourcefulness* is the ability to identify problems, prioritize them and effectively address them by mobilizing available resources. Norris and colleagues (2008) revised this model to include three rather than four elements: *robustness, redundancy*, and *rapidity*. While robustness and redundancy remained the same, they claimed that the dimension of rapidity includes the resourcefulness. In the revised model, it was also speculated that one of the three elements is sufficient for the creation of resilience.

Ganor and Ben-Lavy (2003) used another model with similar components to examine how various groups and organizations worked together in the South Jerusalem neighborhood of Gilo, which struggled to cope with Palestinian terrorist activities and shootings. They identified six Cs as ingredients of community resilience: communication, cooperation, cohesion, copying (taking action), credibility (which depends on grass-root organizations), and credo (i.e. a positive and hopeful community spirit regarding the future).

Experts agree that communities are more likely to be resilient and bounce back from adversities if they experience a short exposure, perceive it as a lower-level threat, have access to formal and informal human, social, physical, financial and natural resources, and competence to use them effectively, as well as public and corporate policies designed to increase resources (Kimhi & Shamai, 2004; Shamai, Kimhi & Enosh, 2007). Of utmost importance are adequate and well-coordinated housing, transportation, energy, water, educational and health care, and psychosocial services. Communities that are more developed and better equipped are also better situated to recruit help and use it, and thus are more likely than poor and weak communities to regain their pre-stressor state and achieve resilience.

An able and trusted leadership is also critical in times of community disaster. Aldrich (2011) used case studies to analyze patterns of recovery in various communities after the 2004 tsunami in Southeast India and the 1923 Great Kantō earthquake in Japan. Villages with organized local leaderships that were able to convey the needs of the communities were more successful in recruiting resources from donors and governmental organizations and received greater amounts of assistance faster than other communities. Communities where people trust the leadership and its ability to guide towards solutions are more resilient. Reliable information sources and open communication are also helpful in achieving positive outcomes because they allow dissemination of details about the event, and recommendations for addressing it. Specifically, people tend to trust familiar local sources of information more than they do an unfamiliar, distant one (Longstaff, 2005). However, there is no consensus as to how much information is effective for keeping people advised without evoking unnecessary panic.

That resources exist is not sufficient; not less important are the equity and effectiveness of their distribution, how well they fit what the affected community feels it needs, and whether they are offered in a way that the community values. Vulnerable and marginal groups of minorities, outcasts, and non-members are often discriminated against and excluded from the assistance process. Numerous relief workers share anecdotal tales of army and official forces kidnapping supplies meant for a suffering population in disaster areas rather than allowing it to reach their target recipients. One typical instance was the report by Mackey and Fisher (2010) about problems in distributing food in Haiti after the horrific 2010 earthquake, which killed an estimated quarter of a million people, cut the supply of food, clean water, communications, gas and medical aid, and caused the spread of disease, fires, and destruction. Similar reports accompany most catastrophic community events in all parts of the world.

No less crucial than tangible resources are strong social networks with emotional connections, a sense of bonding, belonging and shared activities, active local voluntary associations, stable local organizations, and pre-event stability (Adger, 2000; Breton, 2001; Zautra, Hall & Murray, 2008). Connections among people, groups, and organizations, and the ability to reach consensus regarding goals, priorities, and strategies have been conceptualized as social or human capital and focus on the ability for collaborative problem solving, willingness to work together (citizen participation), and commitment to invest in activities designed to address the challenges of the stressful event and its aftermath. For example, while no systematic research has been conducted, narratives of people whose neighborhood suffered serious damage from the 2011 Irene and the 2012 Sandy hurricanes in New York pointed repeatedly to help from neighbors with food, shelter, clothes, kitchen equipment, and encouragement as instrumental in their recovery.

Norris and colleagues (2008) analyzed the role of social capital in community trauma and concluded that while many believe that the more social capital is available, the more resilient is the community, the optimal amount of collaboration and cooperation is the happy medium. They posited that if ties and connections are too tight, the failure of one link may bring down the whole system, whereas if the ties are too loose, the system becomes fragmented. I witnessed the latter when I had an opportunity to learn about the activities of some not-for-profit welfare organizations in West Africa, where each individual organization appeared to do their own thing. The lack of coordination seemed to create overlap of services in some areas while needs in other areas were neglected and the use of resources ineffective.

Finally, cultural focus on the collective, i.e. the extended family and the community, and the existence of a community narrative of resilience prior to the stressful exposure are helpful (Kimhi & Shamai, 2004). Accordingly, Clauss-Ehlers and Lopez-Levi (2002) found in American Latinos and in Mexicans that community structures and cultural values of *familismo* (the centrality of family), *respeto* (treating others, especially those in authority status, older people, and men with dignity), and *personalismo* (partiality for close personal relationships) shaped reactions to stress.

Correlates of Community Outcomes

Like with individuals and families, the outcomes of a community trauma are shaped by prior characteristics of the community, the nature of the event, and its construction by the community. Community size, composition, degree of connectedness, and social cohesion, as well as access to resources, are major factors determining the response to stressor events. Smaller communities tend to have more cohesive social ties, which allow for faster and better coordinated response to stressor events, as was demonstrated following the December 2012 shooting in Newtown, Connecticut. Weaker social networks, limited access to resources by the affected community and the broad society within which it resides, and limited diversity of such resources and inequity in their distribution are associated with more negative effects on a community's post-trauma functioning (Norris et al., 2008). Thus, poor and challenged neighborhoods and developing countries with a limited menu of resources, which are not easily mobilized and unevenly distributed across various sub-groups, are more vulnerable to the negative effects of collective trauma. These characteristics compromise their ability to be ready for the event and recruit means for addressing an emergency situation when it occurs, and result in a slower recovery from the event's effects (Halpern & Tramontin, 2007; Norris et al., 2002). For example, when large numbers of community members are immigrants and lack proficiency in the dominant language, they may not have access to accurate and clear information about available resources such as crisis centers that provide food, shelter, and other types of help. Unfortunately, both within and across communities, rather than mobilizing and distributing support based on relative need, such that those most hurt receive most help, often those who are the neediest, less able, weaker, and lack political connections are in a worse position to raise awareness of the negative effects and receive help in a timely manner or at all.

The magnitude, proximity, and duration of the event and the scope of damage to community infrastructure are also predictors of the extent to which a community suffers negative consequences following the exposure. Kimhi and Shamai (2004) studied how residents in four communities in Northern Israel with different levels of exposure to political violence on the Lebanese border viewed their communities. Residents of communities close to the events and with the longest exposure rated their communities as weaker than those in more distant communities that experienced shorter exposure to the stressful events. While the findings reflect the subjective perception of those who lived the experience and thus may be contaminated by fears, anxieties, and personal projections, they support the intuitive assumption that the most intensive exposure begets the most extreme negative effects. Finally, the narrative that the community develops about the event, i.e. the way in which it interprets and gives meaning to the event, is similar to what Lazarus (1966) calls appraisal (Chapter 3) and Tedeschi and Calhoun (1996) describe as the new schema (Chapter 4). This collective meaning making and interpreting of the event also determines how bad its effects will be.

Part III

Understanding Stress and Trauma from Developmental and Cultural Perspectives

The struggle with highly stressful and potentially traumatic events is shaped by developmental aspects and cultural contexts. Clauss-Ehlers (2008) addressed the combination of these aspects to describe how socio-cultural aspects are related to the development of coping with adversities in children and youths. This part will discuss exposure to highly stressful events and their aftermath in various ages and population groups. It includes two chapters: Chapter 7 addresses developmental aspects of stress and trauma and Chapter 8 examines socio-cultural factors.

7 Developmental Perspectives

Stress, Trauma, and PTG Across
the Life Cycle

The tasks, priorities and functioning of people change over time and differ
in each stage of life. Thus, the exposure to stressful events, its aftermath, and
the ways that people address such exposure have different characteristics at
different ages according to challenges, vulnerabilities, and strengths typical of
each developmental stage. Such changes in stress and coping along the lifespan
depend on the combination of the personal trajectory of an individual from
pre-natal stressors in utero and throughout life, with socio-cultural and other
environmental changes during these years. This chapter reviews the effects of
age on the experience and outcomes of exposure to highly stressful events.
Specifically, it includes content about unique characteristics of traumatic experiences and their correlates in children, adolescents, and older adults.

Trauma in Children

There is more knowledge about the nature and effects of traumatic exposure
in children than any other age group. It has been extensively documented that
exposure to highly stressful events in early childhood may have considerable
short- and long-term negative effects and predisposes children to psychopathology because of the formative nature of these years, including critical development of the neural system, children's vulnerability and lack of the physical and
intellectual capacity to protect themselves, accurately perceive and understand
the event in its entirety, regulate their emotions, or develop appropriate coping
strategies (Chimienti, Abu Nasr & Khalifeh, 1989; Wexler, Branski & Kerem,
2006; Yahav, 2011). These effects can be caused by direct exposure or by the
reduced availability of adults responsible for their care to protect children and
address their needs. Especially devastating is exposure to traumatic experiences
caused by a caregiver, such as abuse and neglect by a parent or a guardian on
whom the child depends.

Recognizing the unique nature of traumatic reactions and outcomes in
children and the need to understand developmental aspects of trauma led to
the establishment of nationwide and regional organizations, networks, services, and research centers committed to raising public awareness of the scope
and impact of traumatic stress on children and adolescents, and promoting a

specific, developmentally informed, accessible continuum of care for traumatized children. It also led a team of experts to suggest that a distinct diagnosis of *developmental trauma disorder* be created for children who have grown up in the context of continuous danger, maltreatment, and dysfunctional caregiving systems (D'Andrea et al., 2012; van der Kolk & Pynoos, 2009). A field trial demonstrated that because childhood traumatic exposure often occurs in the context of numerous adverse experiences and has broad impact on the developing brain, childhood onset of trauma reaction differs considerably from reactions to exposure later in life. Thus, commonly used diagnostic techniques fail to capture accurately the full spectrum of the effects of adverse early life experiences, leaving these children under-diagnosed or misdiagnosed, which may eventually deprive them of access to effective services. The DSM-V (APA, 2013) offers a partial remedy by including PTSD in preschool children as a sub-type of PTSD with distress or intrusive memories where the child feels or acts as if the event is reoccurring or has dissociative symptoms, all of which may be expressed in play re-enactment. The future will show if this solution is sufficient. Children's reactions to trauma are both universal and age-specific.

Universal Reactions

A great diversity is evident in the ability of children who face traumatic events to appraise threat, seek help, express emotions, and employ strategies to regulate stress and cope (Punamäki, 2002). Traumatized children often lack the ability to properly organize, appraise, and process information (van der Kolk, 2003), and may regress to behaviors typical of earlier developmental stages, such as bed wetting after having been toilet trained. They may also appear to have coped well but later overreact to a seemingly minute and trivial situation.

Reactions may be manifested in affective, behavioral, cognitive, social, or physical domains. Typical *emotional* reactions include anxiety, fearfulness, phobias, irritability, sleep disturbances and nightmares, poor emotion regulation and impulse control, guilt, depressive symptoms and crying, and the loss of a sense of security, safety, and identity. Common *behavioral* manifestations are aggression towards others and self, temper tantrums and risky conduct, as well as rocking and self-comforting actions. Frequent *cognitive* symptoms are dissociation (not being there, "the world is unreal," "things are not really happening to me, they are happening to someone else"), loss of concentration, poor academic performance, cognitive distortion (e.g. believing that they did something to cause the event), and memory problems. *Social* reactions may include withdrawal from or clinginess to caregivers, and problematic peer relationships. *Physical* phenomena comprise of somatic complaints such as headaches, stomach aches and cramps, and vague pains, or nervous behaviors including hair twirling or pulling, chewing and sucking, and biting skin and fingernails (Alkhatib, Regan & Barrett, 2007; Klein et al., 2009; Little, Akin-Little & Somerville, 2011; Sagi-Schwartz, 2008; Wooding & Raphael, 2004; Yahav, 2011). In addition to the aforementioned symptoms, traumatic exposure may also disrupt children's development and cause failure to meet age-appropriate milestones.

While most negative effects of childhood exposure to trauma are temporary and short-lived, some studies suggest that traumatic experiences in childhood may have long-lasting effects on cognitive and emotional development, and some studies have suggested that exposure to severe adversity in childhood may lead to faster decline in functioning in old age (Shrira, 2012). Persisting adverse effects that may continue to be manifested later in life include difficulties with memory, integration of sensory experiences, and emotional regulation, dissociation, lack of the ability to develop interpersonal relationships, poor social functioning, lowered self-esteem, and psychopathology (Kaiser, Gillette & Spinazzola, 2010). Survivors may have difficulty reading social cues and speaking up for themselves, have few friends, and allow people to exploit or abuse them, or they may be overly demanding and controlling (Copeland et al., 2007; Kendall-Tackett, 2002; Yahav, 2011). Related possible symptoms include substance abuse, self-mutilation, obesity and eating disorders, high-risk sexual behavior, smoking, sleep disturbances, suicide, delinquency, and violent criminal behavior.

Comparable to adults, children may begin to manifest problems after a significant latent period (Wooding & Raphael, 2004). Maria was 12 years old when she was referred to the social worker in her middle school by her home class teacher, who noticed that she had changed from being a bubbly girl and an excellent student to being unhappy and disengaged. Her grades slipped and she barely participated in academic or social activities. Initially, the girl and her parents denied any problems and were reluctant to participate in any type of counseling. As she gradually began to trust the worker, who persistently tried to engage her, the girl started to share her recollections of the challenging journey from Mexico four years earlier. She reported nightmares of the starvation and threats to their life that the family endured crossing the desert and the river, and the airless and crowded truck that smuggled them into the US.

In addition to severe potential immediate and long-term negative reactions to trauma, children also have remarkable resilience (Kimhi et al., 2010). Sagi-Schwartz (2008) conducted a systematic review of published research and showed that traumatic exposure does not always affect negatively the well-being or functioning of children, and that most show impressive resilience.

Furthermore, though limited in scope, some studies have offered support to the idea that children may manifest PTG. For example, Kilmer and Gil-Rivas (2010) documented outcomes and abilities related to PTG in 7–10 year olds impacted by hurricane Katrina, and Cryder and colleagues (2006) found the same in children who experienced hurricane Floyd and the subsequent flooding. Qouta, Punamäki and El Sarraj (2008) reported PTG in pre-adolescent Palestinian children in Gaza who experienced political upheavals, war and violence, and Salter and Stallard (2004) recounted similar outcomes in children following road accidents. In a retrospective study, adults who in their childhood had a parent sick with cancer reported that the experience led them to appreciate life more and see new possibilities, and strengthened their inter-personal relationships, all of which are dimensions of PTG (Wong et al., 2009). A recent systematic review of 25 studies found that, like with adults, the subjective experience of distress, social support, religious involvement, and the nature of coping are associated with PTG, but it appeared that PTG in youth may decay faster than in adults (Meyerson et al., 2011). However, the few studies that found evidence for PTG in children leave much to be learned before we can safely draw conclusions regarding the existence, nature, pathway, and what supports or hinders PTG in children.

The aforementioned reactions of children to potentially traumatic events have been documented across diverse cultural contexts such as Israel, Lebanon, Sri Lanka, Kuwait, Afghanistan, Australia, Gaza and the west Bank, Uganda, and the US (Betancourt et al., 2009; Elbert et al., 2009; Espié et al., 2009; Hoven et al., 2009; Klein et al., 2009; Llabre & Hadi, 2009; Panter-Brick et al., 2009; Wexler, Branski & Kerem, 2006; Wooding & Raphael, 2004; Yahav, 2011). Comparative cross-cultural studies are rare. One effort to compare long-term effects of trauma exposure in two cultural contexts is currently in progress by Hoven and her colleagues (2009), who have been conducting a longitudinal bi-national study of children in New York public schools who experienced the 9/11 terrorist attacks and Israeli children exposed to consistent terrorist attacks. This study will take years to complete and findings are not yet available (Teichman, personal communication, May 2011).

In addition to characteristics and outcomes common to diverse types of exposure, children also manifest reactions unique to particular kinds of experience, specifically childhood traumatic grief (CTG). Mannarino and Cohen (2011) found that traumatic loss, such as the death of a close person in traumatic circumstances, combines grief and trauma and has distinctive features in children. Kuwaiti children manifested traumatic reactions after losing friends in a non-war-related bus crash but not following the Gulf War (Norris et al., 2002). Common reactions may include waves of intense sadness, crying, refusal to spend time with friends, difficulties in eating, sleeping, concentrating and performing academically, as well as failure to progress along the normal age-appropriate developmental path and maintain earlier patterns, behaviors, and emotional reactions. A major aspect unique to CTG is being stuck on the traumatic aspects of the death of a loved one, manifested by denial, over identification, self-blame and revenge or rescue fantasies, and difficulty processing the experience, achieving reconciliation and negotiating effective bereavement. Re-experiencing reactions to trauma or loss reminders and exaggerated avoidance may interfere with the child's ability to go through the normal bereavement process and appropriately mourn the loss.

The DSM-V (APA, 2013) includes two trauma-related disorders in children. *Reactive attachment disorder* is an internalizing disorder with depressive symptoms and emotionally withdrawn behaviors (e.g. the child rarely seeks and responds to comfort, support, nurturance, and protection from an attachment figure).

These children are often fearful, sad or irritated. *Disinhibited social engagement disorder* is marked by externalized undifferentiated and overly familiar behavior with relative strangers, and violating social boundaries without caution or hesitation. These children readily hug, kiss, and go with people whom they do not know.

Age-Specific Reactions

The effects of age on trauma exposure and its outcomes are many and complex as children understand the world differently at different ages (Beauchesne et al., 2002). In addition to reactions that exist in children of all ages, certain effects are more typical in certain developmental phases. Very young children who cannot express their reaction in words manifest it in their behavior (such as trying to stay away from or become agitated at the presence of an abusive adult), and effects may persist for a long time. They may lose their trust in adults and are at risk for developing an attachment disorder. Pre-school children may present regressive behaviors of clinging, bed-wetting, thumb sucking, baby talk, fears, and decreased verbalization. They may hide when they hear loud noises and act out their reaction in playing police officers, firefighters, and rescue workers, or building tall structures and repetitively destroying them. They may also be obsessively busy with organizing and reorganizing their toys, crayons, and other possessions in an effort to recreate order in their world. Feldman and Vengrober (2011) observed in children at the ages of 1.5–5 multiple posttraumatic symptoms and concluded that future development and adaptation was at significant risk. School-age children can figure out how events fit together and the meaning of loss but lack long-range perspective. They often believe that certain realities are their fault and may feel responsible and guilty ("it happened because I behaved/misbehaved in a certain way"). They are curious about and often become obsessed with details of the experience, including morbid ones, have difficulty concentrating and performing academically, present interpersonal problematic behaviors, and suffer from anxiety and depression. They may manifest repetitive play and retelling, refusal to go to school, exaggerated reactions to minute issues (such as extreme anxiety when a parent is ten minutes late), whining and crying, or fascination with monsters. Garbarino et al. (1998) documented such negative impact on children from consistently affected war zones as well as those who live in violent inner-city neighborhoods.

Correlates of Children's Reactions

While for most children the effects of exposure to highly stressful events decrease rapidly and eventually diminish, sometimes negative reactions persist, increase, or have a late onset. Because not all children report traumatizing experiences, symptoms may go unnoticed or be misunderstood, leading to failure to stop the traumatizing conditions. For example, if the environment does not realize that a child is being abused, symptoms may be misinterpreted, with no action taken to end the abuse and thus a vicious circle may occur of abuse-misunderstanding of responses–ineffective intervention–further abuse.

Outcomes are shaped by characteristics of the traumatic event, the child, the family, and broader caregiving systems. Children's outcomes are affected both directly by exposure to the event and indirectly by its impact on the systems that care for them, whose ability to protect and support the child may be compromised and further exacerbate the child's reaction. Factors that mold children's reactions are similar to those affecting reactions in adults. Children who were exposed directly, were closer to the event, faced a threat to life, lost a relative or a friend or knew somebody directly exposed, especially a family member, or whose caregivers were involved in the event being traumatic are likely to develop more severe problems than others (Furr et al., 2010; Hoven et al., 2009; Neria, Nandi & Galea, 2008; Panter-Brick et al., 2009; Wexler, Branski & Kerem, 2006; Yahav, 2011). Nevertheless, a longitudinal study of Australian children who were exposed to a 1983 wild bushfire, which caused numerous deaths and injuries, found a decrease over time in the effects of proximity and dose on outcomes (McFarlane & Van Hooff, 2009).

Exposure to multiple or frequent stressors as well as long-term family or community disruption creates cumulative effects and becomes a risk factor for emotional, behavioral, and psychological problems. Therefore, children exposed to chronic or early life stress, or those who live in poverty, violent neighborhoods or are being bullied in school might become more vulnerable to subsequent stress (Masten & Narayan, 2012; Wooding & Raphael, 2004; Yahav, 2011). Fazel and Stein (2003) found that refugee children in England who suffered prior atrocities in their home country, and then multiple losses and discriminations related to relocation, manifested more signs of distress than other children, including those from similar ethnic minority groups with no previous exposure. Similarly, Salloum and colleagues (2011) found that at the ages of 7–12, the probability of distress following hurricane Gustav was amplified in children who had experienced prior trauma during hurricane Katrina or community violence. Catani and colleagues (2010) documented more severe negative reactions in school-aged children in Sri Lanka who experienced the 2004 tsunami in combination with war or family violence than those who suffered the effects of the tsunami with no exacerbating community or familial circumstances. Sagi-Schwartz (2008) concluded his review of the literature on children's reactions to living in a chronic war zone by stating:

> Although acute danger might be very damaging, we still might observe responses that can be considered as *situationally adaptive* because of their short-lived duration. Chronic exposure to danger, however, may have more far-reaching and enduring implications for developmental adjustment, with possible alterations of personality, major changes in patterns of behavior or articulation for making sense of ongoing danger – all of which

lead to *negative* conclusions about the worthiness of the self, the reliability of adults and their institutions, and the most appropriate approaches to adopt to the world.

(p. 323).

I witnessed first-hand the effects of cumulative stresses on Israeli children who live in the town of Sderot, which is heavily populated by immigrants and suffered continuous shelling and bombing from neighboring Gaza. For a decade they spent numerous nights in crowded shelters and lost friends and relatives. Consequently, they are considerably more anxious and distressed than Israeli-born and immigrant children who live a relatively safe distance from the border.

Personal and familial correlates of the effects of trauma exposure include the child's general intelligence and cognitive flexibility, social and self-regulation skills, self-efficacy, agency and a sense of competence, and previous trauma exposure (Copeland et al., 2007; Hoven et al., 2009; Masten & Narayan, 2012; Wooding & Raphael, 2004; Yahav, 2011). In addition, there is increasing evidence but no conclusive findings that neurobiological characteristics shape stress responses in children.

The literature is inconclusive regarding effects of age and gender on children's reactions to stressful events. Studies have shown that children may be impacted even before they are born by trauma that their mothers experience. Thus, in New York, babies born to women who were close to the site of the 9/11 terrorist attack and suffered from traumatic reactions had a significant elevated risk for neurodevelopmental problems (Engel et al., 2005). Exposure in certain early critical developmental phases may compromise physical, emotional, intellectual, and moral development, leading children to become fixated in a specific developmental stage without continuing the normal trajectory. This may carry severe psychological distress and functional impairment, hindering the development of basic trust, and eventually leading to a chronic dissociative identity disorder, which is a risk factor for psychiatric hospitalization. Some (e.g. Punamäki, 2002) view young age as protective because young children cannot fully grasp the meaning of the event and its possible implications, whereas others believe that because they lack the cognitive abilities to process the experience properly, younger children are likely to be more vulnerable (Alkhatib, Regan & Barrett, 2007; Comer & Kendall, 2007). Kronenberg and colleagues (2010) found that younger children (ages 9–11) manifested symptoms of depression and posttraumatic stress more than did adolescents (ages 12–18) following hurricane Katrina.

The picture relative to gender is similar. Several studies suggest that girls manifest more symptoms of fear and posttraumatic stress than boys; some report more severe symptoms in boys, but others do not (Laufer & Solomon, 2009, 2010). Most studies found in girls more emotional problems of distress and anxiety whereas boys tended to exhibit more behavioral problems such as aggression (Chimienti & Abu Nasr, 1992; Kronenberg et al., 2010; Pine and Cohen, 2002; Ronen, Rahav & Rosenbaum, 2003). In part, inconsistencies in research findings may be related to methodological issues including measuring different outcomes and using different measures, as well as limited diversity of the age groups studied (Yahav, 2011), and the more complex ways in which gender may affect responses to adversity (Masten & Narayan, 2012).

Key to determining children's reactions to traumatic exposure is the reaction and coping of significant adults around them such as teachers, neighbors, and particularly parents and caregivers. Children learn to understand events and react to them by social referencing, i.e. in ambiguous situations they look to the parent to decide which emotions and actions are appropriate. Even very young children can read their parents' emotional reactions and shape their own responses according to it. Thus, a child who witnesses a parent reacting with fear to a dog in the street may become afraid of dogs. Specifically, studies agree that children's reactions to highly stressful events are shaped by parents' emotional availability, their ability to cope with the stress effectively and provide a sense of security, as well as the consistency of parenting and the quality of parent–child relationships (Comer & Kendall, 2007; Panter-Brick et al., 2009; Stuber et al., 2005; Yahav, 2011). "The buffering effect of proximity to parents and other attachment figures for children in the midst of terrifying experiences is one of the most enduring findings in the literature on war and other life-threatening disasters" (Masten & Narayan, 2012, p. 229). A repeated finding in studies is that symptoms are more closely related to separation from parents than any other factors and that children whose parents cope well with the stress are more likely to manifest less negative outcomes both short- and long-term. Slone, Shoshani and Paltieli (2009) studied the effects on Israeli settlers of forced evacuation from the Gaza Strip, which in some cases included forcible dragging from the home and violent clashes with evacuating forces. They reported that children were more resilient when they perceived their parents as emotionally available, communicating confidence and a sense of support and security.

However, if parents become over protective, the development of children may be inhibited. Working with children who experienced traumatic events, it was not unusual for me to encounter parents who limited their children's freedom to be involved in social activities that were previously permitted. Some parents insisted on accompanying their children to school, refused to allow their participation in sleepovers, and constantly inquired about every minute detail of the child's activities. Children typically responded with resentment, anger, and sometimes acting out. They felt ashamed of being "babied" in front their friends and rebelled against what they perceived as their parents' exaggerated concerns.

In agreement with this connection between parental, especially mothers', reactions to stress and their children's outcomes, parents also tended to report stress-related problems in their children more than teachers did (ElZein & Ammar, 2010), perhaps because they are more attuned to their children's reactions and project some of their own reactions onto their children. Children whose parents exhibit posttraumatic symptoms are more likely to develop negative reactions, and a correlation exists between PTSD in parent and the likelihood that their children develop the disorder (Wooding & Raphael, 2004). Furthermore, a child who is dependent on an abusive parent may learn to dissociate the experience from conscious awareness in order to maintain an attachment to that parent. Specific risk has been identified in children of first responders, including police officers, fire fighters, emergency medical team personnel (Hoven et al., 2009), and those from families with high pre-event vulnerability.

When both parent and child have been exposed to a traumatic event at the same time, the child needs the parent's help and support at a time when the parent is the least capable of providing them. For example, if a parent dies, the remaining parent, who has lost a spouse, is negatively affected and is the least equipped to help the child. Beauchesne et al. (2002) reported how parents who were shattered by 9/11 needed to comfort their children and help them to cope with a situation with which the parents themselves had difficulty coping. This may lead caregivers to feel guilt and shame because of their inability to care for their traumatized child. Consequently a sense of helplessness and inadequacy as well as anger may develop, further limiting the caregiver's efficiency.

Whereas parents' stress reactions may increase the risk of distress in their children, a supportive family environment may contribute to a better adjustment. Effective family functioning and parenting practices provide a protective environment, while a family environment with disorganization, domestic violence, parental conflict, parental substance abuse, criminality, or divorce or separation contributes to negative trauma reactions in children (Gewirtz, Forgatch & Wieling, 2008). Particularly important in determining the effects of trauma on children is the availability of positive relationships (Luthar, Sawyer & Brown, 2006). Secure attachment relationships can serve as a buffer to the negative effects of a stressful event (Wooding & Raphael, 2004). Social support from family and the community can moderate children's reactions in the aftermath of a highly stressful event, and help enhance their sense of self-efficacy and of some degree of control (Sagi-Schwartz, 2008; Williams, 2007; Wexler, Branski & Kerem, 2006). In addition to familial support, children's outcomes following an encounter with a potentially traumatic event are safe schools and community organization, which help re-establish routines in a child's life both directly by providing guidance, supportive adults and peers, and indirectly by providing to parents respite, thus allowing them to regain their own ability to support their children.

In summary, early reviews of research on trauma exposure in children reveal a mixed picture of continuing vulnerability and resilience. While the effects of such exposure are typically temporary, they could be long-lasting in some children; the loss and injury of family and friends has greater effects than material losses, and parents' availability, level of functioning, and support significantly shaped the outcomes of the exposure for children (Garmezy & Rutter, 1983). Many of these conclusions are still valid. Trickey and colleagues (2012) analyzed what we know about 25 risk factors for PTSD in children and adolescents aged 6–18 years, across 64 studies published between 1980 and 2009. Their analysis suggests that the availability of social support, amount of fear, perceived life threat, social withdrawal, and comorbid psychological problems, as well as poor family functioning, trauma symptoms immediately following the exposure, and thought suppression had the maximum effects on the likelihood for developing PTSD. Meanwhile, personal features (gender, intelligence, pre-exposure psychological issues), family characteristics (socio-economic status, parents' psychological issues), and event variables (time since the exposure, severity, exposure to the event by media) had some effects, whereas race and younger age had limited impact. In a recent comprehensive review of the theoretical and empirical literature on the effects of mass trauma on children, Masten and Narayan (2012) concluded that "younger children exhibit acute symptoms of distress or trauma, especially when they are separated from parents, when their parents have intense reactions, or when they are exposed to intense media reports" (pp. 240–241). They also reported that, in addition to traditionally documented linear association between traumatic experiences and outcomes for children, some non-linear association may exist as well, such that "adaptive behavior declines as adversity exposure rises and then at extreme levels begins to rise again" (p. 237).

Possible outcomes for children have been summarized by Sagi-Schwartz (2008) in the aforementioned review of the literature. He concluded that

> despite the debilitating effects of exposure to chronic political violence and traumas, various protective factors have been described. Some children and youth seem to be resilient even when exposed to adversities, and it is proposed that the majority is able to cope effectively with the after effects of their trauma exposure, especially when supported by the family and by other facilitative factors in the community. Children in war zones who are competently cared for by their own parents or familiar adults were reported to suffer far fewer negative effects than those without such support. Moreover, the community (e.g. schools, community centers, various religious activities) can be conceived as a safe haven, especially when there are opportunities for interaction with people and environments that are positive for development.
>
> (p. 334)

Trauma in Adolescents

Adolescents are particularly susceptible to traumatic exposure because they are prone to experimenting with risky behaviors and pushing the limits. They have a better understanding of the stressful event and its potential outcomes and thus often feel more realistic fears and manifest more adult-like responses, while refusing to share these feelings with adults (Pine & Cohen, 2002). Although they are better able to articulate distress and utilize cognitive responses to process their experience, they are also more responsive to stressors and slower than other age groups to let go of the stress reaction (Pattwell et al., 2012). Furthermore, their trauma reactions may interact with age-related developmental stress and their sudden helplessness in the face of a traumatic exposure may conflict with the age-appropriate struggle for autonomy. Reactions may include premature closure of identity formation and entering the adult world, or a dissociative identity disorder at the extreme. They may manifest indifference, hypervigilance, and extensive following of media coverage of the event. Some talk about joining the military and seeking revenge and others may be looking for ways to help. Common symptoms reported in several studies include depression, anxiety and being constantly on alert, somatization and physical complaints (especially headaches and stomachaches), emotional withdrawal, apathy (e.g. neglect of appearance and grooming), negative coping and loss of hope manifested in involvement in risky behaviors such as substance abuse and sexual promiscuity, eating, sleep, concentration and relationship problems, behavior problems, uncontrollable anger, and tantrums (ElZein & Ammar, 2010; Pine & Cohen, 2002; Swick et al., 2002; Wooding & Raphael, 2004). They also may lose trust in the adult world and develop an apathetic or angry rejection of authority, act out, join violent groups or gangs, feel worthless and hopeless ("I am going to die young"), refuse to go to school, or see their grades drop suddenly (de Jong, 2002; Sagi-Schwartz, 2008; Williams, 2007). Because adolescents experience highly stressful events as they are developing their identity, such exposure may lead to lifelong behavioral and emotional problems (Swick et al., 2002).

An article about a 16-year-old survivor of the 1999 Columbine high school massacre provided the following description: "'I experienced nightmares all night, every night . . . I wanted to be around people, but I didn't want people around me . . .' She found herself searching for exits and formulating an escape plan every time she entered a room. A friend followed her around with a box of Girl Scout cookies to make sure she ate something" (Quenqua, 2012). However, like with children, most adolescents are resilient, and while some may remain with emotional scars, the vast majority recover and go on to develop and lead normal lives. The aftermath of adolescents' trauma exposure depends on a variety of personal and environmental correlates.

Correlates of Adolescents' Reactions

The best predictors of adolescents' reactions to traumatic exposure are the level of exposure, the presence of pre-exposure psychological problems, and disruption in social support networks (Pine & Cohen, 2002). Like with other age groups, higher exposure is associated with higher levels of PTSD symptoms (Bokszczanin, 2008). However, 15 months after 9/11, very little effects related to exposure were observed on adolescents' mental health, suggesting that in spite of high initial exposure, recovery may have already occurred in many cases (Gershoff et al., 2010). Emotionality, natural resilience, faith, and religion were significant in determining adolescents' reactions to stress

(Masten & Narayan, 2012). Consistent with rumination as a pathway to benefits from struggling with a highly stressful event, according to the PTG model, positive outcomes were enhanced by rumination in adolescents exposed to the adversities of hurricane Katrina (Kilmer & Gil-Rivas, 2010).

The literature provides extensive compelling evidence that adolescent girls report more posttraumatic symptoms than boys, and when no differences in frequency of reports existed, the manifestations were different, with girls showing more anxiety, guilt and mood symptoms whereas boys exhibited more worry, externalized behavior problems, and concentration and academic difficulties (e.g. Godeau et al., 2005; Kronenberg et al., 2010). However, it is difficult to know to what extent these differences are affected by cultural norms that discourage the manifestation of certain symptoms ("boys don't cry").

Although adolescents depend on their parents less than younger children, parental reactions and symptomatology, love, care, and attention, and the quality of adolescent–parent relationships moderate youths' PTSD and depression symptoms following a traumatic exposure. In a study of 325 adolescents aged 12–19 and their mothers in two Sri Lanka villages after the 2004 tsunami, Wickrama and Kaspar (2007) found that mothers' mental health and the parent–adolescent relationships were critical in determining the effects of the traumatic exposure on adolescents' mental health. The researchers concluded that positive mother–child relationships have a compensatory role and serve as a protective mechanism. In addition to shaping negative reactions, parental functioning affects also adolescents' resilience. Parents' self-reported PTG was a significant predictor of a growth reaction in adolescent after the 2004 tsunami in Thailand (Hafstad et al., 2010).

While parental coping and support as well as level of family conflict were important in shaping adolescents' outcomes, studies also found that parental over involvement, over control and infantilization of adolescents for a long time after the exposure may present a potential obstacle for recovery and be associated with negative outcomes (e.g. Bokszczanin, 2008; Bonanno et al., 2010; Masten & Narayan, 2012). Such parental reactions may conflict with the age-related developmental task of achieving autonomy and thus interfere with the adolescent's ability to bounce back from the traumatic exposure and continue the developmental journey towards maturity.

Outcomes of trauma exposure for adolescents are also affected by immigration status and its related challenges, such as level of language proficiency. Immigration in general and refugee status in particular are challenging for adolescents because the combination of developmental and cultural transition-related tasks, which mutually exacerbate each other, places them at an intersection of multiple risks (Berger, 2008). They experience immigration-related losses, social, economic, and cultural insecurity, and numerous changes in all aspects of their lives, often following pre-immigration experiences of war, natural disaster, torture, oppression, and persecution. At the same time, immigrant adolescents also struggle with age-related physical, cognitive, emotional, and social changes, and new roles, responsibilities, and expectations within

an unfamiliar social and cultural context. Many also experience marginalization and discrimination because of their minority status. This combination of
stressors makes adolescent immigrants a particularly vulnerable population
group, potentially leading to mental health problems of anxiety, identity crisis, decreased self-esteem, insecurity, frustration, anger, loneliness, and depression. Because their parents may also struggle with their own immigration
challenges and their natural support systems have been lost to immigration,
these youths often have few sources for help. Nevertheless, research and clinical
experience show that immigrant and refugee adolescents from diverse cultural
backgrounds and with various relocation experiences also manifest resilience
(Berger, 2008; Suárez-Orozco, Hee Jin & Ha Yeon, 2011).

Trauma in Older Adults

With few exceptions, trauma in older adults has received little attention and
knowledge is sparse, although both trauma and posttraumatic stress are frequent and significant problems in this growing population group. Recently, as
veterans in the US have been aging, knowledge about the aftermath of trauma
in the later phases of life began to emerge and the *American Journal of Geriatric Psychiatry* dedicated its May 2012 issue to lifelong prevalence, comorbidity,
trauma, stress, and resilience in those who are 60 and older.

Like adolescents, older adults are at the intersection of stressors presented
by the age-related reality of losing loved ones and friends, retirement, and failing health combined with lifelong accumulated stress and traumatic events.
This combination positions them at risk for biological changes that may accel-
erate the aging process, physical and cognitive decline, and chronic mental
impairment, and cause substantial negative reactions and decreased functioning. This is especially true for those who were previously exposed to stress
and are therefore at a greater risk for reporting high and increasing levels of
depressive symptoms and low levels of quality of life, thus potentially render-
ing them more susceptible to other physical and mental disorders and suicidality (Shrira, 2012).

There is not yet a clear picture of the relationships among traumatic reactions and age-related conditions. On one hand, because adverse events generally tend to co-occur and their combined impact is greater than that of a
single event, cumulative life stressors may lead to the decline of brain regions
that control emotional inhibition and regulation, intensify emotional memories, dismantle adaptive coping mechanisms, and shape how people handle
additional stressor events. However, old-age related neurological changes (e.g.
dementia) may also fog emotional memories and thus alleviate posttraumatic
stress (Shmotkin, Shrira & Palgi, 2011). Findings of studies have been inconsistent. For example, more somatic PTSD symptoms were reported in senior
than younger veterans (Owens et al., 2005), more veterans were diagnosed with
late age-related diseases like Alzheimer's, and more chronic hospitalizations
occurred in Holocaust survivors with dementia (Shmotkin, Shrira & Palgi,

2011); however, older respondents (age 70 and older) reported fewer trauma-related reactions than did younger individuals in response to similar intensity of exposure to missile attacks (Cohen, 2008) and other stressors (Creamer & Parslow, 2008; Pietrzak et al., 2012). Experts offered several explanations for these results. First, that conceivably many older adults had more opportunities to develop effective ways of coping and enough time to recover since they were exposed to the traumatic event; second, that older people may be less likely to remember past trauma or may perceive past events as less traumatic; finally, that feebler traumatized older adults are more likely to die at a younger age and thus those who are old and well enough to participate in studies are a select group with a disproportionate number of resilient individuals with unique bio-psychosocial characteristics.

Concurrent with trauma reactions, studies have also shown that a large portion of older persons, including those who endured trauma in early life, demonstrate resilience and posttraumatic growth following an encounter with adversity, and that some psychosocial resources may be maintained or even augmented if they are meaningful for the individual. Such resources can buffer traumatic effects and allow growth. Dobrof (2002) interpreted resilience of seniors after the 9/11 terrorist attacks as evidence of their inoculation by previous stress exposure including wars, the Depression, terrorism, and the Nazi concentration camps. The Swedish sociologist Lars Tornstam (2011) documented positive transformation of self-definition, interpersonal relationships, and connecting to the world in response to challenges presented by the realities of old age and coined the concept *gerotranscendence* to describe them. He posits that challenges that people face as they age can trigger a process of deconstruction and reconstruction of reality, which may generate positive changes in defining the self, relating to others, and connecting to the universe, and achieve improved life satisfaction.

Characteristics and Correlates of Trauma Reaction in Older Adults

Older adults may manifest negative reactions to a recent stressor, a chronic, continuing, lifelong response to traumatic exposure earlier in life, or re-emergence of trauma memories related to previous experiences (remote PTSD) that left them more susceptible to subsequent adversity. Furthermore, age-related reductions in attention and the increased tendency to reminisce may augment the likelihood that distressing memories intrude into the person's consciousness. Thus, reports exist of individuals who began to manifest posttraumatic symptoms later in life, after having lived symptom-free for decades, although some claim that actually the traumatic reaction was present all along but remained undiagnosed (Hiskey, 2012). Lingering trauma reaction may disrupt the ability of older individuals to manage their life narrative as well as triggering a range of other problems such as phobias, adjustment and dissociative disorders, enduring personality change, and psychosis (Hiskey, 2012; Shmotkin, Shrira & Palgi, 2011) but findings are inconclusive.

A summary of what is known about PTSD in older adults (Lapp, Agbokou & Ferreri, 2011) shows that manifestations of the disorder in this population group include significant impairment in daily life, decreased satisfaction, receiving lower-level care, and feeling older than their objective age, all of which are associated with more health problems including heart disease, depression, and anxiety. Because changes in the levels of stress hormone and in brain structures and some symptoms of PTSD such as difficulties in attention and memory are similar to those of normal aging, they may be exacerbated when older adults are traumatized and the task of differentiating which symptoms are trauma induced and which are age-related becomes challenging.

While correlates of trauma reactions in older age are similar to those in other adults (the nature of the traumatic event, life circumstances such as homelessness, coping strategies used), some unique aspects have emerged. For example, gender-based differences decrease when people age (Hiskey, 2012), and the social context and meaning of the stressor event are significant in determining outcomes (Shmotkin & Litwin, 2009). Correlates of resilience include high social capital as manifested in quality of relationships with family and friends, social support, social integration with the community, and the use of solution-focused rather than avoidant coping (Hildon et al., 2010). In addition, resilience in older adults has been explained by using their experience and lessons learned throughout life to prepare for predictable losses and other difficult events as well as the tendency to de-emphasize negative experiences and selectively optimize positive experiences (Shrira, 2012). Thus, older adults with previous trauma may view later stressors as less threatening as they have developed a hierarchy of suffering ("this is nothing compared with what I have already endured").

8   Cultural Aspects

Culture shapes the experience of trauma and thus plays a major role in understanding and addressing it. Race, ethnicity, sexual orientation, religion, and additional cultural affiliations serve as lenses through which people perceive, conceptualize, interpret, make meaning of, and respond to stressor events, as well as seek and use help. Historically, cultural and traumatic aspects of human experiences have been addressed separately. However, the growing recognition of the importance of interpreting traumatic experiences within cultural contexts led to the establishment of the specialty of cultural psychiatry in 1969, the dedication of the December 2010 special issue of the journal *Traumatology* to culture and trauma, and the updating of the DSM regarding cultural aspects of trauma. DSM-V (APA, 2013) addresses three issues regarding the effects of culture on trauma-related mental health: *cultural syndrome*, i.e. the cluster of co-occurring patterns of distress found in specific cultural groups; *cultural idioms*, i.e. how the disorder and its manifestations are conceptualized in various cultural contexts; and *cultural explanation* of its etiology. Accordingly, DSM-V includes detailed structured information about cultural concepts of distress, criteria for cross-cultural variations in symptom presentations, and a clinical interview tool to help assess cultural factors in clients' perspectives of their symptoms and treatment options. In spite of recognition of the importance of culture, development of culture-specific models for the assessment and treatment of trauma has been recent and slow, and most studies examine trauma effects within specific cultural contexts while comparisons of traumatic exposure and its aftermath in individuals from diverse backgrounds are scarce.

Cultural context affects which stressful life events are likely to befall people, standards of normality and the understanding of the nature, etiology, causes, onset, course, and outcomes of trauma reactions, acceptable ways of seeking help, treatment alternatives, suitable providers, and consequences of coping strategies (Marsella, 2010).

Cultural Aspects of Nature, Etiology, Manifestations, and Negative Outcomes

Some traumatic exposures are more predictable in certain groups. Inner city residents are more likely to encounter community violence, while gay youth are more prone to being bullied. A group of researchers from medical schools and organizations nationwide (Harris et al., 2010) found that data about the frequency of traumatic experiences in various cultures were inconsistent and estimates of the prevalence vary by cultural context. In a large Australian study (Creamer, Burgess & McFarlane, 2001) prevalence of PTSD was 1.33 percent, which is significantly lower than the estimates of about 4 percent (after one year) to 9 percent (lifelong) typically reported in North American studies such as the seminal large survey conducted by Kessler and colleagues (1995). Nevertheless, a comparison of the American and Australian studies showed similarities in rank ordering of the degree of traumatic experience associated with various stressor events in the two cultures. However, these two cultural contexts are similar in their western value orientation and emphasis on individualism, self-reliance, personal freedom, and independence, although Australia is a more secular society (Shakespeare-Finch & Morris, 2010). Such similarities would not necessarily be true in more traditional environments.

Types of traumatic exposure are also culturally related. Traumatic reactions following child maltreatment were identified more frequently in African Americans and Hispanics, whereas war-related trauma was more common in Asian Americans, African American men, and Hispanic women. PTSD was diagnosed in African Americans more frequently than in other groups, which may be caused by minority status, experiencing racism, living more often in less safe neighborhoods, and limited access to mental health care (Roberts et al., 2011).

Explanations of etiology of trauma also differ culturally. Latino cultures explain trauma as loss of the soul (*susto*), fright or terror sickness (*espanto*) caused by bad spirits, luck (*suerte*), the evil eye (*mal de ojo*) or enemies' curses (*maldiciones*), and traumatic reactions are viewed as related to vulnerability to stress (*nervios*). Cambodians view symptoms as *khyal* attacks whereas in the Ethiopian culture emotional issues, including trauma reactions, are considered an incurable sign of craziness or character weakness, associated with madness and violence from supernatural origins such as spirit possession. Some Ultra Orthodox Jewish communities tend to explain mental health issues in social-religious rather than psychological or medical terms (Pirutinsky, Rosmarin & Pargament, 2009).

People from diverse cultures manifest diverse trauma reactions. For example, outcomes of exposure to missile attacks differ between Israeli Arabs and Jews (Yahav & Cohen, 2007), Holocaust survivors manifest the concentration camp (KZ) syndrome unique to former prisoners of the Nazis (Ryn, 1990), and children displaced by war in Northern Uganda present culturally distinct distress symptoms (Betancourt et al., 2009). Eight months after the 9/11 terrorist attacks, Thiel de Bocanegra and Brickman (2004) found in China Town in Manhattan, which is close to the attack site, a relatively high rate of PTSD symptoms in general (21 percent), and of intrusive symptoms in particular (92 percent). Marsella, Friedman and Spain (1996) reported that African Americans and Latinos manifested more posttraumatic stress symptoms and fewer intrusive symptoms than other groups, and that Latinos experienced more intrusive symptoms and fewer arousal symptoms than African Americans. The researchers interpreted these differences as evidence that intrusive symptoms are a universal response to trauma whereas avoidance, numbing, and hypervigilance may be culturally dependent.

Some cultures accept physical symptoms of pain and feeling lightheaded, unfocused, and dizzy but not psychosocial trauma symptoms, as documented in Latinos (Joyce & Berger, 2007), Cambodian Killing Fields survivors (Uehara, Morelli & Abe-Kim, 2001), Vietnamese (Cardeña & Nijenhuis, 2000), Georgians in the Caucusus (Makhashvili, Tsiskarishvili & Droždek, 2010), and other non-western cultures. Behaviors considered abnormal by DSM criteria were viewed as normative by Bosnian Muslims (Weine et al., 1995). Western-trained professionals interpreted somatic symptoms as indicating psychopathology in Cambodian survivors of the Killing Fields, but the survivors viewed them as "authentic embodied pain" (Uehara, Morelli & Abe-Kim, 2001).

Cultural norms and taboos regarding treatment and providers also vary. In most traditional cultures, turning to God for help is a dominant norm. In cultures receptive to seeking help, there is often preference for folk healers, who are viewed as having greater power than mental health professionals, although sometimes such help is used in combination with modern professional services (Berger & Weiss, 2010). Following the ethnic war in Sri Lanka in the 1990s, survivors sought help from medical providers of general health services or traditional healers for somatic complaints rather than psychological traumatization (Somasundaram, 2004). While talking about traumatic experiences is the core of certain types of western therapies that emphasize disclosure and discussing of traumatic events as part of the healing process, some cultures discourage such conversations as inappropriate. Few words exist in the Amharic language to describe emotional issues, which are treated as a black box that should not be discussed, and people refrain from seeking treatment for them. In Israel until the late 1970s, expressions of fear and anxiety in response to war and terror were unacceptable, and trauma-related diagnoses were sparsely ascribed and highly stigmatized; however, in recent decades an open conversation about such reactions and a more accepting public atmosphere exist.

The absence of well-developed culturally sensitive models for understanding trauma and its aftermath in non-western and non-white populations raises questions about the accuracy of available research. Some differences in findings may be due in part to the fact that early models of stress and trauma had a Eurocentric emphasis and heterosexual two-parent bias (McCubbin, Thompson & McCubbin, 1996), potentially compromising the ability to recognize, understand, and address trauma-related issues from an inclusive perspective. Many of the studies have been conducted by western researchers, employing methods based on western assumptions, conceptualizations, norms, and criteria that are not culturally informed and pathologize indigenous reactions and behaviors considered normal and healthy within their cultural context. For example, some mourning practices in certain Jewish Moroccan communities and Latin cultures may be viewed as hysterical when observed through a western lens.

In the 1990s preliminary efforts began to address the hegemony of Euro-American approaches to trauma and studies began to focus on the nature and meaning of trauma through a culture-sensitive lens. As this book goes to press, such efforts are still limited and focus on a few communities such as Native Americans or ethnic enclaves within western environments, although some researchers have also examined the process of healing from trauma through local and traditional methods in Mozambique and South Africa (Hill, Lau & Sue, 2010). However, much of the knowledge about traumatic exposure, means and principles for assessing its effects, and strategies for addressing them remains insensitive to ethno-cultural variations and the field is dominated by what Marsella (2010) conceptualized as the "tyranny of Western expertise" (i.e. assumptions about the universality of understanding trauma and attending to its aftermath).

Cultural Aspects of Resilience and PTG

Culture and diversity have an important role in the development of resilience. Coll and Lamberty (1996) and Clauss-Ehlers (2008) described cultural background, traditions, legacies, and values as critical to successfully negotiating stressful situations because they shape the nature and process of coping and resilience in individuals of diverse socio-cultural and racial/ethnic backgrounds. In a book about PTG around the globe (Weiss & Berger, 2010), authors from a dozen diverse cultures including Japanese, German, Israeli, Australian, Chinese, the Spanish speaking world, Turkish, Palestinian, Kosovar, and Dutch discussed the meaning of stress, crisis and growth in their respective cultures, and reviewed research conducted in theses cultures about resilience. A cross-cases analysis revealed that PTG is a universal phenomenon, which was reported by researchers and practitioners in all the cultures and subcultures that were examined; however, its specific nature, dimensions, manifestations, and correlates have unique culture-specific characteristics. Thus, what constitutes resilience in traditional societies such as Latino and Bosnian culture differs from its meaning, manifestations and correlates in modern, individualistic societies such as Australia and Germany (Weiss & Berger, 2010).

Cultural Aspects of Help-Seeking Behavior and Service Utilization

Cultures vary in what is viewed as acceptable help and who is viewed as a suitable help provider. Racial and ethnic minorities are less likely to seek treatment for issues associated with traumatic exposure because of the stigma attached to mental health, limited access to services, and perception of providers as lacking sensitivity and being biased (Roberts et al., 2011). When they do seek help, these groups often prefer to turn to family members, religious leaders, traditional healers, and folk medicine rather than psychiatrists, psychologists, and social workers. Because of the cultural aspects of trauma, effective interventions cannot be universal. Rather, trauma practice must be culturally enlightened, taking into consideration race, religiosity/spirituality, sexual orientation, and class in understanding nuances of stress reaction; use concepts that do not pathologize culture-specific ways of trauma manifestation and coping; and offer services congruent with the recipients' ethno-cultural contexts by employing models that are compatible with their norms (Betancourt et al., 2009; Joyce & Berger, 2007; Dubow, Huesmann & Boxer, 2009; Weiss & Berger, 2010). Projects that focus on translating intervention strategies commonly used in the western world (depicted in Chapters 9–11) to other cultural contexts demonstrate that such transfer is effective when the original ideas and models are filtered through the cultural lens of the implementation society, and integrate local traditions and people in planning and executing the intervention (Saltzman et al., 2003). Culturally competent trauma practice can mitigate risk factors for the disorder, and prove effective with people who traditionally might not seek treatment.

One strategy for enhancing service utilization by people from diverse cultural backgrounds is the development and delivery of services in collaboration with indigenous experts such as shamans and traditional healers, as well as religious and spiritual leaders, to whom people affected by traumatic exposure typically turn for help. Such collaboration can help achieve two major goals. First, it capitalizes on natural mental health providers to adapt modern services to the indigenous setting and enhance tailoring interventions to become compatible with the characteristics and norms of service recipients. Second, because they are developed jointly with local leaders, helpers and services enjoy a legitimate status, potentially reducing non-compliance and dropout. For example, a study of mental health services in sub-Saharan Africa and in Aboriginal communities in Canada (Alem, Jacobsson & Hanlon, 2008; Zahradnik et al., 2009) documented the importance of collaboration between modern medicine and traditional healers who are trusted by the community. My own practice experience taught me that such collaboration is fruitful when I provided services to an Ultra Orthodox Jewish community in Israel and often teamed with the particular rabbi whose moral authority the client respected to plan and implement interventions. Those services that received the blessing of the rabbi became popular and utilization rates increased.

Part IV

Addressing the Outcomes of Stress and Traumatic Exposure

Understanding the possible effects of highly stressful events in their cultural contexts and across the life cycle provides a basis for the development of interventions to address these effects on the life of individuals, couples, families, and communities. Such interventions are designed to enhance healing, prevent negative outcomes, and foster PTG, though the emphasis varies in diverse approaches. *Healing* seeks to help people calm down extreme emotions in the first phase and normalize their reactions (i.e. help them to understand that their reactions are common and they are not weak or "going crazy"), followed by gradually helping them get their life back, regain a sense of safety, efficacy, control, connectedness and hope, and restore their viable beliefs about themselves and the world. *Prevention* seeks to anticipate future issues and enhance coping with additional exposure; however, Wittouck, van Autreve & De Jaegere (2011) found that in cases of complicated grief, preventive interventions are less effective than those meant to heal. *Fostering PTG* helps gain benefits from the struggle. In recent years the focus in treating trauma-related problems has been changing. As more interventions have become available and shown to be effective, the emphasis of trauma treatment has shifted from symptom management and reducing of suffering to recovery-oriented treatment and seeking cure.

To be effective, services need to be accessible, easy to negotiate, well coordinated, evidence-based, culturally relevant, and informed by relevant historical, social, economic, and political contexts (National Institute of Mental Health, 2002). To understand, assess, and treat trauma, systems of care must be aware of histories of abuse, domestic violence, terrorism, life-threatening disease or combat, racism, sexism, and classism because socio-political factors intersect with interpersonal experiences to shape trauma reactions, especially among the working class, women, people of color, LGBTQ, immigrants, those with disability, and other oppressed groups (Quiros & Berger, 2013). It is critical to understand how people explain traumatic situations and their beliefs about them and to tailor interventions to help individuals, families, and communities that agree with these views and which interweave local folklore knowledge passed through generations in the development of interventions. Thus, many of the western strategies to address the aftermath of trauma include some component of verbal processing of the experience and its emotional effects. However, the relevance of such strategies is quite limited in cultures where expression of emotion is considered rude and speaking about the dead is taboo as it is believed to create negative energy and bring about bad consequences. Similarly, for many years in Israel, mental health professionals were discouraged from processing the "Pandora Box" of Holocaust experience with survivors as such interventions contradicted the future-oriented culture of the developing nation state.

Interventions to address the aftermath of traumatic events may be offered on individual, family and community levels. Following recent wars and natural and human-made disasters across the globe, numerous guidelines and protocols for the management of psychosocial effects of traumatic exposure have been published (e.g. Kearns et al., 2012). While treatment of individuals has been supported by research, interventions with systems of families and communities are mostly based on consensus among experts as research of effective systemic treatments is scarce. The next three chapters address interventions with individuals (Chapter 9), couples and families (Chapter 10), and communities (Chapter 11) affected by trauma.

9 Helping Individuals Affected by Highly Stressful Events

Prior to planning and implementing the most appropriate treatment it is crucial to conduct a full assessment of trauma history within a culturally informed framework, taking into consideration the recipient's beliefs in relation to their culture of care. Failure to assess traumatic experiences via the proper cultural lens and within individual contexts may lead to over-diagnosis, under-diagnosis, and/or misdiagnosis (Joyce & Berger, 2007), and pathologizing of behaviors that were originally used for coping with trauma exposure (such as the use of drugs).

Irrespective of the specific intervention, major components in helping individuals affected by traumatic exposure are safety and stabilizing, processing of the trauma, and reconnection and integration. Most approaches include providing accurate relevant information, guidance in problem solving, developing ways for escape, and battling helplessness. As evident from their definitions (Chapter 1), crisis and trauma are two separate though related entities with similar components. The same is true for the interventions designed to address them, of which the most common ones are crisis intervention and trauma treatment. Crisis intervention is time-limited and focuses on immediacy and short duration, where assessment is performed and resources mobilized as quickly as possible to offer rapid access to help during the active state of crisis (Rapoport, 1962). Crisis intervention may become the only action needed to allow those exposed to continue to recuperate on their own and regain independent functioning, or it may become the first step in trauma treatment, which can last from a few weeks to many years. Disaster management models adopt a similar three-stage approach of acute support typically provided within the first week, intermediate support (after a month), and ongoing treatment.

Crisis Intervention

As noted, not all encounters with highly stressful events lead to traumatic reactions. Often, a short and immediate intervention, which focuses on addressing the most pressing needs, is sufficient to reduce the acute stress and help people to restore their ability to function effectively and resolve the crisis. Most existing guidelines recommend that delivery of Early Psychological Intervention

(EPI), sometimes called defusing, follows three basic principles of proximity, immediacy, and expectancy. While variations exist, emphasis is typically on an active, time-limited, goal-focused, and directive process to help people mobilize resources as soon as possible and recruit their inner strength to address the imminent situation.

Roberts (2002) developed one of the most widespread approaches to crisis intervention, which incorporates elements characteristic of most models. Its acronym, ACT, stands for Assessment, Crisis, and Trauma treatment. The Assessment of the situation and those affected must be conducted prior to any intervention. While the nature of the assessment may vary by the circumstances and the approach, in most models, it includes two phases: *triage*, i.e. identifying those in imminent danger with the most urgent needs and ranking priorities, and *evaluation* of those affected and their environment in terms of danger and safety, stress level, trauma reactions, availability of resources and support, history of coping with prior crisis situations, and cultural context. The Crisis aspect of the model refers to connecting to relevant resources and providing for immediate needs by exploration of alternative courses of action, developing an action plan, and following up. The Treatment component includes the interventions discussed below in the section on trauma treatment.

Roberts' (2002) model includes seven stages, which in different combinations and variations exist in all models of crisis intervention: rapid assessment, establishing rapport and helping relationships, identifying major problems, addressing emotions, generation and exploration of alternative plans of action, developing an action plan and mobilization of resources, and follow-up. In the development of an action plan, it is beneficial to adopt a collaborative approach with the recipient, to the degree that the person is amenable to it, and to focus on strengths and possibilities rather than on pathologies, without minimizing and making vague positive statements ("everything will be fine"). Practitioners providing crisis intervention should be non-intrusive and compassionate, have no assumptions regarding the experience, and carefully seek and follow cues from the survivor as to the direction and pace that the interaction should take.

Hobfoll and colleagues (2007b) built on the principles of crisis intervention and developed Psychological First Aid (PFA). They identified five broad core elements: 1) promoting a sense of safety, 2) calming and reducing distress, 3) connectedness, 4) fostering adaptive coping and a sense of self and community efficacy, 5) enhancing resilience and hope. Initial steps for all survivors include provision of comfort, information, and practical and emotional support, and reuniting with relevant resources and services (Forbes et al., 2010), which can be offered by first responders, mental health professionals, disaster volunteers, and school personnel in a broad range of emergency settings including shelters, schools, and family assistance centers. Clearly, safety is a relative condition, especially in situations of community disaster when the event has an engulfing effect and no place is really safe. However, even in war or natural disaster zones, there are some places that are more protective than others. A place or a situation needs both to *be* and to *feel* safe, such that the intervention should make a situation safe and restore people's confidence in its safety. The National Child Traumatic Stress Network and the US National Center for Posttraumatic Stress Disorder developed a comprehensive manualized guide for PFA that highlights eight components: contact and engagement, safety and comfort, stabilization, assessment of needs and concerns, practical assistance, information on coping, and connecting with social support and relevant services.

Psychological Debriefing is a model for early intervention designed for secondary prevention, i.e. minimizing negative outcomes of trauma exposure. It was developed as part of the Critical Incident Stress Management model and was originally applied by the military in the two world wars, when commanders asked soldiers immediately after combat to share their personal experience, with the expectation that discussing horrific encounters in the war zone and processing the emotional experience would enhance morale and preparedness for future fighting. Psychological Debriefing is based on the assumption that those exposed to a potentially traumatic event are at risk of developing a stress reaction and that sharing the experience and expressing one's thoughts and feelings soon after the exposure can bring relief and help to prevent or reduce this risk. The method was later applied to rescue workers and eventually more widely. It has been used commonly and some say indiscriminately as a blanket intervention for an entire population of people exposed to mass disasters and warfare.

Of the several available models of debriefing, the most famous is the Critical Incident Stress Debriefing (CISD), which was later developed into Critical Incident Stress Management (CISM). It is a one-time, seven-stage, semi-structured intervention, designed as first aid to diminish the potential for posttraumatic negative reactions and facilitated by mental health workers and trained peers within a few days after the traumatic exposure. It can be administered to either an individual or a group (Foa et al., 2005). The focus is on cognitive processing of the traumatic event and ventilating emotional reactions evoked by it, and educating participants about typical stress reactions, normalizing them, and teaching ways to cope. It also allows the identification of those who manifest more severe trauma reactions and need longer and more intensive help (Ireland, Gilchrist & Maconochie, 2008; Litz et al., 2002).

Conceptually CISD is based on the notion of catharsis, i.e. the assumption that an opportunity to vent emotionally following traumatic exposure promotes psychological healing and reduces the likelihood of developing PTSD. Because the intervention is typically done in a group setting, the opportunity for participants to share with others the trauma experience normalizes it, and provides social support and information about additional available resources.

CISD includes a combination of didactic and experiential components. It comprises of an introduction to the process, contracting for confidentiality, asking participants to recall the details of the situation that they experienced (the fact phase), share the thoughts and feelings they had during the experience as well as when they recount it, and give their view and interpretation of it (appraisal and meaning making). The goals of the intervention are to normalize reactions and symptoms, provide information about available services, discuss strategies for addressing additional outcomes of the encounter, avoid over exposure (e.g. by excessive exposure to media coverage of the event and its aftermath), and draw practical conclusions. Participants are encouraged to employ strategies for self-soothing (exercising, yoga, using breathing techniques, being involved in favorite activities) and use social support, and, if needed, referral to professional mental health practitioners is offered.

CISD was originally intended for use with very specific groups, particularly those whose professional occupation involves interaction with trauma survivors, such as emergency services personnel, firefighters, police personnel, paramedics, physicians, and nurses, and those who are tangentially affected, including witnesses, bystanders, and co-workers. For example, following the 9/11 terrorist attacks, I responded to a call for professionals with experience in trauma work to volunteer to facilitate debriefing groups with individuals who witnessed the attacks or worked in companies that lost employees. However, a review of the literature reveals that over the years CISD has been employed with a wide variety of groups, including direct trauma victims such as survivors of rape and of cancer.

CISD evoked a heated debate in the field of trauma practice and is one of the most controversial approaches. It has been critiqued on several grounds (e.g. Bisson & Andrew, 2007; Bonanno et al., 2010; Gist & Woodall, 2000; National Institute of Mental Health, 2002). First, it has been claimed that its core concepts lack clarity, especially due to the implied focus on a trauma as a single isolated event. The model has been viewed as failing to specify what qualifies as a critical event and how to distinguish direct victims from others. Would a firefighter who on Christmas Day 2011 ran into a building in flames in Stamford Connecticut to find two grandparents and three children burned to death and their horrified daughter/mother, who barely escaped, be considered a direct victim, for whom the intervention is discouraged, or a witness, for whom it is suggested? Additionally, the assumed potential of CISD to reduce risks for developing delayed negative reactions has been questioned. Furthermore, concerns have been raised that requiring people to revisit the stressful event without providing enough time to digest the experience, come to terms with it, and regain some balance, is potentially harmful and may exacerbate distress. Critiques claim that increasing arousal at the very time that individuals seek calming down and restoring their balance after the traumatic exposure may overwhelm individual defenses, interfere with natural adaptive coping mechanisms, and cause a secondary trauma by pathologizing normal reactions.

Studies to date have failed to find evidence for the effectiveness of the intervention in preventing traumatic responses. Furthermore, according to some experts and based on several studies, such a "one-time shot" may put some at heightened risk for adverse outcomes (Jacobs, Horne-Moyer & Jones, 2004). In particular, encouragement to revisit horrific exposure may endanger those who use a repressive coping style by ignoring or diverting attention from a potentially traumatizing event, which has been found to play a protective role in dealing with stressful exposure (Ginzburg, Solomon & Bleich, 2002).

The practice of including as a facilitator a layperson who is a peer of group participants (e.g. a co-worker or human resources personnel from the same workplace), in addition to a professional with training in mental health, has been criticized for several reasons. The rationale for this practice is that providing the service by somebody familiar with a participant's background, culture, and circumstances may be supportive and enhance the credibility and legitimacy of the intervention; however, it can also compromise the feeling of safety, limit willingness to share private information, and be viewed as unethically breaching confidentiality. Furthermore, because CISD is often organized by employers, participation in it may be experienced as implicitly coercive such that people feel that they were expected to take part rather than opted to do so (Litz et al., 2002). In the aforementioned post 9/11 group, I found myself unintentionally collaborating in such a situation when some participants expressed a mixture of gratitude and being gently pushed into attending the group. However, Dr. Jeffrey Mitchell, who originally put CISD on the map in the early 1980s, and Hawker, Durkin and Hawker (2011), who studied the intervention, claim that much of the unfavorable conclusions were contaminated by methodological flaws, failure to follow the principles and protocols, and misapplication of the intervention to groups for whom it was never designed (e.g. individual civilians and direct victims) and under inappropriate circumstances (Everly & Mitchell, 2000).

Currently no consensus exists regarding the effectiveness of CISD. Because studying it presents severe methodological challenges (the discussion of these is beyond the scope of this book), it is difficult to reach conclusions based on rigorous research. Critical reviews of available research (e.g. Litz et al., 2002) suggest that there is little evidence to support its continued use, especially in an indiscriminant manner, to non-prescreened victims of traumatic exposure, and that based on available knowledge it was premature to decide that CISD is helpful in secondary prevention of negative outcomes. However, there is also not enough research that evaluates the model when it is applied with high fidelity to the populations for which it was designed and thus its effectiveness cannot be ruled out. This inconclusiveness concurs with the results of two Cochrane reviews (Bisson & Andrew, 2007; Rose et al., 2002), as well as studies in the UK (Ireland, Gilchrist & Maconochie, 2008) and Australia (Magyar & Theophilos, 2010). While the benefits and risks of CISD are unclear, it remains widely used worldwide.

The following case example illustrates principles of crisis intervention. As a social work consultant to a neighborhood medical clinic, I was called urgently to the house of a young mother of two children, aged five and eight, who was informed in the middle of the night that her husband was killed in a road accident on his way from military reserve service. I entered a noisy house packed with relatives and friends bombarding with contradictory ideas the young widow, who had given in to pressure from her family to not share the news with the children and had sent them to school. She was now conflicted about their participation in the funeral. In a private room she shared with me her concerns about breaking the news to the kids. She was afraid that they may learn about the tragedy from other children in the neighborhood before she could tell them herself, and that they would lose their trust in her; however, she did not know how to tell them and how to "get off her back" the pressure from her parents and in-laws to delay telling them until after the burial. I was able to offer her information about children's short- and long-term reactions to the death of a father and to secrets in the family, help her assess the benefits and disadvantages of different options, and reach a plan of action. In our dialogue it became quite clear that the children needed to hear from their mother as soon as possible what had happened. She decided to take the family dog, which was a source of warmth and comfort for the children, retrieve first her older son, and give him the option to decide whether to attend the funeral, and then go together with him to get his young sister and tell her. She also decided that the funeral was too much for the girl to handle and that a visit to the grave a few days later would be a better choice. At her request, I took her in my car to the school, where in collaboration with the principal and counselor, each child met individually and privately with the mother. We then contacted a close family friend to whom the girl was attached and who agreed to watch her as the rest of the family headed to the funeral (in Israel the dead must be buried as soon as possible and funerals are rarely delayed). After leaving the girl and the dog at the friend's house, we returned to the family's home, where the new widow now felt more confident and ready to confront the pressure from relatives. A few days later I came to visit during the traditional week of mourning and we developed a plan for preparing the girl for the visit to the cemetery. Periodical follow-up interactions confirmed that the woman was able to effectively and resiliently address the challenges that followed, including processing the loss with her children, rearranging family finances, childcare arrangements and daily tasks, and dealing with insurance companies, social security, and administrative issues. In retrospect, she was convinced that she handled matters with the children in ways that were appropriate to them and stated: "Thank god you were there to help me think, plan and execute rational decisions at the moment when I was so confused and overwhelmed and yet crucial decisions with potential long-term ramifications needed to be made."

Trauma Treatment

Two major types of approach exist in the treatment of trauma survivors. Trauma-specific interventions are designed to address the outcomes of a particular traumatic exposure whereas trauma-informed interventions adopt an overarching comprehensive approach that takes into consideration trauma-related issues in all aspects of the lives of those affected (Quiros & Berger, 2013). Traditionally, approaches of both types are used individually or in concert with psychopharmacological and psychosocial interventions. While they do not pre-scribe medication, social workers, psychologists, and other healing profession-als often work in teams with psychiatrists and medical personnel monitoring the pharmacological treatment, and must be cognizant of changes in symp-toms and of side effects to make appropriate referrals. This chapter focuses on psychosocial interventions, which are the cruxes of trauma treatment.

Two principles have gained general agreement across all intervention approaches. First, there is consensus that when a traumatic stressor hits, before any psychosocial issues are targeted, basic needs must be addressed to secure shelter, food, safety (also called demobilization by removing away from the scene of the event), medical help and other instrumental care, and reunifica-tion of families (as much as possible), because the absence of basic resources may endanger lives and create stress, mistrust and violence. It is important that resources to the needy are sufficient, reaching those for whom they are intended, and that distribution is done in a fair way without excluding vulner-able groups. Special attention must be given to children, older and sick people, those with disabilities, immigrants, and excluded communities. Unfortunately, historically this has not always been the case because those who are physically and socially stronger often receive more than their share and are able to negoti-ate priority in addressing their needs. Therefore, strategies need to be in place to maximize the coordination among organizations that provide the help to secure effective and fair allocation of supplies, including providing accurate information about the location, times and procedures of distribution. Once some degree of safety is achieved, the focus can shift to core elements of recov-ery from trauma, including calming, fostering social connection, promoting a sense of efficacy, i.e. confidence in one's own ability to regulate reactions and solve problems related to the traumatic exposure, and instilling hope.

The second general principle is that an effort should be made as soon as possible to identify and carefully reach out to those most at risk due to pre-existing events, personal and environmental circumstances, lack of effective social support, isolation, or the manifestation of immediate negative reactions to the traumatic exposure. However, general formal screening or early uni-versal intervention have not been recommended because of the considerable logistical, organizational and financial challenges involved in such an opera-tion, with no systematic evidence to its efficacy (Bisson et al., 2010). Rather, careful, targeted, selective interventions are indicated using a model of stepped care such that appropriate services are offered on the basis of identified specific needs. Because there is a critical window of opportunity to reverse detrimental effects before problems become stabilized, an early intervention may play a critical role in the prevention of future, more severe, problems. This requires walking a fine line between neglecting signs of distress and need for help, and misinterpreting and pathologizing normal reactions to traumatic exposure.

Because one symptom of trauma reaction is avoidance (Chapter 4), those who do not seek help are sometimes the ones who need it most but are too depressed, afraid, or ashamed to pursue it. It is the responsibility of the professional community to put in place measures to identify them and make efforts to prevent the falling through the net of these individuals. Research and my clinical experience with domestic and international immigrant communities suggest that such underutilization of services for addressing psychosocial problems following an encounter with potentially traumatic events is common in these populations. For example, Thiel de Bocanegra and Brickman (2004) found that residents of China Town NY who manifested very high prevalence of PTSD following 9/11 refrained from using counseling services. Therefore, efforts directed at such communities to ensure that their needs are not overlooked, and routine screening for trauma exposure (i.e. was the individual exposed to stressor events? Which? When? How many?) and trauma symptoms are very important.

Once triage is done, it is important to choose the most appropriate intervention and provide it within a non-stigmatized context (e.g. not all veterans choose to use VA facilities and may prefer community-based services). Numerous and diverse practice models exist for the treatment of those exposed to highly stressful events and experiencing traumatic reactions. The task of identifying what works for whom is complicated by the diverse effectiveness of interventions depending on the individuals involved, the particular combination of symptoms they manifest, and the time elapsed since the traumatic exposure. Certain strategies may help whereas others may not, and the same intervention may have positive short- but not long-term outcomes and vice versa. An accurate and specific map of what helps who and when is yet to be developed. Furthermore, it is useful to remember that knowledge about effective practices for trauma work has been evolving and what may have been considered the approach of choice at one point may become obsolete later.

In agreement with Foa and colleagues (2005) and DiMaggio and Galea (2006), at the time of this book going to press, there is still no strong evidence that any particular treatment approach is superior to others. A review of the available research suggests that no intervention can be recommended as the best for routine use following traumatic events and that all interventions may have an adverse effect on some individuals (Roberts et al., 2010). However, several individual studies and meta-analyses indicate the effectiveness of individual and group trauma-informed treatments, i.e. interventions that include a specific focus on trauma (Bradley et al., 2005; Foa et al., 2009; Powers et al., 2010). Compatible with the principles of evidence-based practice (EBP), which currently is increasingly accepted in the field of psychosocial practice (Berger, 2010a), the choice of intervention needs to be guided by considerations of treatment availability, feasibility, existing infrastructure, and client preference (Foa et al., 2005). This conclusion has been reiterated especially relative to non-traditional populations (NATO, 2012).

In recent decades, various professional associations in different countries have developed protocols and guidelines for treating those affected by exposure to traumatic events. Experts from three continents joined forces to conduct a comparative review of various guidelines for the treatment of trauma and offer recommendations relative to their use (Forbes et al., 2010). They concluded that although developed for different constituencies by diverse professionals who used various methods, there is a high degree of consensus among the different guidelines relating to what works for whom, and recommended that practitioners select and apply a particular intervention on the basis of three criteria. First, supportive evidence for the effectiveness of the intervention with the specific problem and the particular client's characteristics including age, gender, cultural background, personality traits, and emotional status circumstances; second, their clinical assessment of a client's strengths, challenges and preferences; finally, their own expertise and available resources (to enable proper application of interventions with supportive evidence).

Hobfoll and colleagues (2007b) reviewed knowledge about trauma practice and concluded that the main foci of leading interventions include promoting a sense of security, self and collective efficacy, connectedness, calmness and hope, validation, processing of feelings of guilt and self-blame if culturally appropriate, raising awareness of the wide range of available options, and helping find ways to move on as acceptable to each individual and compatible with their beliefs, values and cultural context. An analysis across dominant treatment approaches conducted for this book supported these conclusions.

In addition, helping individuals who are so inclined to achieve spiritual change that fits them may provide those affected by trauma with the opportunity to rewrite their life narratives within a spiritual framework. One commonly used strategy for working with trauma survivors seeks to help search for meaning, such as self-sacrifice to save life. "He died to help save many people/ the country" is a frequent expression by family members of fire fighters who went into dangers zones, and rescuers in the 2012 Colorado theater shooting and in the Fukushima Daiichi 2011 nuclear disaster in Japan. To maximize the effectiveness of the intervention, practitioners must be aware of clients' spiritual beliefs and how they affect the perception, interpretation, and response to the trauma. However, for many, the sole meaning of a loss is the waste of life. Thus, contrary to common assumptions, Davis and others (2000) posited that a review of published empirical literature and their own studies of individuals coping with the loss of a child or a spouse showed that the search for and finding of meaning is not universal. Practitioners need to find ways to help these people learn to live with the sense of unnecessary waste and minimize their anger with the lost person, society, the world, and if they are not atheists or agnostics, God.

Summarizing best practice for helping individuals suffering from trauma-related problems, Courtois, Ford and Cloitre (2009) offered an all-encompassing picture that effective interventions are "safety-focused, strength-based, self-defining, self-regulation enhancing, self-integrating, avoidance challenging, individualized" (p. 101), delivered by responsible, well-trained practitioners with specialized training and professional resources. However, in resource-poor countries, trained professionals are not always available. To provide effective help to those affected by trauma in diverse contexts, it is of utmost importance to develop resilient intervention strategies that are easy to master, and train local educators and religious leaders to provide them in collaboration with indigenous healers (NATO, 2012).

Trauma-related interventions are typically characterized by two main foci: first, the alleviation of pain to allow adaptation and well-being such that the traumatic exposure is integrated and no longer disrupts functioning or causes distress, as well as prevention of chronic negative effects; second, fostering post-traumatic growth. There tends to be a consensus that the more complex the traumatic experience and its aftermath, the more multisystemic, multicomponent, and multimodal interventions are called for to effectively address the diverse dimensions of the situation.

Interventions to Alleviate Pain and Prevent Negative Effects

It is widely recognized across practice models that trauma shatters trust and feelings of safety and thus rebuilding and solidifying helping relationships is the bedrock of trauma treatment, which can help people to move away from the feeling of powerlessness and regain confidence and the ability to function. A major goal of helping individuals who struggle with the effects of traumatic experience is helping them to gain some closure and, while the traumatic memories are always there, make the trauma part of their past history rather than a painful and constant part of their present lives, and move towards seeing themselves as survivors (connoting resilience) rather than victims (connoting powerlessness). Both individual and group interventions are helpful in achieving this target.

Individual Intervention Strategies

A task force of the International Society for Traumatic Stress Studies initiated a survey to identify best practice for the treatment of PTSD and Complex PTSD (Cloitre et al., 2011) and sought expert opinion from 50 mental health professionals specializing in these disorders. The results showed that consensus existed regarding the benefits of a phase-based treatment approach, although the sequencing of the phases should remain flexible and adapted to the particular individual and circumstances. Experts also agreed that practitioners should employ interventions to target specific aspects including emotion regulation (i.e. approaching emotions associated with the trauma in a way that they are tolerable), describing trauma memory and construction of the trauma narrative, cognitive restructuring, anxiety and stress management, and interpersonal skills. Because many intervention strategies share some elements, such as therapies that focus on exposure tending to include cognitive processing, the resulting overlapping does not allow for creating a classification of the rich plethora of therapies with distinct categories. The most commonly used approaches to address trauma-related issues are discussed below.

Cognitive Behavior Therapies (CBT)

Strategies employed for helping individuals following encounters with potentially traumatic events tend to include at least some cognitive-behavioral components, which target the main issue typical of traumatic reaction, i.e. processing the traumatic experience, its aftermath, and the related emotions such that they can be integrated into one's life in a tolerable, meaningful, or neutral way. CBT interventions are informed by learning theory and emotional-processing theories. The assumption is that when clients are helped to identify negative (sometimes automatic) thoughts about the event and maladaptive coping behaviors and substitute them with more realistic perception and more effective coping strategies they feel safer and less distressed. Research and clinical practice suggest that emotional and cognitive processing of traumatic experiences contribute to better outcomes and interventions that enhance such processing, and demonstrate better efficacy in helping traumatized individuals than non-directive, supportive counseling and community therapy approaches (National Institute of Mental Health, 2002). Cognitive-emotional interventions are typically short (12–15 sessions) and can also be delivered via new media technology (such as Skype, email and computerized programs) and telephone.

All CBTs share the effort to identify, evaluate, and challenge dysfunctional beliefs (specifically about the world being a dangerous and threatening place and devaluative views of self as incompetent), automatic and irrational thoughts, emotions, and behaviors associated with trauma reaction, and reframe dysfunctional cognitions and substitute them with more realistic, balanced, rational and functional perceptions of the world, self and future. Emphasis is placed on instilling a sense of self-efficacy, control (rather than helplessness), and hope by encouraging individuals to be active in their own therapy and by teaching them strategies for doing so.

Core elements that are used with different combinations in various models of CBT include disclosure, countering avoidance, psychoeducation, cognitive restructuring, and teaching skills, as well as encouragement to get involved in pleasant activities and limit exposure to anxiety-provoking media (e.g. news). *Disclosure* refers to sharing details of the traumatic experience – what the person saw, felt, thought and did, and how she or he reacts to their own reaction, such as, "when I remember what happened, I feel ashamed because I panicked/ran away/did not help as much as I should have . . ." Disclosure offers the opportunity to construct the trauma narrative in one's own terms with the pace and level of detail that are tolerable at any given point. Typically, people are able to share more as they progress. *Countering avoidance* means gently and supportively blocking the efforts of the survivor to run away from discussing what happened. *Psychoeducation* is providing knowledge about common trauma reactions and normalizing them with statements such as, "many people with experience similar to yours tend to feel, react . . ." *Cognitive restructuring* is helping the individual to understand the role of misperceptions and misinterpretations in maintaining the problem, and teaching them to identify distortion of key elements and modify automatic thoughts by replacing those that are dysfunctional with more helpful beliefs, e.g. "it is true that you were assaulted by your boss but not all bosses are aggressive and abusive." Guided actual or imaginary exposure of the traumatic event can also be helpful in restructuring (Foa et al., 2005; Sharpless & Barber, 2011). *Teaching skills* include training in relaxation, yoga, and deep breathing exercises to prevent hyperventilation and reduce anxiety symptoms, contextual discrimination to differentiate a given situation from the traumatic one, cognitive rumination to seek possible meanings in the traumatic event, rational self-talk to tell oneself things that help mitigate the anxiety, and utilizing grounding to help stay in the here and now by focusing on sounds, smells, and sights in the present rather than drifting away to the traumatic past experiences.

Studies have shown that generally cognitive-behavioral approaches, especially those that are trauma focused (TF-CBT), are effective in reducing the frequency, duration, and severity of acute stress disorder and posttraumatic stress disorder, as well as depression in trauma survivors (Bryant et al., 1999, 2008; Gidron et al., 2001); however, findings relating to the efficacy of specific cognitive-behavioral interventions are inconsistent. For example, adding cognitive structuring to exposure improved outcomes according to some studies but not others (Bryant et al., 2008). Cognitive-behavioral interventions commonly used to address trauma reactions are discussed below.

Cognitive Processing Therapy (CPT)

CPT was originally developed in the early 1990s by Dr. Patricia Resick of the Center for Trauma Recovery, Department of Psychology, at the University of Missouri, St. Louis to treat rape victims. It has since been applied to treat those who suffered from PTSD following 9/11, childhood sexual abuse, combat-related experience, and other types of traumatic exposure. The treatment is offered in individual, group or combined individual and group formats and there has been a successful pioneering effort to deliver it via video teleconferencing (Morland et al., 2011). Its core assumption is that when a traumatic exposure causes people to face new information derived from it, which conflicts with their previous thinking (somewhat similar to the idea of shattered assumptions discussed in Chapter 4), they get stuck. For example, the new information "I just got hit in a road accident" may conflict with the existing schemata that "Careful drivers do not have accidents."

CPT combines cognitive restructuring and emotional processing of trauma-related content to help resolve these stuck points and is executed in three phases typically lasting 12 sessions. In the first phase, individuals are educated about processing information, the symptoms of PTSD, and the practice model, and are guided in examining the meaning that they ascribe to the causes of the event, and its impact on their beliefs about themselves, others, and the world. The goal is to identify distorted beliefs, denial, self-blame, and extreme overgeneralized beliefs. The practitioner then helps to distinguish between thoughts and emotions, and between emotions triggered directly by the event and those that reflect later interpretation of it. Special attention is given to explaining the role of avoidance in maintaining symptoms and the importance of confronting fears. The second phase focuses on efforts to identify points where clients got stuck in thinking about the event because of fear, shame, or guilt, and to counteract the tendency to suppress or avoid the emotional experience associated with the event. This is done by guiding the individual to write detailed reports about traumatic experiences and the emotions that accompanied them, read these reports, reflect on them, and revise and share them with the practitioner, who uses Socratic questioning to challenge beliefs specifically relative to issues of safety, trust, power, esteem, and intimacy, such as "What is the evidence that supports your belief that if you go to a certain place, you will be in danger/ that a particular person does not respect you?" Daily worksheets are filled out to practice the identification of negative automatic thoughts and challenge the distorted beliefs and assumptions underlying them. The third phase is dedicated to helping clients to develop a more balanced and realistic approach to the traumatic event and reconstruct its meaning, thus achieving better integration, ability to self-monitor, trust in others, self-efficacy, and the capacity to express anger without losing control, be intimate with others, and gain higher self-esteem. CPT has received support from research as effective in decatastrophizing, i.e. using facts to counteract the maladaptive expectation of the worst, correcting erroneous cognitions, changing negative self-labeling as a failure, and enhancing hope that things can and will be better. In a trial with 60 veterans, CPT was shown to effectively reduce PTSD symptoms (Monson et al., 2006).

Exposure Therapy

This type of intervention focuses on emotional reliving of a traumatic experience and attempting to change dysfunctional reactions to it. It is conceptualized as exposure therapy in cognitive behavioral terms and abreaction in psychodynamic terms. It is based on the assumption of emotional processing theory that emotional experiences may create a pattern of avoiding the trauma memory and can continue to affect behaviors long after the original event that triggered them is over (Foa & Kozak, 1986). Avoidance is a major mechanism of maintaining the traumatic reaction and controlled exposure can help battle it by activating affective and cognitive processes associated with the trauma. The intervention includes actual, imaginary, or virtual exposure to the stimuli that creates negative responses, including memories, smells, visions, and sensations associated with the event, and learning to strip them of fear, anxiety, and additional negative reactions. Because each traumatic event consists of numerous small, traumatic mini-events, in building the narrative it is important to understand what the person thought and felt during each of these specific mini-events.

Models that use exposure share the assumption that at the time of the original event irrational association between images, people, and stimuli was created, yielding symptoms which are maintained through the distortion of the autobiographic memory about the event and cause the narrative of the traumatic memories to become fragmented. For example, a song that a woman heard while being raped may cause her to shiver and panic whenever she hears it played. To help people regain a sense of safety, this irrational association needs to be interrupted by reliving the experience and teaching the brain to eliminate or dissolve the association that was engraved at the time of the traumatic exposure. Exposure to the original traumatizing experience allows revisiting and processing it emotionally, putting the pieces together, and eventually gaining mastery over thoughts and feelings related to the event, and lowering traumatic reactions and symptoms.

Various models employ the principles of exposure, and most combine elements of pre-exposure preparation and assessment, exposure, and processing. The idea that guides many, though not all, exposure interventions is built on Wolpe's (1958) approach of systematic desensitization for treating anxieties and phobias. The principle is that as the person repeatedly revisits the traumatic event it becomes less emotional and scary. Exposure can be intense flooding or gradual. After learning relaxation techniques and constructing a hierarchical list of conditions that trigger the traumatic reaction, the affected individual is exposed to these conditions in an escalating order (from the least alarming to the most). In some models, the person is guided to practice during the exposure relaxation techniques that were learned beforehand. For example, when I was a young social worker, I was treating a soldier who developed traumatic reactions in the 1973 war, when all his peers were killed by an Egyptian bomb, and he was spared because he left the bunker to go to the nearby bathroom. Under my supervisor's guidance, I educated him about relaxation techniques and then instructed him to imagine the situation and act it out to allow him get in touch with the experience and the emotions that accompanied it, while practicing the relaxation techniques he learned.

Therapeutic exposure to the triggers can be imaginary, actual, or virtual. *Imaginary exposure (IE)* includes teaching the person about common reactions to trauma, calm breathing and the rationale for exposure, obtaining a narrative of the traumatic memories, guiding them as they repeatedly relive the event and the sensory and affective responses involved to allow time for habituation, processing of the experience, supportive counseling, and strategies designed to prevent relapse. *In vivo exposure (IVE)* includes, in addition to similar psychoeducational steps, gradually entering the feared situations and remaining in them until the anxiety decreases. *Virtual exposure (VRE)* uses computer-generated visual, sound and smell simulations to create a virtual reality when in vivo exposure is not feasible (e.g. combat conditions overseas, disaster), or the person has difficulty imagining vividly the traumatic event (McLay et al., 2012). There is software available that can create highly individualized virtual environments tailored to the unique experience.

Prolonged exposure (PE) is probably the most well-known and supported by solid evidence relative to a wide range of traumatic experiences with very low relapse.

Furthermore, because it is simple and resilient, non-experts can be trained and apply it effectively and thus large population groups can be helped even in resource-poor communities. It is designed to reactivate the traumatic reaction through exposure and then introduce information that disagrees with the traumatic reaction to facilitate new learning and changing maladaptive beliefs associated with the trauma. The intervention was developed by Professor Edna Foa of the University Of Pennsylvania School Of Medicine and consists of a manualized short-term treatment package, typically 8–15 weekly 90-minute sessions, structured around specific activities for a pre-determined duration. First, an assessment is completed and the individual is trained in relaxed breathing and instructed about common trauma reactions. Then, she or he is guided in repeated imaginary exposure and reliving the trauma memory and its triggers by providing increasingly more detailed description of the trauma during sessions, listening to recordings of these descriptions between sessions, and, if applicable, in vivo exposure to trauma reminders (such as visiting places, people and objects that have been avoided but are safe) between sessions. To change how the traumatic event has been processed, the practitioner uses strategies for identifying and self-monitoring thoughts and emotional reactions triggered by distressing experiences, and self-talk to stop negative automatic thoughts and cognitive restructuring. Revisiting and reliving the traumatic memories and repeatedly retelling and discussing disturbing and anxiety-provoking aspects of the event ("hot spots") reduce avoidance of feared memories, help to organize the memory more effectively, modify dysfunctional cognitions and allow learning of new corrective ones, differentiate reality from thoughts and emotions, and help to gain a better perspective on the trauma and a sense of mastery over one's reactions and symptoms. Through the process individuals realize that the fear that haunts them was based on unrealistic expectations and the consequences that they feared but do not occur and thus they acquire a more sensible approach that allows them to go on better with their lives (Foa & Rothbaum, 1998).

Narrative Exposure Treatment (NET) builds on the same principles as other exposure models. Based on the assumption that a distortion of the autobiographic memory about traumatic events leads to a fragmented trauma narrative, which results in maintenance of PTSD symptoms (Neuner et al., 2004), it uses a combination of exposure therapy with a narrative approach to help the individual confront the memories of the traumatic event and integrate it. As the traumatized individual tells their story, the therapist continuously verbalizes and mirrors sensations and behaviors to help process cognitions, emotions, and meanings. A variation is *Cognitive Behavior Writing Therapy (CBWT)*, which was developed for using the internet as a vehicle for treatment and includes elements of exposure, cognitive restructuring, and social sharing. *Structured Writing Therapy (SWT)*, which relies on writing assignments, was also found to be helpful in buffering the negative effects of exposure to potentially traumatic events (van Emmerik, Kamphuis & Emmelkamp, 2008).

Sometimes, it is beneficial to add to exposure therapy *Stress Inoculation Training (SIT)*, which is a combined set of skills designed to improve the management of anxiety and stress, bolster coping abilities, and enhance confidence in these abilities to combat future stressors (Meichenbaum, 1985). It is typically comprised of teaching about PTSD and using modeling, role playing, and *in vivo* exposure to feared situations to teach deep muscle relaxation and problem-focused coping strategies such as self-talk, positive thinking, and thought stopping. Such interventions help enhance self-efficacy (the belief in one's own ability to accomplish things) and hope. For example, a stress inoculation training (SIT) was provided by teachers *prior to* the exposure to rocket attacks and other community trauma in Northern Israel. Children who learned to identify and regulate emotions, work through experiences, cope, make decisions, communicate effectively, and balance tension manifested fewer posttrauma and stress symptoms (Wolmer, Hamiel & Laor, 2011).

The efficacy of various types of exposure interventions in ameliorating symptoms of PTSD and depression has been demonstrated in studies (Bichescu et al., 2007; Powers et al., 2010; Resick et al., 2002, Sharpless & Barber, 2011). Both CPT and PE have demonstrated enduring gains in client outcomes, which remained positive five years after treatment (Karlin et al., 2010). Exposure focused on the "hotspots", i.e. the parts of trauma memories that cause high levels of emotional distress and which are often re-experienced, has been specifically emphasized (Nijdam et al., 2013). Furthermore, because evidence has started to emerge that it is transferable into the community (Sharpless & Barber, 2011), PE has potentially broad applicability. However, success of these strategies in children and particularly in adolescents has been more limited (Pattwell et al., 2012). Based on these findings, exposure therapy has been identified as effective by several leading organizations, including the American Psychological Association and the Substance Abuse and Mental Health Services Administration (SAMHSA), and adopted as a treatment of choice for PTSD by the Administration of Veteran Affairs (Board on Population Health and Public Health Practice, 2008).

Third-Wave Behavioral Treatment

This is a heterogeneous group of treatments that includes such models as dialectical behavioral therapy (DBT), mindfulness-based cognitive therapy, and acceptance and commitment therapy (ACT). Positive outcomes have been reported of DBT, which combines cognitive behavior interventions with validation, distress tolerance, affect regulation, and mindfulness, i.e. non-judgmental acceptance of experiences in the moment. The focus on the here and now allows clients to learn to turn off their mind and avoid the fear-producing past and the anxiety-generating future, thus promoting feelings of safety. The client learns to observe what is real in the given circumstances rather than import to a current safe situation feelings of fear associated with the original event. Acceptance and commitment therapy (ACT) teaches individuals to experience their thoughts and feelings rather than attempting to avoid or alter them. Its core elements include acceptance, cognitive diffusion, being present, self as context, values, and committed action (Hayes et al., 2006).

Psychosensory and Sensorimotor Therapies

Several trauma therapies focus on the mind–body connection and use sensory input to alter brain function and encourage psychophysiological reorganization of the traumatic experience. They seek to activate the mind to revisit the memory of the stressful event and use sensory input to free this memory of its traumatic meaning. The non-verbal components of these approaches allow access to traumatic experiences that are not yet available for cognitive or verbal processing. The goal is to identify and reorganize the non-verbal encoding of a traumatic exposure in body sensations, movements, smells, sounds, and images. Verbal and physical strategies are used to increase awareness of the somatic aspects, i.e. the bodily sensation connected to a traumatic memory during an imaginary re-exposure to the event. Once the sensation is acknowledged, various forms of sensory input, such as touching, tapping on acupressure points, and movement are used to change these sensations and gain a sense of mastery over one's reactions. Ruden (2011), a New York based internist specializing in trauma, called these the *third pillar* in addition to psychosocial (first pillar) and pharmacological (second pillar) traditionally used approaches. Reports about these interventions have appeared in well-respected professional journals and there are current efforts to evaluate them; however, most have not been tested rigorously and therefore, other than clinical experience and theoretical knowledge, evidence to support their efficacy is yet to be developed. Included in this group of therapies are Eye Movement Desensitization and Reprocessing (EMDR), Havening, Emotional Freedom, Callahan's Thought Field Therapy (Callahan & Callahan, 2000), and Peter Levine's (1997) Somatic Therapy. Some sensory therapeutic approaches (such as yoga and reiki) are general and others are more trauma-specific.

Eye Movement Desensitization and Reprocessing (EMDR)

EMDR is an eight-step intervention technique based on the Adaptive Information Processing (AIP) model developed and introduced in the 1980s by the psychologist Francine Shapiro (Shapiro & Laliotis, 2011) to reduce the distress of traumatic memories. It combines elements of CBT, mindfulness, body-based approaches, and person-centered therapies (Shapiro & Laliotis, 2011; Sharpless and Barber, 2011). The assumption is that exposure to a highly stressful event can create emotional bruising and the memory of the experience, if not adequately processed, is stored in its original form with the accompanying emotions, sensations, and beliefs in the brain within a network of dysfunctional memories that are disconnected from where adaptive information resides. These capsulated memories become the basis for later responses and behaviors and the primary cause for the development of pathological reactions. Subsequent encounters with a similar experience trigger the unprocessed memories, lead to actual re-living of the original experience, and shape the perception of later experiences (Shapiro & Laliotis, 2011).

Activating the traumatic memory in a safe and supportive context while connecting it with visual or tactile cues is believed to help unfreeze the originally stored memory. Subsequently, the negative experiences are reprocessed and connected with adaptive information that was previously inaccessible. This allows restoring of non-pathological processing and integration of information, and eliminating dysfunctional emotions, distorted perceptions, and physical sensations inherent in the memory and changing them into appropriately stored memories, leading to the removal of symptoms. The intervention is designed to address the etiology of, triggers for, and templates for coping with traumatic exposure. Bilateral stimulation is used by eye movements, tactile taps, or auditory tones, while processing memories of traumatic experiences. The individual is guided to invoke and hold the original experience and hold in mind positive cognitions while simultaneously focusing on rhythmic lateral finger movements by the therapist in front of their field of vision.

Studies of the biological mechanism underlying EMDR suggest that a wide variety of mild brain stimulation through sensory inputs is effective in erasing the physical basis for a fear memory in the brain (Harper, 2012). However, EMDR has been controversial. Some studies found that it produced substantial and sustained reduction of PTSD symptoms (van der Kolk et al., 2007) and that EMDR and trauma-focused cognitive behavioral therapy were equally effective in reducing PTSD symptoms (e.g. Seidler & Wagner, 2006), but others concluded that it has not received strong support in objective research (Bisson & Andrew, 2007; Board on Population Health and Public Health Practice, 2008; National Institute of Mental Health, 2002). Proponents of the method blame the use of inappropriate populations and insufficient amounts of treatment for the failure of some studies to support its effectiveness (Shapiro & Laliotis, 2011). Several approaches have built on EMDR. For example, Knipe (2010) developed the method of constant installation of present orientation and safety (CIPOS), which focuses on alternating between the establishment of safety in the present situation and accessing the traumatic material in a highly controlled and predictable way.

Havening

Like shamans and faith healers, this approach uses touch to heal (Ruden, 2011). The approach de-traumatizes events, which were encoded as traumatic during the original encounter, by using guided imagery to identify and retrieve the event when symptoms began, and reactivate the emotion attached to it or a similar relevant emotion if access to re-experiencing the event itself is impossible. Once the emotion is recalled, it is de-encoded or erased as the practitioner or the traumatized individual gently applies touch (tapping) to the face, the arms, or the hands, to create a sensation of a safe haven (from which the name of the intervention derives). Simultaneously with recalling the disturbing memory, the individual is also instructed to focus on a continuous visual or auditory stimulus such as counting steps or humming a tune. Guided by the idea that a working memory can only hold one item at a time, the new stimulus introduces a distraction and its benign content is implemented to substitute the charged memory associated with the stressful event.

Self-soothing and relaxation techniques build on the body–mind connection. Because hyperarousal has been documented as a predictor for PTSD and mindful meditation has been shown to impact brain functioning, specifically increasing activity in the area of the brain that dominates attention, it has been suggested that training in arousal management by relaxation exercises and yoga may contribute to minimizing risk (Litz et al., 2002). Furthermore, after a while, the practice of meditation and self-soothing may become an automatic reaction that interrupts the stress reaction before it fully develops and may help buffer such reactions. Similarly, Peter Levine's (1997) *Somatic Experiencing* is a body awareness approach to treating trauma based on the belief that human beings have an innate ability to overcome its negative effects. Like the approaches discussed above, it includes the creation of an environment with relative safety, providing corrective experiences, helping to regulate high arousal states and restore dynamic equilibrium, and reorienting to the here and now.

Additional Treatment Models

Several other approaches have been suggested, with some supportive evidence for their effectiveness. Examples are *Trauma-Focused Hypnosis* and *Interpersonal Psychotherapy (IPT)*, which focuses on enhancing social skills and sense of agency, reducing feelings of helplessness, providing a corrective emotional experience, and learning effective coping skills, and has also produced promising results (Ibbotson & Williamson, 2010; Sharpless & Barber, 2011).

Evidence exists that combining intervention models rather than using individual models exclusively may yield better outcomes. For example, a team from New York University showed that a phase-based treatment that combined training in affect regulation and interpersonal skills (STAIR) was more effective in reducing PTSD symptoms than treatments that excluded either component (Cloitre et al., 2010). Najavits (2001) developed the manualized program *Seeking Safety* with documented effectiveness of modified CBT paired with an emphasis on teaching safety skills and future solution-focused orientation, especially for those with both trauma and substance abuse related issues. Recently, with the growing awareness of neurological aspects of trauma responses, the *Observed and Experiential Integration (OEI)* model has been developed, combining experiential, neurobiological, cognitive, affective, and educational elements from the approaches discussed earlier (Bradshaw, Cook & McDonald, 2011).

In addition to verbal interventions, expressive arts therapy using painting, sculpturing, writing, and dance can also be helpful in processing trauma and coping with it, as was demonstrated in a collection of articles in the April 2009 special issue of the journal *The Arts in Psychotherapy*, which was dedicated to art therapy with trauma survivors. Because of its sensory-based nature, art-making activates the non-verbal brain and promotes linking verbal and non-verbal brain functioning (called hemispheric integration). Thus, it allows access to dissociated experiences and feelings for which it is hard to find words and may facilitate healing negative neurological effects of the trauma reactions that were described in Chapter 4. The active nature of the process of creating art is potentially helpful in reversing the helplessness felt during traumatic experiences and it can offer a vehicle for catharsis, telling the narrative of the trauma and restoring positive memories, while the product of the process allows for articulation of both conscious and unconscious content.

Strategies for Addressing Complex PTSD

No consensus exists as to whether interventions recommended for the treatment of PTSD are also useful and sufficient for treating complex PTSD, or if the latter requires specialized strategies. While treatment of PTSD is often designed to process the traumatic exposure and its aftermath, treatment of the more pervasive complex PTSD may require attending to the broad array of personality and relational issues associated with it before the trauma can be accessed.

Because of the need for a balanced and gradual approach, there is agreement across the literature that treatment of complex PTSD should be phase-oriented and include three steps (Bethany et al., 2011), even though the specific nature and focus of these phases vary in individual practice models. Recognizing how important is the context of behaviors, in agreement with Herman's (1992a, 1992b) *Recovery-Focused Model*, typically the first step seeks to create conditions favorable for directly addressing the traumatic experience. It includes interventions designed to achieve stabilization, symptom reduction, and a sense of security, as well as efforts to establish a collaborative client–practitioner relationship and develop an organized daily routine by using social support. The second phase involves carefully and sensitively processing traumatic memories and reconstructing the trauma story. Finally, strategies to enhance integration, reconnection, and rehabilitation are employed to help the individual gain skills for connecting with and management of daily functioning. These phases do not necessarily occur sequentially and may periodically alternate.

Treatment models for complex PTSD include various combinations of psychosocial and pharmacological strategies. While different in emphasis and the sequence of interventions, models share the focus on facilitating the transition from the helplessness, self-blame and alienation typical of complex PTSD to collaborative, trusting relationships, sense of self-worth, and agency. One such model is contextual therapy, which is based on the idea that complex PTSD is often associated with growing up in families that failed to provide the supportive and secure environment necessary for healthy development, leading offspring to be vulnerable to traumatization. Therefore, just as the disorder is pervasive, so the intervention needs to be comprehensive and address many domains. Rather than adopting a narrow trauma focus, in preparation for readiness to address the trauma the intervention targets changing the current life context as a means to develop more functional behaviors, teaching practical skills for non-addictive self-soothing, staying focused on the here and now, and participating in collaborative relationships. Many studies found that cognitive behavioral therapy, which was described above, is effective in reducing complex PTSD symptoms, specifically those related to emotional regulation and interpersonal relationships (Jackson, Nissenson & Cloitre, 2009). Additional variations of approaches that emphasize clients gaining the ability to recognize, process, express, and utilize emotions in an adaptive way are also useful.

Of special importance are psychopharmacological treatments. Some of the aforementioned interventions, such as relaxation to mitigate hyperarousal and experiential psychotherapy to increase awareness of bodily reactions, can help to ameliorate certain physiological aspects of traumatic reactions. However, they do so indirectly, whereas medications directly address physiological symptoms. The use of psychopharmacology in combination with psychotherapy has been recommended strongly and universally because numerous medications are effective in alleviating symptoms and facilitating improvement. However, some medications have been shown to be helpful in the immediate term but are also associated with negative effects and heightened risks in the long run (Hobfoll et al., 2007a). A discussion of specific medications is beyond the scope of this book.

Group Interventions With Traumatic Exposure Survivors

In addition to implementing some of the aforementioned strategies in the context of a group setting, group is the main tenet of interventions in several approaches to helping traumatized individuals. For example, a structured group intervention that has been developed at the Royal Air Force Hospital in Wroughton, England (RAF), and adjusted by the British Ticehurst PTSD Treatment Program, used intensive group processes, some of them in a short-term residential setting, to aggressively address symptoms of trauma reactions in veterans and released hostages (Busuttil, 2006).

Groups give those affected by trauma an opportunity to share their stories with others with similar experiences who can understand them, have access to role models and guidance, learn practical skills and modes of coping, as well as receive feedback about their own coping, in the context of a safe, non-judgmental, supportive relational environment. Consequently, groups allow participants to feel validated and empowered, regain hope, and recover a sense of self. The emphasis on commonalities lessens feeling of stigmatization and enhances a sense of belonging and connectedness, which has often been lost to the trauma. Groups can also enhance PTG. Antoni and colleagues (2001) found that learning cognitive-behavioral stress management strategies in the context of a group helped reduce prevalence of depression and increase reports of gaining benefits and optimism in women diagnosed with breast cancer.

Access to supportive group services is important because trauma reactions often involve feelings of isolation and social disengagement, and social support has a documented role in coping with and recovery from traumatic exposure. Litz and colleagues (2002) emphasize how crucial it is to assess if survivors of traumatic events have both access to social support and the knowledge necessary to elicit and use this support. The role of practitioners is to expand the supportive network by organizing groups and ensuring that survivors are aware of them and know how to access them, because traumatic exposure may compromise people's ability to seek and use help from others. Furthermore, if the situation forces evacuation and relocation, efforts to keep people in natural groups are essential, and if informal support systems collapse, interventions for reconnecting should become a priority (de Jong, 2002; Norris et al., 2002). For example, in a report about the use of unions to support families of workers who were missing following the 9/11 terrorist attack, Boss and her colleagues (2003) emphasized the effectiveness of groups that were community-based, multiple-family, and cross-generational in creating a cohesive environment that provided support for regaining strength. Two elements were underscored in the report: first, involving the older generation of grandparents was very helpful in modeling resilience and successful coping; second, the respect for diversity and the view of all ways of coping that were not life-threatening as acceptable.

Ford, Fallot and Harris (2009) reviewed existing knowledge about using groups with individuals diagnosed with PTSD following exposure to various types of traumatic events and at different ages, such as survivors of childhood abuse, intimate partner violence, rape, HIV, incarceration, and combat. Improvement in functioning, adaptation and interpersonal relationships as well as reduction in symptoms and in stress were associated with participation in long- and short-term groups that used various group modalities including psychodynamic therapy, psychoeducation, mutual support, dialectic behavior therapy, narrative, memory processing, trauma-focused therapy, and combinations of elements from these and other approaches; however, no modality showed superiority over others. Because there are inconsistencies in reported outcomes, it is not yet clear if including a component that requires group members to revisit a traumatic event (such as in exposure therapy or trauma memory retelling) is helpful in recovery or contributes to dropout from the group, or to negative outcomes.

The use of groups has been recommended even for the most traumatized individuals who are diagnosed with complex PTSD (Ford, Fallot & Harris, 2009). Groups are potentially effective with this population because of two main reasons. First, participating in a group allows individuals to offer supportive feedback to other group members and realize that they have something valuable to give, contrary to their self-loathing perception as worthless, associated with the diagnosis; second, because in the vast majority of cases of complex PTSD, the original traumatic experience was within an interpersonal relationship, the experience of a warm and supportive relational system provides a corrective experience and potentially leads to reparation of psychological wounds caused by the original traumatic exposure.

However, groups are not suitable for all those affected by traumatic exposure. For some, hearing other people's experiences is too painful and may take them back to places that they cannot tolerate. For others, the posttraumatic symptoms are such that they do not have the patience or are not emotionally available to listen to and focus on other individuals' struggles. Some traumatized individuals are so needy for intense personal attention that they tend to take more than their share of the group's space and time and become a source of distress to other group members. A group member who manifests severe trauma-related symptoms, especially in the domains of interpersonal relationships and affect regulation, can lack empathy for what others have to say or can exhibit emotional outbursts, especially of aggression, challenging other group members' ability to contain these behaviors in addition to their own pain. Therefore, the decision whether to offer an individual with trauma-related problems a place in a group, as well as determining the specific type of group that may be useful, requires thorough consideration of the potential benefits and risks on a case by case basis.

While practice wisdom suggests that group therapy is helpful in the treatment of trauma survivors, a committee appointed to assess the efficacy of various interventions (Board on Population Health and Public Health Practice, 2008) concluded that no sufficient rigorous empirical evidence is available to support this idea. Unfortunately, only four studies that were evaluated as methodologically strong were available for this review, limiting the validity of the conclusions.

Multisystem Interventions

Several comprehensive models for healing the effects of traumatic exposure combine different modalities such as individual, family, group, and environmental strategies. Specifically, mindfulness is widely used in combination with other therapies. One such model is the wraparound psychosocial, multisystemic, multimodal rehabilitation approach, which is holistic and employs a wide menu of strategies to address emotional, social, educational, health and psychological needs, and has been documented as beneficial, especially with those who have experienced complex traumas, present multiple needs and are hard to reach. Based on empowerment, the intervention is designed to build on the strengths of affected individuals and their immediate (family) and broad (community) environment, all of whom are encouraged to be active participants in the planning and execution of the interventions (Kira, 2010).

Intervention for Fostering Resilience and PTG

The question as to whether and how practitioners can help individuals become resilient and receive benefits from the struggle with highly stressful events has been debated extensively (e.g. Tedeschi & McNally, 2011). Resilience typically occurs naturally and evolves out of an individual's coping; however, practitioners can nurture and foster the process by promoting sense of control, cohesiveness and connectedness (Reich, 2006). While professionals cannot and should not push those who are traumatized towards perceiving growth following a struggle with highly stressful events, they can help to develop conditions that enhance PTG and remove barriers to it, such as stirring the client from counter-factual and self-blaming to deliberate and productive rumination. For example, because higher problem-focused coping was associated with greater PTG in cardiac patients, Senol-Durak & Ayvasik (2010) suggested developing programs for teaching strategies to enhance such coping and the probability of PTG.

Calhoun and Tedeschi (2013) advocate that mental health professionals act as expert companions, who bring knowledge and expertise about possible impacts of traumatic exposure and strategies for coping with them to the encounter with the individual, who brings his or her own circumstances, beliefs, experiences, and preferences. The combination of these mutual contributions informs the path for the client to address the adversity and potentially grow. How exactly this potentially growth-enhancing encounter works is not yet clear. However, based mostly on practice wisdom and theoretical understanding, several principles for facilitating PTG have emerged. Including a PTG perspective in clinical practice does not mean adding a specific protocol, practice model, or intervention technique. Rather, it involves adopting a certain mindset and approach to healing, which may be integrated with and implemented in the context of various commonly used types of therapy. It is of utmost importance to clarify with clients the norms of their culture relative to the possibility of growth, expression of emotions, and self-disclosure. In some cultures (e.g. Japan), sharing a greater sense of resilience, which is an aspect of PTG in western cultures, is considered negatively as arrogant and inappropriate; thus, the personal experience of growth may clash with such norms. In those situations, it is the role of the clinician to help the individual to sort through how compatible beliefs and changes associated with PTG are with notions about the social environment, and develop strategies for effectively addressing discrepancies.

The process of facilitating growth involves several steps. First, the practitioner needs to help identify clues for forthcoming surges of uncontrollable sensations. Second, clients need to be psychoeducated about normal trauma reactions, effective ways to move from intrusive automatic to deliberate rumination, and strategies for emotion regulation. Third, client and practitioner need to figure out which parts of the clients' assumptive world are no longer useful in light of the traumatic experience, how to substitute them with more relevant beliefs (narrative revision) and with a new sense of purpose that allows them to live meaningfully rather than just exist or endure, and how to make the necessary changes in behavior. Throughout the process, it is important to emphasize that growth is a result of the way in which one chooses to respond to the traumatic event rather than the event itself. Practitioners should refrain from challenging a client's worldview and core beliefs (e.g. the existence of a god who dominates world's events), use a collaborative rather than an expert approach, employ language that focuses on clients' successes, and normalize difficulties, reframing them as opportunities for becoming more proficient in effective strategies for improving their situation. PTG is not a universal experience for all those exposed to potentially traumatic events and patterns vary such that a client may experience growth in some domains but not in others. Therefore, practitioners should not convey expectations for PTG to occur or to take a specific form. Such expectations may create additional pressure and if growth is not achieved clients may become disappointed, intimidated, and more distressed. All experiences of trauma involve a sense of loss of control and consequently of confidence in one's own ability to cope and perform. Therefore, it is beneficial for fostering growth to maximize the ability of clients to make choices (e.g. how much and what to disclose to whom) and battle the experience on their own rather than prescribed terms, thus enabling them to regain a sense of mastery over life.

As part of the process, the practitioner teaches the client breathing exercises, imagery that the client controls (rather than guided by the practitioner), and strategies for managing external distractions. Various measures may be helpful in addressing the challenges involved in the traumatic experience and facilitate the rumination process, which can mitigate distress and eventually pave the way to PTG. Examples include verbal and creative means, such as writing a personal dairy, literary (i.e. short stories, poems, a memoir) or scholarly works (e.g. a survivor of an earthquake who begins to research the effects of earthquakes on people), drawing and sculpting, acting, and additional expressive strategies. In a talk in NY on October 2012 about his journey following a severe brain injury in combat, the Israeli geologist Yoram Eshet-Alkalai discussed writing a book about the experience as his way of gaining ownership, recognizing, framing, demarcating ("organize my murky world"), assigning meaning to chaotic memories, seeking reconciliation, and defining an attitude towards the trauma ("I now accept that this is who *I* am and this is what happened to *me*"). He emphasized the importance of focusing on one's own narrative rather than on "how much of it really happened or was fabricated."

Even when PTG does occur, it is manifested later rather than sooner in the process, after the stressful experience has been processed and related losses mourned. Affected individuals must have as much time as they need to process the traumatic experience and acknowledge their pain. Specifically beneficial are the cognitive measures described above, such as education about typical symptoms and normalizing reactions. The environment may pressure to "get over it already", be reluctant to recognize losses, and overlook, dismiss or minimize the agonizing nature of the experience. In a study of women who struggled with infertility (Berger, Paul & Henshaw, 2013), participants shared their frustration with reactions, which they perceived as insensitive, such as "most people want us to adopt or move on and not talk about it any longer" and "no one acknowledges how stressful and hurtful infertility is." The same is true for immigrants. Even if relocation improves their personal safety, living conditions, and medical, financial, educational and social circumstances, the loss of the past is real and needs to be acknowledged before they can move forward. Similarly, abused children experience loss and long for their abusive parents from whose care they were removed. While the change improves their life and safety, the sense of a hole is still present. It is imperative that practitioners exercise patience to allow the time necessary for processing the loss and pain before being ready for the possibility of growth.

Because PTG may co-exist simultaneously with distress (Dekel, Ein-Dor & Solomon, 2012), it is important to remain attentive to indications of both. Easing posttraumatic stress symptoms does not necessarily lead to growth and the clinician must be trained and ready to offer interventions that are designed to ameliorate pain and cope with the distress as well as those that foster growth. In addition to helping traumatized individuals to reduce trauma-related pain, it is important also to encourage them to actively engage in activities that give them joy and pleasure.

While timing is important in all interventions, it is critical in fostering PTG. It is imperative that the practitioner listens carefully and is attentive to emerging intimations and signs of potential growth rather than actively trying to elicit it, push towards it or convey an expectation for it. Equally important is being attentive and paying attention to even the slightest indication that a client may be beginning to contemplate benefits as refraining from doing so may be interpreted by the client as indicating a negative message from the practitioner about the possibility of growth following a trauma. This means tip-toeing along the tightrope of recognizing the potential for growth and facilitating it while exercising patience regarding signals for growth readiness. Typical indicators are statements using positive, future-oriented language including expression of hope, starting to develop plans, discussing changes in one's life after the traumatic experience in positive terms, and hints of personal strengths and improved relationships (e.g. "since the accident I have a better relationship with my family, it is easier for me to understand what really matters, and I am less worried about small things"). Only when indications are manifested that the individual is beginning to reconsider their own beliefs can the practitioner begin to foster growth by highlighting statements that address changes the client identifies in his or her views and beliefs. The practitioner should stay close to the client's original statements, and thus cultivate, validate, and acknowledge potential for growth without denying distress and vulnerabilities or pushing an agenda. In doing so, it is crucial to remain sensitive and non-judgmental, and ask questions that allow the individual to redefine basic concepts and explore successful coping with previous traumatic events.

Part of the intervention is indirect and focuses on creating conditions conducive to growth, identifying potential barriers, and working in concert with the client to remove these barriers within themselves (e.g. fear that others fail to understand, empathize or support reports of growth) or in the environment. For example, Sonya, whose husband died of pancreatic cancer, shared in a bereavement support group that she constantly encounters judgmental remarks when she attends parties or goes to the theater in her small, tight-knit neighborhood. Before losing her husband, she was mostly focused on her work and family and did not take part in such activities; however, now she wanted to become more active socially as her husband's death made her realize how limited her social interactions were. She expressed the feeling that she was "living under the microscope" and that her attempts to create for herself a life which was not exclusively focused on her role as a widow met with unfavourable criticism. In a discussion that the group facilitator instigated, other members shared similar experiences. Following a brainstorming session, the group developed a plan that required several steps. First, they went out as a group for social activities, which were processed in group sessions. After participating in several such outings, Sonya invited three group members to accompany her to a party in her neighborhood. She reported that their presence provided a supportive safety net, which allowed her to withstand critical looks and remarks. When she felt ready, she decided that she was able to establish her status as an active participant in neighborhood social activities, in which she enjoyed a gradually increased attendance. In this case, the group facilitator served as a catalyst to mobilization of resources that enabled Sonya to grow from her struggle with the traumatic experience.

Furthermore, because social support is critical to the development of PTG, it is of utmost importance, if culturally acceptable, to simultaneously help the individual to enhance their ability for self-disclosure as a way to become more open with others, and at the same time create an environment that recognizes and is receptive to the possibility of growth and can foster reflective rumination, which may eventually lead to growth. This can be done by encouraging participation in groups that provide opportunities for interaction with mentors and others who have experienced similar traumatic stressors, achieved personal growth, and can serve as role models. Although limited in number, studies have shown that mentoring can enhance academic achievement and employment success and contribute to decreasing substance abuse in teens. The same is applicable to achieving PTG. Recruitment of support from family, friends, and relevant informal reference groups in the community, such as the church, social clubs, and sports teams with which the individual is affiliated, is potentially helpful in enhancing the possibility for growth. Volunteers and practitioners may use their own traumatic exposure and growth experience to guide and encourage clients in their efforts to gain benefits from their highly stressful endeavor. This requires sensitive and careful walking of a fine line between lending the mentor's own learning and being tolerant of the path and pace that the client opts to follow.

Calhoun and Tedeschi (2013) called attention to the need to use nuanced and sensitive language when recognizing growth. It is important to talk about positive outcomes of *struggling* with adverse circumstances rather than an outcome of the circumstances themselves. Furthermore, while PTG is a universal phenomenon, it has unique characteristics in different cultures and therefore, like with all interventions, one must remain mindful of the perception of coping with trauma and of PTG in the individual's culture, religious and spiritual contexts, and its interpretation by the particular client. While religious beliefs may help in finding new meanings following a trauma, the exposure may also lead some individuals to question these beliefs, a reaction that must be normalized.

The principles and strategies used to heal from trauma exposure and to promote PTG in direct survivors are also useful with those who struggle with secondary traumatization. Concluding a review of literature relative to secondary traumatization, Galovski and Lyons (2004) recommended focusing on interventions that directly address the needs of significant others and seek to improve the psychological well-being of spouses, children and other family members, rather than the traditional focus on bettering relationships and reducing victims' symptoms exclusively. Fostering PTG in practitioners can be done using similar measures, as well as using peer support from colleagues (Hernandez, Gangsei & Engstrom, 2007).

Treating Children

In the decade that followed the 9/11 terrorist attacks, protocols and guidelines for addressing posttraumatic responses in children mushroomed. Two of many examples were the initiative of the Federal Emergency Medical Administration (FEMA) to develop, pilot, and disseminate guidelines for helping traumatized children in the welfare system (Berger et al., 2002; Berger & Joyce, 2010), and a report produced by The American Psychological Association based on a presidential task force to advise about helping children exposed to trauma (American Psychological Association, 2009). In a summary of available research relating to children facing highly traumatic events, Masten and Narayan (2012) concluded that intervention efforts should have a double focus, addressing negative outcomes and fostering resilience. A third goal that has been emerging on the basis of the immunization approach (see Chapter 4) is the preparation for exposure to future events as a protective measure (Wolmer, Hamiel & Laor, 2011). One strategy used to choose intervention goals is the Neurosequential Model of Therapeutics (NMT), which is a structured assessment of a child's history and current functioning that allows identification of key systems and areas impacted by adverse developmental experiences, and helps select and sequence therapeutic, enrichment, and educational activities rather than focusing on any specific therapeutic technique (Perry, 2009).

In spite of the shortage of research on effective interventions with children following the exposure to potentially traumatic events (Masten & Narayan, 2012), a review of the flood of guidelines reveals consensus regarding some broad principles. Most interventions with traumatized children have been modified from treating traumatized adults or children with related symptoms, such as anxiety and depressive symptoms. The first critical steps are early detection, correct identification of symptoms as trauma-related, discontinuing the presence of a stressor in a child's life, and reunification with their parents, family, and natural support systems, such as a close grandparent or caretaker, as soon as possible if the event separated the child from them (Gammonley & Dziegielewski, 2006; Wooding & Raphael, 2004; Yahav, 2011). However, eliminating the stressful situation may sometimes create new stresses. Thus, if a child is removed from a war zone or from an abusive home as a measure of protection, the relocation itself may involve multiple new stressors such as losing relationships with non-abusive family members, familiar daily routines, neighbors, friends, and school environment.

One aspect of discontinuing exposure is limiting access to media, such as monitoring the amount and type of TV coverage that a child watches. Younger and more sensitive or anxious children may be especially affected negatively by media reports because they are unable to sort and understand the meanings of what they hear and watch (Bonanno et al., 2010; Comer & Kendall, 2007; Lengua et. al. 2005; Masten & Obradovic, 2008). For example, young children do not understand that the fire or plane crash that they see are reruns of the same event and are often terrified by seeing what they perceive as numerous disasters. Riding an elevator after the World Trade Center was attacked in 2001, I overheard a little girl fearfully telling her mother who came to fetch her from a play date that she saw on her hosts' TV more and more buildings collapsing and asked if their building would also fall down. Because of her tender age, she was unable to understand that what she was witnessing was repeated broadcasting of the same footage, and she was terrified. On the other hand, older children may have more severe negative reactions because they have better access and clearer comprehension of what they are watching and its potential danger. The effects of social networks on media exposure are still unknown (Masten & Narayan, 2012).

Because of the unique nature of trauma reactions and their manifestations in children, parents are not always able to identify signs of distress in their traumatized children and negative effects may go unrecognized and therefore not be addressed in a timely manner (McDermott & Palmer, 1999). Identifying and assessing the child's reaction to a potentially traumatic event is a delicate balancing act between being alert to changes in the child's behaviors, which may indicate a negative reaction, and refraining from pathologizing normal reactions. The task becomes even more complicated for two reasons. First, some changes may seem minute, so that the child appears unaffected. Second, immediate family members may be so overwhelmed by their own reactions that they fail to notice alarming changes. When practitioners seek to assess trauma reactions in young children, they must often rely on observing behaviors rather than verbal reports about internalized reactions because the child may not have mastery of the verbal skills necessary to describe emotions.

Once the effects of the exposure on the child are identified and understood, interventions should be geared toward the child's developmental stage and the way he or she perceives and interprets the traumatic event. In addition to securing that basic needs for shelter, food, and acceptable living conditions are met, the work with children needs to focus on creating a sense of safety, normalcy, clarity, and trust, as well as preparing for future stressors. Most researchers and practitioners agree on the need to provide age-appropriate information about the event, its causes and ways of coping, normalize reactions, and adopt a multi-faceted, holistic approach that addresses diverse aspects of the child's life (Cohen, Berliner & March, 2000; Ehntholt & Yule, 2006; Yahav, 2011). One effective way to provide information is by generalizing reactions with statements such as "many children who shared a similar experience to yours were in an accident/lost a father/had to be evacuated from their home, feel like you [anxious/confused/angry] and find it hard to sleep/learn/play with friends; however, these feelings and thoughts often go away after some time." When the upcoming stressor is normative and known (such as a loved one dying or an anticipated major medical treatment that the child is facing), it is useful to prepare children by telling them what may happen, thus mitigating the effects of unpredictability. However, it is important to assess carefully the amount and level of detail given and adjust them to the age and abilities of the individual child because both too much and too little information may be stress producing.

Strategies for Working with Traumatized Children

Special attention should be paid to children with the highest level of exposure and with pre-exposure mental health issues because these are strong predictors of negative outcomes. To help traumatized children, development of specialized strategies and adaptation of strategies used with adults are required to make them compatible with the age-dependent ability to process experiences, regulate emotions, and react. General principles for working with children include creating a trusting relationship, rapport and a holding environment for their efforts to test limits, blaming, regression and acting out, which often occur, encouraging them non-intrusively to talk about their reactions, acknowledging and validating their feelings, and encouraging them to find their own solutions (e.g. ask what they feel like doing). In doing so, it is important to follow children's lead and be sensitive to clues that they provide in their talk, drawing, or play, such as repeated violence in games or checking to see if doors are locked. Language that children can understand should be used, such as "People are working hard to make us feel secure," "There are millions of buildings in the country, and only three were attacked."

Diverse approaches to help children have been suggested and many of the methods for treating adults have a children's version. Two of numerous examples are KidNET, an adapted narrative exposure for children (Van der Oord et al., 2010) and the Multisystemic, Multimodal, Multicomponent Model With Children (SDTAS), which includes individual trauma-focused therapy, group training in social skills, problem solving, conflict resolution, anger management and stress reduction, psychoeducation, art therapy, and medications within a therapeutic structured environment.

Many of the available treatments to help traumatized children have been shown to be effective. Although most approaches have been documented to reduce trauma-related symptoms and improve children's outcomes, evidence that a specific treatment is superior to others is yet to be developed. Yahav (2011) conducted a systematic review of available knowledge about the effects of war and terrorism on children and identified the following treatments as beneficial: brief trauma-focused therapy, cognitive-behavioral therapy (CBT), narrative exposure therapy, testimonial psychotherapy, meditation-relaxation techniques, and eye movement desensitization (EMDR).

Cognitive approaches received the most extensive empirical support as helpful in addressing traumatic reactions in children (Deblinger, Behl & Clickman, 2012; Pine & Cohen, 2002). Various models of CBT include similar components in different dosage, sequencing, and "how to's", and all are seeking to substitute distorted cognitions with realistic ones and enhance effective coping. The main elements are normalizing a child's reactions to the event, processing the experience and its meaning, facilitating mourning of losses, teaching ways of coping, fostering resilience, and strengthening social networks. One of the most effective models for helping traumatized children is *Trauma-Focused Cognitive Behavior Therapy* (TF-CBT), which is a highly structured intervention that integrates sessions with the child and the parents (Cary & McMillen, 2012). It was developed specifically to help children who experienced traumatic exposure and is effective following diverse types of events. Rather than a rigid protocol, it includes eight core components that can be tailored flexibly to individual needs. These components are relaxation training, review of the event, restoring trust, psychoeducation to parents about reactions typical to the child's age, parenting skills designed to address behavioral problems, and effective family communication. Research has shown that this model has the potential to help reduce PTSD symptoms and behavior problems, as well as the emotional distress of their caretakers, in children from racially and culturally diverse population groups in the US, Sri Lanka, Indonesia, Thailand, Zambia, Israel, the Netherlands, Germany, Norway, Russia, and Pakistan (Ford, 2009; Little, Akin-Little & Somerville, 2011; Mannarino & Cohen, 2011; Weiner, Schneider & Lyons, 2009).

The four-session *Child and Family Traumatic Stress Intervention* (CFTSI) that was developed recently also shows promise as an early intervention to help prevent the development of chronic PTSD in children aged 7 to 17 who were exposed to potentially traumatic events (Berkowitz, Stover & Marans, 2011). This model focuses on two key factors: social and familial support, and coping skills. As discussed in Chapters 4 and 7, the personal characteristic of good coping skills and the environmental aspect of available support are instrumental in determining and shaping reactions in children exposed to events that may be traumatic. The model attempts to ameliorate the risk for a chronic traumatic reaction by enhancing communication about feelings, symptoms, and behaviors between the child and the caregiver, thus increasing the support that the caregiver gives to the child, and by teaching both of them cognitive skills for coping with symptoms, such as guided imagery, thought stopping, and distraction techniques.

Additional successful models also exist. The modified version of CBT (CBT-CTG), which includes in addition to the trauma-focused components a grief-focused component, was developed by Cohen and colleagues (2006) to address traumatic grief in children, and was shown to generate significant improvement in PTSD, depression, anxiety, behavior problems, and grief. Van der Oord and colleagues (2010) found that the children's version of *Cognitive Behavioral Writing Therapy* helped to reduce trauma symptoms in children after various traumatic experiences and Kira (2010) documented that SDTAS produced a decrease in PTSD, complex PTSD, anxiety, and depressive symptoms. Although cognitive-behavioral therapy has received the most empirical support, Yahav (2011) concludes from her critical review of the diverse approaches that "other techniques are commonly used" (p. 90).

A model that specifically targets children exposed to multiple traumas is Attachment, Self-Regulation, and Competency (ARC). This is a comprehensive, milieu-based, phase-oriented intervention designed to enhance safety, stabilization, trauma processing, and functional reintegration (Arvidson et al., 2011). The model addresses three core domains that are typically harmed by exposure to continuous interpersonal trauma: attachment, self-regulation, and developmental competencies. The practitioner works with the child and the caregivers, such as parents, relatives, school staff, or residential facility personnel, to improve their ability to mutually read each other. In addition, the caregiver learns to interpret the child's behavior in the context of traumatic exposure (e.g. behavior of avoidance and aggression may be normalized), employ a consistent and appropriate response pattern, create predictable structure, and use soothing and co-regulating of the child's emotional reactions. This allows the building of a secure attachment that supports the development of the child's ability to identify and manage emotions, participate in problem solving, develop a sense of self, and learn effective strategies for coping. It also gives the child an opportunity to catch up in acquiring age-appropriate competencies, the development of which had been delayed by the traumatic exposure. Research shows that the model is effective in helping to improve behavior problems in children of all ages from diverse ethnocultural backgrounds who were involved with child protective services because of maltreatment (Arvidson et al., 2011).

Often a combination of strategies derived from various approaches is employed to achieve the most optimal outcome. For example, the Stanford Cue-Centered Treatment for Youth Exposed to Interpersonal Violence showed that a hybrid trauma intervention merging diverse theoretical approaches was helpful in reducing posttraumatic reactions. Specifically, while the results have not yet been published, mindfulness training with children in California who live in devastated communities and experience community violence, a high crime rate, and homelessness also seems to be promising in reducing the negative effects of trauma on executive functions, and enhancing youth cognitive functioning (Victor Carrion, MD, personal communication, March 2014).

Using drawing and other non-verbal techniques in trauma work can be helpful in allowing children to express, process and communicate their emotions in relation to the traumatic events, and play out their anxieties, anger, fear, and confusion, which they cannot express verbally. Creative means of play, drawing, books, enactment, and music for processing trauma have been claimed to be useful because they target the right hemisphere of the brain, where traumatic memories are stored (Arvidson et al., 2011; Crenshaw & Hardy, 2007; Haen, 2005; McNamee & Mercurio, 2006). As traumatized children repeatedly act out in their play an overwhelming experience, it gradually reduces the anxiety attached to the event and they regain a sense of mastery. For example, medical play is commonly used to help familiarize hospitalized and severely sick children with their disease and frightening medical procedures. Research has shown that this helps to reduce anxiety, alleviate stress, and enhance relationships with others and meaning making of their medical condition, thus contributing to growth (Jones & Landreth, 2002).

Creative therapeutic means help children to process diverse traumatic experiences in various cultural contexts. For example, an international, interdisciplinary program was organized by mental health professionals to help Mayan children in Guatemala process traumatizing experiences during the war and state-sponsored terror in the 1980s and 1990s. Indigenous cultural traditions of drawing, storytelling, collage, and dramatization were used in groups to allow participants to express their emotions, share their experiences, and learn ways of coping (Lykes, 1994). Most recently, a group of Israeli mental health professionals developed a sad-faced dog doll called Hibbuki (Hebrew for a little hug) that has been anecdotally reported to successfully help children who were exposed to political violence in Israel and to the atomic disaster in Japan to negotiate the effects of the traumatic experience. These and other creative strategies are especially useful when used in combination with additional techniques such as cognitive-behavioral strategies. Creative interventions can also be combined effectively with family, community and school-based interventions to facilitate children's expressions of grief and their coping with traumatic experiences (Webb, 2011).

Using Groups to Help Traumatized Children

Groups allow the creation of a secure and safe place, normalization and universalization of reactions to the stressor event ("I am not the only one experiencing this and thus, I am not crazy"), rebuilding a sense of community and supportive relationships, mitigation of feelings of isolation and loneliness, gaining better understanding of the negative effects and opportunities for growth from the experience, and the processing and overcoming of feelings of helplessness, guilt, shame, and despair (Aronson & Kahn, 2004; Haen, 2005; Malekoff, 2008). Leek Openshaw (2011) summarized and offered case illustrations for the skills and structure of providing group interventions to elementary and middle school children. However, providing services to children in groups has been found to be helpful in some but not all studies. For example, a group intervention, which combined verbal and experiential strategies, led to alleviation of grief symptoms in children who had lost a primary family member such as a parent or a sibling (Tonkins & Lambert, 1996), and a play therapy group was successful in helping children to process and cope with the death of their teacher (Webb, 2011). In contrast, Thabet, Vostanis and Karim (2005) failed to find that group intervention had a significant impact on posttraumatic or depressive symptoms in children in refugee camps in the Gaza Strip during ongoing armed conflict.

Groups are especially successful when conducted in schools by social workers, guidance counselors and psychologists to help children who share exposure to a traumatic event such as community violence or a disaster. A model with documented success is the *Multimodality Trauma Treatment (MMTT)*, which was developed by Amaya-Jackson and colleagues (2003) as a group intervention to be administered in schools to treat children and adolescents exposed to single-incident trauma resulting in PTSD. It is based on empirically validated cognitive-behavioral methods of treating PTSD in adults and anxiety and aggression in children. The model focuses on providing psychoeducation about anxiety management, telling the story of the trauma, processing of the experience, and learning strategies for preventing relapse. A British team (Fazel, Doll & Stein, 2009; Stein et al., 2003) found that short-term cognitive behavior interventions provided by trained, school-based mental health clinicians to small groups (5–8 participants) of vulnerable children, such as refugee children and middle school inner city youngsters who were exposed to violence, helped to reduce negative effects of traumatic exposure. Students who received the intervention reported significantly less PTSD and depression symptoms and their parents reported less psychosocial dysfunctions than the non-participating counterparts, but there were no differences among the groups in class performance and behavior. That the difference disappeared when those who did not receive treatment participated in a later similar group intervention supports the view that the change in symptoms was an outcome of the intervention. Similarly, Salloum and her colleagues (2009) reported that short-term structured groups with elementary school children after hurricane Katrina were useful in promoting strengths, coping, safety, and resilience.

Groups are particularly useful in helping children from predominantly collectivist communities and cultures because of the central role that relational systems play in their lives. Clauss-Ehlers (2008) found that connecting children influenced by traumatic exposure to a peer group was helpful to Latino children, echoing the finding by Belgrave and colleagues (2000) that group activities designed to increase feelings of self-worth, Afrocentric values, ethnic identity, and gender identity helped promote resilience in African American young adolescent girls. These research findings support my own experience as a consultant to psychosocial services in schools in areas of Brooklyn, New York, that became heavily populated with immigrants from the former Soviet Union after the collapse of the Communist regime. I supervised youth workers who facilitated groups for adolescent immigrants and witnessed the positive effects that group participation had on the ability of the youth to cope with stresses and challenges related to their relocation to a new and unfamiliar culture (Berger, 1996).

Two of the many group models with documented success in helping traumatized children are the *Cognitive Behavioral Intervention for Trauma in Schools (CBITS)* and the *Trauma Adaptive Recovery Group Education and Therapy (TARGET)*. CBITS was developed after hurricane Katrina to address PTSD, depression, and anxiety symptoms in children aged 10–15. It involved group and three individual sessions with traumatized children, their parents and teachers, and focused on psychoeducation about trauma reactions, relaxation training, cognitive therapy, real life exposure, and social problem solving. Research showed its efficacy in diverse ethnic groups following exposure to various potentially traumatic events (Cohen et al., 2009; Little, Akin-Little & Somerville, 2011; Morsette et al., 2009; Stein et al., 2003). TARGET is a non-exposure intervention that builds on the importance of attachment in coping with traumatic experiences and emphasizes the shift from a survival mode to a focus on personal growth in interpersonal relationships with family, friends, and community by addressing issues of self-esteem, anger, grief, shame, guilt, and spirituality (Courtois, Ford & Cloitre, 2009).

Settings for Working with Traumatized Children

Services for traumatized children function best when they are community-based, stigma-free, and cost effective. Thus services delivered in the context of schools and community centers rather than mental health facilities are often more appealing to children and families, especially in cultures that discourage sharing private and family issues with strangers. For example, Berger, Pat-Horenczyk and Gelkopf (2007) evaluated a school-based intervention program and recommended a two-stage approach. The first stage is universal and targets all children in an affected area, such as where a natural disaster occurred, a bomb exploded, or a nuclear accident happened. It includes psychoeducation and training in coping skills, which has shown to decrease trauma-related reactions. The second phase focuses on those who fail to show significant improvement within a reasonable amount of time and offers them specialized trauma-related therapeutic interventions, preferably in stigma-free settings. Jaycox and her colleagues (2010) found, in a project designed to offer free cognitive behavior trauma-focused services to children in New Orleans 15 months after hurricane Katrina, that most families preferred to access services through their children's schools rather than similar services at community clinic settings to avoid the stigma of mental health. Findings in other cultures were similar. McDermott and Palmer (1999) observed that a large-scale, school-based Australian project for the screening of children who suffered from psychological symptoms following the exposure to a bushfire was effective and acceptable to the public. These findings echo my own experience with immigrants from the former Soviet Union. Because mental health services were abused in their country of origin for political oppression, residents of the Russian enclave of Brooklyn were reluctant to use services identified as psychological and preferred to utilize counseling offered in the context of schools or community centers (Berger, 2005). Thus, it may be useful to maximize the offering of services in or adjacent to children's schools in communities that struggle with a collective stressor or a disaster.

Working with Parents of Traumatized Children

In working with traumatized children, it is important to include their parents, if they are available and able, because they are potentially their children's most helpful sources of support and are those who need to offer as much as possible reassurance and safety to prevent frightening feelings from becoming overwhelming. Parents should be encouraged to spend time with their children, listen to them and offer opportunities to express their concerns, use physical soothing such as picking them up, hugging, stroking and uttering comforting words, and validating ("I can understand that seeing something like this can scare you"), relating to previous successful coping ("you remember when you were afraid because . . . and you did . . . and it helped? Why don't we try it again?"). In addition, explanations in language and level of detail that are appropriate to a child's developmental ability can help children to regain a sense of security and feel that things are under control.

The more support and guidance parents, families and others in the immediate environment receive in restoring routines and creating a feeling of safety, the better they are equipped to help children to understand what is happening and cope with it, the more confident they feel, and a better outcome for parents and children is likely, whereas confused, overwhelmed and panicked parents may exacerbate children's negative reactions. It is especially important to help restore parental roles and a sense of competency, which may have been compromised during the struggle with the traumatic exposure.

Depending on the age of the child and the parent–child relationships, work can be done with parents alone or in diverse child–parent combinations. Examples of such combinations are conjoint play therapy, behavioral parent–child interaction therapy, family-based cognitive behavior therapy, psychodynamic child–parent psychotherapy (CPP), and child–parent interaction therapy (CPIT). Some of these models target the effects of a specific type of trauma and a certain age group (for example, CPP was developed for young children who had witnessed domestic violence), whereas others are more universal and applicable to different situations.

Parents need to be calmed and educated about developmentally appropriate, nurturing, and responsive ways to help their children. Of special importance is guiding parents and children in creating a joint narrative of the traumatic events. For example, Comer and his colleagues (2008) trained mothers in strategies to provide sensitive care-giving and modeling in addressing threatening exposure and found that their children showed fewer trauma-related symptoms, anxiety, and sadness, as well as better cognitive performance. Similarly, Sandler and colleagues (2010) found that programs to strengthen families of traumatized children have been successful in reducing mental health issues and improving academic and social functioning. Specifically, children can benefit from their parents learning strategies for soothing their kids, helping them to feel safe and express their reaction to distressing experiences, and maintaining a family life that is as normal as possible. Finally, Gewirtz, Forgatch & Wieling

(2008) advocate a first-line universal intervention for families exposed to a mass trauma event, the Oregon Model of Parent Management Training (PMTO), which trains parents in skill encouragement, limit setting, monitoring, interpersonal problem solving, and positive involvement, and has been implemented within diverse cultures and in several countries.

While it is very well understood that parents' reactions shape children's outcomes, the opposite is also true. Koplewicz and colleagues (2002) studied children who were in the World Trade Center building when it was bombed in 1993 but their parents were not. Although children were the only ones at the disaster site, parents' long-term reactions were strongly influenced by their children's distress, and the extent of intergenerational concordance in levels of PTSD symptoms increased over time. Therefore, practitioners who serve traumatized children will do well to assess their parents' reactions and be ready to offer help, if necessary, to enhance parents' ability to help their children.

Working with the Environment

There is abundant evidence that the return to familiar conditions benefits children's recovery. Therefore, it is recommended that services to traumatized children involve working with their environments, including extended family, neighborhood, and school, to activate support from kinship networks and social, spiritual and community systems. The logic of such intervention is that if their environment functions better and copes effectively, it is equipped to foster better grounding and coping in children by providing them with psychological and practical help and bringing much needed stability to their lives. Comprehensive, wrap-around, multi-component interventions with the child's environment have the best potential to help all involved to recover.

Interventions to affect the environment have been informed by different theoretical and therapeutic approaches. Trauma Systems Therapy (TST) is a multimodal, phase-based comprehensive method for treating posttraumatic stress (PTS) in children that adds to individual therapeutic approaches, creating trauma-informed milieu to also address environmental aspects. Because the social-ecological environment is critical in helping children to regulate emotions following exposure to traumatic stressor events and thus serves as a protective factor, this approach focuses on the social environment, especially home and school, which impact children's symptomatology. This approach has been developed in the Boston Center for Trauma Psychology and may include decreasing environmental stressors by changing school placement and case management assistance to improve the family's living conditions, which will eventually increase the child's capacity to regulate emotions and thus improve traumatic reactions. Research supports the effectiveness of this approach and shows that interventions to increase the stability of the environment indeed lead to significant improvements in stress-related symptoms (Ellis et al., 2011). Many other interventions include some effort to reshape the environment to become better holding and more supportive.

Treating Adolescents

Parents and educators should not be misled by reactions of adolescents that may appear adult-like, or underestimate the potential devastating long-term effects of traumatic exposure (Schonfeld, 2002). To address such effects, practice models have been developed specifically for this age group or adopted from models used with adults. In addition, some of the models discussed above as effective with children, such as *Trauma Systems Therapy*, apply also to adolescents. Numerous models exist, most of which include some combination of strategies based on cognitive behavior, psychoeducation and sometimes psychodynamic principles, as well as trauma-focused content, and are delivered individually or in groups. For example, the *Trauma-Focused Cognitive Behavior Therapy* described above is helpful for adolescents too and research has shown that a school-based ten-session cognitive-behavioral therapy group intervention helped to reduce symptoms of PTSD and depression, and improve psychosocial functioning and classroom behavior in traumatized middle school students (Stein et al., 2003).

Most of these approaches are effective in various cultural contexts. For example, in a project supported by UNICEF, school counselors provided trauma and grief-focused group services to secondary school adolescents in post-war Bosnia. Outcomes evaluation showed that participation led to reduction in distress and depressive symptoms as well as better psychosocial adaptation, school attendance, and compliance with rules (Layne et al., 2001). Rynearson (2001) successfully employed restorative storytelling, which includes the use of a healing narrative experience and reconnecting. The cognitive-behavioral model called *Thought Field Therapy* (TFT), which utilizes self-tapping of specific acupuncture points while recalling a traumatic event, was applied by Callahan and Callahan (2000) in a community-based program for adolescents orphaned during the genocide in Rwanda, and Sakai, Connoly and Oas (2010) reported that it led to a significant decrease in PTSD symptoms. A benefit of this model is that it gives adolescents a great amount of control over the treatment of their symptoms and thus is compatible with the search for autonomy and self-reliance ("I can do it on my own rather than depend on adults") typical at this age.

Like with children, groups offer an effective way for providing services to traumatized adolescents. Because of the central role that peer relationships play during adolescence, with the affiliation with natural groups providing a major source of support, the use of groups is very helpful. A group of youths with similar experiences may provide role models and substitute for relationships lost to a stressful event such as immigration or forced relocation. Research and clinical experience support groups that: (1) are short-term (6–12 sessions); (2) focus on content directly related to trauma (rather than general pathology) such as processing the experience, sharing it, and learning techniques for relaxation and strategies for coping; and (3) use cognitive behavior principles. Goenjian and colleagues (1997) reported good results in treating young adolescents following the 1988 earthquake in Armenia with a brief, school-based trauma and grief-focused group psychotherapy combined with a few individual sessions. Processing of the traumatic experience, learning coping skills, and relaxation techniques helped to alleviate PTSD symptoms and prevent the worsening of depression. Similarly, *Structured Psychotherapy for Adolescents Respond-ing to Chronic Stress (SPARCS)*, which is focused on trauma and uses the cogni-tive approach of dialectic group psychoeducational intervention to teach skills, yielded positive outcomes (DeRosa & Pelcovitz, 2008). Layne et al. (2001, 2008) found in a randomized controlled study in post-war Bosnia that a 17-session group intervention tailored specifically to address grief reactions in adolescents who experienced traumatic loss and severe adversity was effective in reducing symptoms of PTSD and depression. Another successful program is *Trauma and Grief Component Therapy (TGCT)*, which combines interventions that are consid-ered effective in helping adolescents who have been exposed to traumatic expe-riences including psychoeducation about typical reactions of adolescents to trauma and loss, teaching coping and problem-solving strategies, skill building, in-depth processing of the traumatic experience, grief reactions and related feelings, and building social support.

Although most effective groups for trauma treatment apply cognitive-behavior principles, other types of groups have also been used successfully to treat traumatized adolescents. For instance, Aronson and Kahn (2004) have developed a manualized group therapy, which is based on psychodynamic perspectives and addresses issues of separation-individuation, anger, identity, and interpersonal relationships. A team of mental health experts from the Netherlands, Sudan, Indonesia, Burundi, and the US (Jordans et al., 2011; Jordans, Tol & Komproe, 2011) collaborated in an effort to develop guide-lines for choosing effective intervenions and tested it in particular for low- and middle-income countries. The results suggested that a modular intervention that combines therapeutic elements from community mobilization, parent-management training and cognitive behavior therapy, and includes local cul-tural beliefs and practices, is effective in reducing trauma-related symptoms (Saltzman et al., 2003).

Non-verbal interventions with traumatized adolescents have also received some support from research, although this is non-conclusive. For example, New-man and Motta (2007) found that adolescent girls aged 14 to 17 who lived in a residential facility and participated in aerobic activity three times a week for eight weeks demonstrated reduced symptoms of PTSD, depression and anxi-ety. Similarly, Jordans and colleagues (2010) examined a five-week, 15-session, classroom-based group intervention (CBI) informed by concepts from creative-expressive and experiential therapy, cooperative play, and cognitive behavioral therapy. Techniques of psychoeducation, socio-drama, movement and dance group activities, stress reduction, and drawing were used. The outcomes were improved interpersonal skills, especially among girls, reduction in psychological difficulties such as hyperactivity, peer-related, emotional and conduct problems, and aggression among boys, and increased sense of hope for older children. The authors concluded that because the nature of the intervention is active, it is compatible with externalized expressions of distress, which is typical for boys.

Like with children, working in concert with the family, teachers, sport group leaders, and other adults involved in the life of the adolescent is helpful in creating a healing and growth-prompting social environment. Family involvement and strengthening and monitoring by parents may be critical to the successful treatment of traumatized youths. For example, Rowe and Liddle (2008) reported the success of a trauma-focused version of the *Multidimensional Family Therapy (DFT)*, which combines sessions with the adolescent, the parents, the whole family, and systems in the community such as schools and churches. Individual sessions with the teen are used for telling of trauma narratives to examine feelings of abandonment, loss, or guilt and learn to regulate them. The focus is on collaborative setting of goals, generating hope, facilitating life skills, teaching effective ways to cope with stress and to seek support, attending to interpersonal relationships, and providing guidance for recognizing signs that trauma symptoms are activated and addressing them to increase the sense of mastery. In sessions with parents, their own struggles with the stressor are addressed, and they are validated, guided in managing their emotional reactions, taught about adolescents' trauma reactions, and encouraged to take care of themselves, and when they are ready, to become more available and responsive to their adolescent children and try new parenting strategies. With the whole family, work addresses effective interactions and communications, rebuilding mutual support among family members, and talking together in a non-blaming, non-defensive way to construct solutions. In addition, case management by collaboration with social networks, the juvenile justice system, and educational and social service agencies is used to stabilize the environment and develop supports for youths and their families to enhance the recovery from traumatic exposure. Other promising approaches are the Sanctuary Model, Integrated Treatment of Complex Trauma for Adolescents (ITCI-A), the Trauma Affect Regulation Guide for Education and Therapy (TARGET), the Trauma Recovery and Empowerment Model (TREM and M-TERM), and the Structured Psychotherapy for Adolescents Responding to Chronic Stress (SPARCS).

Self-Care for Providers

Practitioners who serve survivors of traumatic exposure must exercise self-care for their own welfare as well as for recharging and maintaining their professional effectiveness in helping their traumatized clients. Such self-care can include individual and environmental measures. On the individual level, self-care is a customized process based on what each practitioner identifies as working for her or him. Relevant strategies include awareness of feelings and behaviors that may indicate secondary traumatization, being tuned to one's own and colleagues' signs of distress, mindfulness of one's own limits, and refraining from being a hero and pushing too hard. Of utmost importance is deliberate taking of action to recover from taxing intensive interactions with trauma survivors (Killian, 2008; Pearlman & Caringi, 2009). These may include physical, emotional, and, if applicable, spiritual measures. Practicing relaxation and yoga as well as making time and plans for leisure and hobbies, listening to music, meeting friends, and traveling that allow taking a break from constant "rubbing" with human suffering are useful. An additional measure is reflexivity to develop a personal narrative of the involvement in the helping process (i.e. what were the nature, phases, challenges, benefits, meanings and "take away" of the process of providing help?). Keeping written notes about professional interactions, documenting and self-analysis of interactions with the traumatized, and monitoring the feelings and thoughts that they trigger in the practitioner help to create a protective distance and maintain the necessary ability to observe from outside rather than become an insider who shares clients' experience and potentially their inability to cope effectively.

On the environmental level, help can come from the practitioner's family, social networks, agency, and fellow clinicians. The family is potentially a valuable source for instrumental help such as providing childcare and household services as well as emotional support. Social networks can be a very powerful source of support for practitioners. They can offer chatting sessions with friends and colleagues, opportunities to process the experience and their own reactions in a non-critical, caring context, as well as recognition and validation of the importance of their contribution by society at large, as reflected through written and electronic media, leadership, and relevant social institutions.

Agencies that serve traumatized clients have the obligation to ensure that they provide conditions that allow workers to perform effectively. Because traumatic situations tend to become chaotic, it is crucial that the agency develop a well-structured and flexible work environment with clearly defined roles, tasks, leadership, and procedures, which are implemented before, during, and after the helping process. The agency must maximize the physical safety of professionals to the degree that circumstances allow as well as securely meeting their basic needs (food, sleep, respite), because the absence of these may compromise practitioners' ability to serve. Because preparation and training are potential buffers against STSD, negative effects on helpers can be lessened by providing appropriate knowledge about clients' normal and pathological stress responses (such as violent outbursts of frustrated individuals), which may become challenging to workers, principles for mobilization of services, a clear protocol for differential assessment and effective interventions with diverse population groups, and developing skills and readiness to help those exposed to trauma. Berger and Gelkopf (2010) documented the effectiveness of participation in a group that provided theoretical knowledge, experiential exercises, and learning of skills for reducing the level of secondary traumatization and increasing professional self-efficacy of practitioners. Craig and Sprang (2010) showed that utilizing evidence-based trauma intervention decreased compassion fatigue, suggesting that agencies should train practitioners in such practice models.

Working in pairs or in teams may afford peer support and alleviate stress, as can changes in size and composition of caseload, such as reducing the number of clients or diversifying types of issues treated to create a more balanced experience, although this may not always be feasible, depending on the nature of the practice context. Even in an agency that serves primarily traumatized clients (e.g. a burns unit in a hospital or a shelter for severely abused women), the intensity or duration of trauma exposure of workers can be modified and thus reduce the likelihood of secondary traumatization. Supervisory and consultation sessions with a senior experienced practitioner may help novice practitioners to reflect on their own and clients' situations, identify issues, and discuss options for solutions. For example, practitioners often become frustrated, hopeless, and angry when a traumatized client does not respond well or becomes aggressive in reaction to their well-intentioned effort for engagement and empathy. An explanation from a supervisor that such a seemingly negative reaction is typical testing by a client scarred by betrayal in the context of a close relationship and may indicate that the client is starting to feel close to the practitioner and is afraid of such closeness because of the previous negative experience, can help to enhance the ability of a practitioner to contain and tolerate a client's behavior and create the necessary holding environment.

In addition to mitigating professionals' stress related to direct and vicarious traumatization, Baum and Ramon (2010) documented reports from Jewish and Arab Israeli social workers that formal and informal, emotional, and practical help from managers, supervisors, and colleagues can foster professional growth, cultivate increased knowledge and intervention skills in situations of crisis, loss and bereavement, and enhance professional identity, pride in professional accomplishments, and team cohesion. Helping providers of services to those whose lives have been affected by trauma to receive reliable information about available resources, promoting of the importance of taking care of practitioners' mental health, and destigmatizing the use of services (Scully, 2011) can minimize negative effects, and assist in combating secondary traumatization.

In situations of shared traumatic reality, the natural support systems of family, colleagues, supervisors, and professional and social organizations with which the practitioner is affiliated are also potentially struggling with the effects of the traumatic exposure, making them less available and capable of offering support. In such conditions helpers' knowledge that their own family members are unharmed enhances their ability to help others. It is important that the environment be sensitive to clues from the practitioner regarding offering help because sometimes well-intentioned efforts to help can produce more stress. For instance, coming home after having facilitated a challenging group of survivors and witnesses following the 9/11 attacks, I wanted to be left alone. My family respected my wish, but it proved to be challenging for friends who were visiting from Israel, who made extensive attempts to get me to share my painful experiences, causing further distress rather than providing support.

10 Interventions with Couples and Families

Interventions with families apply both to those who have been traumatized directly as a system, such as when a whole family lives in a war zone or is involved in a road accident, and those who live with traumatized family members, such as the families of veterans diagnosed with PTSD or a life-threatening cancer. Trauma-related couple and family interventions have several foci. First, members need to be helped to communicate openly about the trauma and its effects in a pace and manner that is acceptable to all. Second, the system needs to be restructured to adapt roles and power allocation to the new circumstances (e.g. if the mother can no longer drive children to school because of an injury, the father, an older sibling, or a member of the extended family needs to take on the responsibility or the family must secure extra-familial help). Finally, the family's ability to provide mutual support to its members must be restored and enhanced. These goals may be achieved by working with an individual couple or family as well as by working with several couples or families who share the traumatic experience in a multi-family group. For example, a community-based, multi-family group was developed to create a supportive, normalizing healing environment that addressed the traumatic loss experienced by families of union members who were missing after the 9/11 terrorist attacks (Ludwig et al., 2006).

Working with Couples Affected by Trauma

As discussed in Chapter 5, traumatic experiences of one or both spouses are often accompanied by challenges to the marital relationships. Couple trauma work can help the relationships directly by improving specific aspects such as communication, sharing of emotions and joint decision-making, and indirectly by helping to achieve changes in the individuals that then feed back into changes in the relationship. Thus, if a practitioner works with a couple to improve their way of giving feedback to each other, they learn better mutual understanding and responding. When a traumatized spouse feels understood due to the couple work, it can lead to less aggressive or avoidant behavior, which contributes to improving intimacy and the quality of the relationships.

This double foci is compatible with recent models of treatment which, unlike the previous focus on improving the relationship or family environment exclusively, target simultaneously improvement in family functioning and individual symptoms (Monson, Fredman & Taft, 2011). Of special importance is helping non-direct victims of traumatic exposure, such as a spouse of an individual diagnosed with PTSD. Sometimes, to shield their loved ones, spouses try to protect them from unpleasant encounters and mitigate the pain involved in treatment. For example, a wife may encourage a husband who struggles with trauma-related problems not to think about the traumatic event and focus on pleasant memories, or she may suggest that the couple refrain from meeting people and going to places associated with the trauma. While well intentioned, such spousal reactions are not helpful because they deprive the partner of the opportunity to learn to cope with the difficulties and may in fact reinforce dysfunctional avoidance and undermine interventions built on exposure (described in Chapter 9). The focus of working with the couple in such situations is on discussing strategies for helping the traumatized partner accomplish the tasks required for the intervention rather than encouraging shying away from trauma-related issues. Thus, a wife may be asked to offer encouragement and support to a husband who is going through the pain of exposure rather than offering him a glass of wine or involving him in a discussion of unrelated topics.

One aspect of helping couples affected by highly stressful events is enhancing their relationship-focused coping, which has been found to increase marital satisfaction, adjustment, and quality (Bodenmann & Randall, 2012). A dominant strategy to this effect is guiding and encouraging partners to use *active engagement*, i.e. teaching them productive modes of open communication and encouraging them to use these modes to have a discussion of their mutual feelings, which can pave the way to the co-development of ways to address the situation.

Several promising models have emerged for helping couples with trauma-related issues. Monson and colleagues (2011a) developed cognitive-behavior conjoint couple therapy (CBCT), a time limited, manualized approach that combines psychoeducation about PTSD and relationships, behavioral interventions to improve communication, and cognitive interventions to modify maladaptive thinking and behaviors. It addresses simultaneously PTSD and intimate relationships, and focuses on sharing thoughts and feelings, conjoint meaning making in relation to the trauma, and developing strategies for problem solving. Preliminary evidence has shown that the intervention led to improvement in couple relationships, more satisfaction, and better couple functioning and adjustment, as well as decrease in PTSD symptoms in the partner diagnosed with PTSD.

Emotion-Focused Therapy, a short-term practice model supported by research, has been the most frequently used intervention to help couples where one or both partners have a history of severe trauma with negative effects on the relationships. The model is systemic in the sense that it combines focusing on the couple's interactions with addressing individual aspects in spouses to help change interaction and communication patterns that erode the relationships.

Response patterns related to the trauma are identified in current interactions and addressed as an external entity to be targeted by both parties rather than an issue that resides in one of them, thus recruiting both to concentrate on the experience rather than get involved in a mutual blaming game. Partners learn to mutually read each other's emotional cues and respond to them in terms of past traumatic experiences, i.e. how present interactions are the manifestation of reactions in previous traumatizing situations rather than the current behavior of the partner, such as a wife's rejecting of sexual approaches by her husband being viewed as shaped by her reaction as a victim to sexual abuse by her father rather than recoiling from her husband. Gaining such understanding helps to de-escalate negative interaction cycles and allows partners to become less angry and more empathic, and develop a more accepting mutual attitude ("this unpleasant reaction is not personal; it is not really directed to me"), such that they become able to better contain each other's emotional scars and attend to mutual needs. Based on this cleansing of the relationships of exacerbating, unconstructive reactions, partners can change the rules for and nature of their interactions to become more mutually supportive, and help to build rather than destroy each other and create a healing relationship. The focus on the impact of emotions on the quality of intimate relationships is useful in helping improve the spousal connection for those whose life becomes chaotic as a result of exposure to traumatic events, where issues of affect-regulation, self-blame, and troubled interpersonal relationship prevail.

Additional models of couple therapy for pairs affected by traumatic exposure include emotionally focused couple therapy, systemic family therapy, couples coping enhancement training (CCET), coping-oriented couples therapy (COCT), cognitive behavioral conjoint therapy (CBCT), and family crisis intervention. Like individual models, most of these interventions comprise of diverse variations of similar components of psychoeducation, practicing different interaction patterns, and mutual nourishing and support. However, we have limited and anecdotal evidence of how well these models work and their outcomes.

Working with Traumatized Families

Practitioners can work with an entire family in conjunction with and as a context for treating one traumatized member, or target the family as the focal unit and employ family work as the sole intervention designed to address the impact on the family of a traumatic exposure experienced directly by one or more members (e.g. a life-threatening diagnosis) or by the whole family (e.g. living in a war zone). For some families, discussing children's issues is easier and may serve as a segue to the discussion of broader family problems. A review of effective strategies for treatment of trauma-related problems by the Institute of Medicine (2007) stressed the importance of understanding and addressing the impact of trauma in intergenerational context. Wells (2006) emphasizes the importance of encouraging families that have encountered a disaster and its aftermath to rely on help from their natural community rather than rushing to offer therapy. In some societies, this recommendation may be culturally inappropriate. For example, during the ethnic war in Sri Lanka many families suffered ambiguous loss (Boss, 2007) due to the disappearance of family members, typically husbands/fathers, whose fate was unknown. The safest strategy was for the remaining members to keep silent, whereas seeking social support could have been dangerous (Somasundaram, 2004).

Major aspects in working with traumatized families are helping them to develop mutual tolerance for differences in response and coping, as well as building the courage and openness to discuss taboo topics which sit in the living room like a white elephant that everybody tiptoes around. Critical in creating an atmosphere favorable to such dialogues are teaching parents to give children permission to discuss their emotional reactions, and supporting the parents in their efforts to do so, teaching all family members to avoid blaming and negotiate the creation of new ways of doing things by accommodating rituals, revisiting role allocation and mutual expectations, restructuring rules and boundaries, and improving communication among family members. Such changes allow families to resume their life in a way that is different, functional, and appropriate for their post-trauma new self.

Parallel to helping individuals discover possible meaning in a traumatic experience, some approaches advocate assisting families to identify a common family ethos of constructing their distress in a more acceptable and positive way. Practitioners can help families to share, bear witness to each other's pain, validate their experiences, and offer love and support. In the tradition of narrative family therapy, clinicians can help family members to discuss and develop an alternative story of the traumatic experience that frames their distress more positively and provides a preferred alternative to the "trauma-centered family story" (Hawley & DeHaan, 1996). Psychoeducation for families about normal grief reactions and validation of different ways of coping are crucial. Such measures can help family members to be receptive to each other's diverse pace and paths of reaction. Furthermore, Johnston, Bailey and Wilson (2014) posit that fostering personal agency, effective communication, relational networks, and rules and exchange of support can enhance multigenerational interdependence, which leads to family resilience. For example, a few months after a couple lost their son in combat, the mother continued to mourn, refused to wear any color but black, see friends, go to movies, concerts or the theater, or attend any social event. The father, while grieving the death of his son, desired to gradually begin to go on with his life and felt that spending time with friends could help to alleviate his pain. This led to animosity between the spouses and mutual accusations. As their therapist, I focused on working with them on developing tolerance and acceptance of their different ways of coping with the loss and learning to live with it.

The aforementioned core principles have been translated into various models of practice with traumatized families. One of the first models of family therapy with traumatized families was developed by Figley (1989). His model seeks to empower the family and provide secondary prevention, i.e. avoid further dysfunction. It builds on the natural healing forces of the family system and is designed to create a situation that allows families to heal themselves by making peace with the past and preparing for future challenges. It included five steps: (1) building commitment to change, and identification of objectives acceptable to the family; (2) framing the problem, i.e. identifying the required change by eliciting all members' views as to what, how, and why the stressor event happened; (3) reframing the problem, i.e. redefining its familial meaning in terms that are more tolerable, such as understanding an unacceptable behavior as attention seeking; (4) developing a theory for healing, i.e. exploring what family members think they can do to resolve the problem; and (5) closure.

Wells (2006) advocates a model for brief family therapy. Similar to helping individuals affected by traumatic exposure, the first step is addressing basic needs as much as possible through the adult couple as a means to reestablish their parental role as protectors and providers. Once basic needs are met, parents are helped to take the lead in recovering routines of bedtime, family norms, and rituals. The final phase in the familial healing process is creating conditions favorable to all family members for sharing their narratives of the stressful event, their individual ways of understanding what transpired, and the meaning they make of it. Young children may express their experience by non-verbal means of drawing, puppets, or play.

Link Individual Family Empowerment Intervention (LIFE) is a model that was developed by Landau (2007) on the basis of Linking Human Systems Approach (LHSA) to initiate and sustain change in families that have undergone a trauma. It is ecologically based, informed by the strengths perspective, and can be adapted to diverse cultural norms. A basic assumption is that people and families are inherently competent and resilient. Facing highly stressful events, they tend to disconnect from each other and respond to the event in different ways and at different paces. This may trigger a transitional conflict manifested in a wide range of problems and risky behaviors including increased drug abuse, mental health issues, and violence. Shortage of resources may exacerbate the conflict. Family interventions based on this model include eight sessions. One family member, typically not the person with the presenting problem, is selected in a collaborative process to serve as a link between the practitioner and the family. First a joint mapping of the family structure and an intervention plan are developed collaboratively by the link person, who serves as the main change agent, and the professional, whose main role is to be a resource rather than intervene directly. The sessions with the family focus on enhancing positive connectedness, exploring and recreating ritual, and re-storying (i.e. developing a family narrative that represents its lived experience) to help the family to change intergenerational themes of vulnerability into themes of resilience.

The model titled *Families OverComing Under Stress (FOCUS)* was developed by the University of California, Los Angeles (UCLA) and the Harvard School of Medicine. This model is structured yet flexible. This six to eight-session trauma-informed, strength-based, family-centered program is designed to facilitate the resiliency of military families encountering stress because of the deployment of a family member to active duty in a conflict or war zone. Some of the meetings are with parents and children separately and some include all available family members. Since its inception, this model has been implemented in bases of the US army, air force, and navy as well as communities in Florida that were impacted by multiple hurricanes, and families facing children's medical trauma in California. The program trains families in communicating effectively, especially about issues related to stress and seeking mutual help, sharing narratives, practicing relaxation strategies, enhancing empathy, stress management, collaborative setting of goals and solving problems, emotion regulation, and mutual fostering of hope and confidence. Preliminary evaluations showed improvements in parents' levels of stress, depression and anxiety, in children's emotional, behavioral, social and coping functioning, and in family communication, role clarity, emotional responsiveness, and problem solving (Beardslee et al., 2011).

Another model supported by research is *Strengthening Family Coping Resources*. This multi-family group, manualized, trauma-specific intervention is tailored for distressed families residing in stress-intensive contexts of low-income urban settings. It involves all family members in the healing process of learning constructive coping strategies during three modules over 15 sessions. Building family routines and rituals, identifying priorities, and developing strategies for addressing traumatic exposure receive special emphasis (Kiser et al., 2010).

Combinations of similar components of teaching family members about typical trauma reactions, strategies for self-regulation, and developing family tasks, rules, communication, boundaries and decision making, as well as identifying and reaching out to potential sources of social support are the crux of additional available models for family-focused trauma interventions.

11 Community Interventions

To heal communities, it is not sufficient to address the needs of individuals within the community. Rather, broad systemic interventions are often necessary. For example, it has been argued that efforts to promote the mental health of Native Americans who have suffered a continuous community trauma must begin with recognition of their fundamental rights as a distinct population group (McLeigh, 2010). Furthermore, because communities are systems, which are parts of larger systems such as the state and the nation, and include smaller subsystems such as families, churches, and schools, any intervention in one part of the community potentially impacts other parts. Thus, a school-based intervention may start a chain reaction of effects on diverse groups, as well as the whole community.

The increased frequency and awareness of mass violence in the world has led to a growing need for the development and evaluation of interventions designed to address the aftermath of collective traumatic events. One effort to address this need took place in 2001, when 58 disaster mental health experts from six countries were convened in a collaborative initiative of The US Departments of Defense, Justice, Health and Human Services, Veterans Affairs (including the National Center for PTSD), and the American Red Cross to evaluate the effectiveness of various strategies for early interventions in situations of mass trauma, identify gaps in knowledge, and make recommendations relative to what works (National Institute of Mental Health, 2002). While the committee used a combination of research findings and expert opinion, conclusions were based mostly on findings from randomized controlled experiments, whereas other types of knowledge, such as practice wisdom and documented clinical experience, were viewed as offering limited support for the effectiveness of interventions. Thus, the perspective reflected in this particular report is that of a narrow hierarchical positivistic approach (i.e. only knowledge generated by certain types of research is considered), rather than an inclusive evidentiary pluralism (i.e. considering all types of knowledge). This selective nature of the sources may result in preferring particular types of interventions over others not necessarily because they are better but because they have been more rigorously researched.

Another initiative was by The European Network for Traumatic Stress (2009), which orchestrated a collaborative effort of experts from 15 European countries to develop recommendations for best multi-agency practice with various levels of intervention following a disaster, and disseminated the conclusions to professionals across the continent. In 2012, the NATO Science for Peace and Security Programme organized an advanced research workshop titled Reaching Vulnerable Populations Worldwide: Applying Evidence-Based Training and Core Psychological Change Processes to Disseminate Effective Services for Trauma Survivors. Trauma experts (myself included) from various countries (the US, Canada, the Netherlands, Germany, Israel, Armenia, Turkey, and Croatia) worked to identify effective strategies for addressing the aftermath of collective trauma, disseminating this knowledge, and training professionals and non-professionals in using it to help traumatized populations. Finally, the Administration of Child Services in New York City commissioned an effort to develop an evidence-based, practitioner-friendly, trauma-related curriculum, with an emphasis on cultural competence, designed for child welfare workers (Berger & Joyce, 2010).

In spite of these and similar endeavors, as Foa and colleagues (2005) posited almost a decade ago, the current reality is still that empirical evidence for the efficacy of interventions with whole communities remains limited and many of the recommendations are based on practice knowledge.

Goals of Community Interventions

Like with individuals and families, panels of experts on best practices for responding to mass trauma have emphasized that interventions should be as immediate as possible and first focus on survival, safety, food, shelter, and providing information on available distribution of clothes, products, and medical supplies (National Institute of Mental Health, 2002; Inter-Agency Standing Committee, 2007). At this phase, one stop shop crisis centers that offer information about the provision of instrumental needs, connect people to relevant resources in a reliable way, and refer to mental health emergency services are effective. Early, brief, and focused interventions have the potential to effectively address the immediate impact of mass trauma by reducing the incidence, duration, and severity of negative reactions, though they do not secure against long-term effects, which may require long-term interventions.

Once the basic needs of the community are addressed, a major goal is restoring the community's collective sense of togetherness and efficacy, i.e. the sense of belonging following a collective trauma, which contributes to the healing of the community and its members (Possick, Sadeh & Shamai, 2008). The critical role of social networks in recovery from disaster has been extensively recognized such that the collective actions of the community have the potential to minimize vulnerability and enhance healing. Especially helpful is affiliation with a group that is likely to cope successfully and achieve positive outcomes in general and specifically in relation to traumatic occurrences and their aftermath (Hobfoll et al., 2007b). This facilitates the recovery of individuals, families and specific age, gender and ethno-cultural groups within the community (such as children, adolescents, older adults, and undocumented immigrants), recovery of the collective sense of efficacy, the revitalization of social agencies and community resources, and the instilling of hope.

A critical component in healing is fostering mutual recognition and acknowledgement of the suffering of members of other groups, accompanied by an effort to minimize the comparative competition of who suffered more, creating opportunities for mourning past painful experiences and taking steps towards forgiveness, as well as helping the community to develop narratives about the event and its aftermath, specifically those that include hope and recognition of the community's strengths (Shamai, forthcoming). Thus, systematic archiving and documentation of survivors' memories that combines recognition of pain, loss, strengths, and bravery can be beneficial in re-storying and generating new empowering narratives, which are conducive to PTG (Somasundaram & Sivayokan, 2013). Similarly, public testimonials of the persecution of Native Americans by white conquerors serve to acknowledge suffering and injustice, while also helping Native Americans to regain their own cultural identity. Intervention with communities should also include a component of enhancing preparedness for future collective disasters.

Strategies of Intervention with Traumatized Communities

Like with individuals and families, community interventions may require both immediate short-term and long-term strategies, because some community traumatic exposures are prolonged due to living for years in a war zone, such as Somalia, or for extended periods in refugee camps following a natural disaster, such as in Haiti. Several strategies for the identification and classification of approaches for working with traumatized communities have been discussed in the literature. For example, Sztompka (2000) analyzed social trauma literature and identified diverse types of strategies used for addressing a community trauma. Strategies of *Adaptive innovation* aim to improve the condition of those affected by raising economic, social, and cultural resources, advancing social networks, and cultivating the modification and transformation of norms. Related to this is *Cultural rebellion* or *Radical contestation*, which involves a comprehensive transformation of a culture to substitute the original traumatizing culture with a totally different cultural set-up. *Sustained optimism* is adopting the belief that eventually dangers will be avoided and solutions found by science, human ingenuity, and technology. People may use *Ritualism*, i.e. seeking a safe haven by affiliation with spiritual and religious movements or other established traditions and institutionalizing systemic memorial and reconciliation rituals such as Memorial Day rites, prayers, and ceremonies. Thus, the screening of a movie that documented multi-generational consequences of a community disaster in a Navajo reservation and the development of a conversation about the meaning and implications of the trauma became part of the healing process. *Retreatism*, also conceptualized as *Pragmatic acceptance*, means ignoring, repressing or denying of the trauma as if it never existed and related to this is *Cynical pessimism*, which refers to focusing on enjoying life here and now before the traumatic occurrence. This can be seen in life in Israel, where people go about their daily life and adopt an attitude of business as usual as if suicide bombs and shelling of towns and villages were not a daily occurrence.

In planning and implementing interventions, several core principles for helping traumatized communities must be observed. First, interventions must be selective based on a needs assessment. Most groups do not need professional treatments and can regain stability with the help of support from immediate and community systems. Therefore, to most effectively help communities to recover, the focus needs to be on activating local powers and natural support systems, while professional services are reserved for those whose situation requires more specialized help. Particularly important is facilitating access to social support by both *bonding*, i.e. micro-level strengthening of social networks (family, kin, friends), and *bridging*, i.e. macro-level connecting to broader systems (e.g. schools and churches). Access to resources should be allocated in a fair and as equitable a manner as possible based on identified needs rather than gender, age, sexual orientation, immigration status, ethnic/racial affiliation, or localities. Efforts to facilitate impartial access to all may encounter pressure from stronger groups, which may claim that they are more eligible because of their history of supporting the systems by paying taxes and fulfilling other civil obligations. In addition, such efforts are susceptible to nepotism and favoritism. Developing mechanisms to limit forceful access to resources and maintain social justice in allocation should be a priority in communities devastated by traumatic exposure.

A second principle is that the endeavor be collaborative on all levels, i.e. between the community and external help providers, between community leadership and members, and among different groups within the community. Collaboration in planning and executing interventions to help the community cope and heal can take different formats with varying degrees of community involvement in the recovery efforts. This involvement may range from the community carrying the dominant role in providing services, to sharing this role with non-local help providers, or serving in a consulting capacity (Inter-Agency Standing Committee, 2007). Whatever role the community plays in the planning and execution of rehabilitation programs following a collective trauma, these efforts are most effective when the community takes an active part in the activities, even when external financial, technical, material, medical, and professional resources are mobilized. Whatever the level of the affected community's involvement, it is important that it has a voice and participates in the planning and implementation of the interventions.

The benefits of community involvement are fourfold. First, community members are best informed relative to who needs what amongst them and thus can best direct the distribution and utilization of resources. Using local human and organizational resources and building their capacities helps to make sure that relief and reconstruction efforts are relevant to the concerns and challenges experienced by the affected population. Second, it has been demonstrated time and again that community members and community-based organizations are invaluable in the development and provision of post-trauma services because they allow the incorporation of local knowledge and indigenous strategies into the responses to traumatic events, and enhance cooperation in the restoration efforts. Joop de Jong, a Dutch professor of cultural and international psychiatry (2002), recommends that those affected take central responsibility in the recovery efforts within their natural cultural traditions and social structures. This recommendation stands on the shoulders of previous scholars who have underscored the importance of early and ongoing participation of community members in planning and carrying out interventions (Harvey, Mondesir & Aldrich, 2007), and building on local assets. Third, community involvement serves to rehabilitate natural local leadership and a sense of self-efficacy, and empower a sense of local control and ownership over decisions that affect community members' lives. Community leaders can play a major role in the efforts to map and re-establish natural social support systems. In many cultures, people tend to listen and be open to receiving guidance and help from informal leaders more than from professionals. For example, Boehm, Enosh and Shamai (2010), who studied communities in Northern Israel at a time of political and military tensions with neighboring Lebanon, found that communities in crisis gravitated towards grassroot leaders whom they trusted and felt close to for direction and support. Therefore, it is crucial to identify who are influential local indigenous key figures in the relevant communities, whose voices are respected, and recruit them for collaborative work to lead the process of rebuilding (Somasundaram & Sivayokan, 2013). Support and empowerment of local leaders and working together with them are keys to helping traumatized communities and can be achieved by creating advisory bodies as well as forums that allow a dialogue for exchanging ideas, assessment of the situation, and examination of possible actions to rehabilitate the community. Finally, while international help efforts are temporary in nature, local resources will continue to be there when the strangers leave, and being partners in restoration efforts contributes to the development of a permanent infrastructure and human capital, and increases the sustainability of the programs as people tend to preserve activities that they helped to develop.

One model that emphasizes the employment of local communities in the development and delivery of posttrauma intervention is the Community Empowerment Model (Harvey, Mondesir & Aldrich, 2007). This model is based on an ecological view of trauma and assumes that human reactions to adverse events are best understood in the context of their social environment, and that effective community interventions are those that enhance the relationship between the community and its members. Formal and informal leaders (e.g. city officials, neighborhood activists) are used to develop strategies that offer the best ecological fit between interventions and the needs of the specific community.

A third principle is maximizing the integration of services and prevention of fragmentation, redundancy, and duplication of services. Better coordination avoids ineffective use of resources and confusion of those seeking help as to where to go for what type of provisions. Community strategies to address the aftermath of trauma and set in place mechanisms for recovery should include networking among governmental and non-governmental organizations to rebuild both formal and informal community structures, institutions and processes, and promote collaboration among the police, fire department, medical and welfare agencies, and citizen groups.

Irrespective of the particular approach to post-trauma community rehabilitation, a critical early step in addressing the aftermath of a community trauma is the reunification and restoration of natural support systems, which are often destroyed during the traumatic event, and employing the remaining community structures to help survivors. When trauma hits, people become concerned, in addition to themselves, about relatives and friends, so identifying and reuniting kin and social systems as soon as possible within a community affected by trauma can serve two major goals. First, knowing where everybody for whom they care is and what is their condition can allow people to focus their energy and resources on the coping and recovery process, rather than splitting their resources between efforts to find out what happened to loved ones and efforts to cope with the trauma. In addition, reunification can equip those affected by traumatic exposure with the support and collaboration needed to start a healing process. The reconstructing of connections with family and friends and the creation of a safety net provide a holding environment, and offer the opportunity to share with and learn from those with similar experiences, especially people who speak the same language, share a cultural background, or have encountered similar experiences. Furthermore, creating self-help opportunities supports continuity and enhances a sense of self-efficacy.

Two additional important aspects of community intervention are using diverse types of media for stress management and making sure that coverage of the events is balanced, organized, not sensationalizing, and delivers accurate, clear information and recommendation for action to identify threat and cope with it effectively (Foa et al., 2005). Exposure to media needs to be moderated carefully in order to provide sufficient information to enhance the sense of control, clarity, and safety, but at the same time refrain from over-exposure to too much information with too many details, which may create excessive public stress.

In addition to providing information, new media technology has become a tool for delivery of psychological interventions in addition to services by providers, especially in situations of community trauma where numerous people are in need of help. Websites are proliferating and offer an evolving channel for providing knowledge, advice, and assistance to communities virtually instantaneously (Benight, Ruzek & Waldrep, 2008) – e.g. Interapy, DeStress and after-deployment.org (for veterans). Providing internet-facilitated, trauma-focused interventions has several advantages including bypassing transportation, scheduling and other logistical aspects of service delivery, protecting privacy, which is especially important where certain stressor events (e.g. rape) and the use of mental health services carry a stigma, flexibility in accessing services and self-pacing in using them, elimination of waiting lists, and the possibility of widely and simultaneously delivering services to a large number of those affected by a stressor event at low cost (Ruzek et al., 2011). Although the evaluation of new technology as a vehicle for providing help to affected communities is in very early stages, the modest body of studies to date provides preliminary support for the efficacy of treatments delivered entirely via technology or in combination with interventions by practitioners who review writing assignments and give feedback and directions to augment adherence and the efficacy of the intervention (Ruggiero et al., 2006; Ruzek et al., 2011; Wagner, Schultz & Knaevelsrud, C., 2011).

Media-assisted services show promise; however, they may be more relevant in communities with access to the necessary resources, including electricity and new wireless satellite technologies, and also carry the risk of disseminating inaccurate and potentially harmful information. Wagner, Schultz and Knaevelsrud (2011) conducted a pilot evaluation of cognitive-behavioral interventions that were translated into Arabic, adapted culturally, and delivered via a combination of technology and in-person interaction with a therapist to Iraqi women traumatized by the death of a relative, exposure to bombing or random shooting, rape, or sexual assault (www.ilajnafsy.org). In spite of considerable attrition rate and logistical barriers (such as frequent electricity break down), the service was feasible and contributed to an increase in self-reported quality of life and reduction of PTSD, depression, and anxiety symptoms. In addition to practical information such as providing guidance about hiring appropriate and reliable contractors to help people to restore their homes, delivery of large-scale community psychoeducation about normal traumatic reactions and strategies for managing anxiety can help communities to restore public calm, help people gain at least some measure of temporary routine, and activate communal resources (schools, churches, community centers, and informal organizations) to support those affected. Consequently, community members may get relief from self-blame and become better positioned to work on rehabilitating their community, gain understanding of the reactions of others, and develop tolerance towards those affected negatively. For example, public education about typical trauma reactions may liberate the community of the idea that stress reactions are indications of weakness of character and that recovery is only a question of strong will and personal effort. At the same time, it is important to avoid ignoring concerns about reactions that are indeed beyond the regular realm and help the public to identify those who manifest potentially more severe outcomes, and encourage them to seek help, or call the attention of appropriate service providers to their distress. Thus, if neighbors notice an individual who appears to neglect hygiene and take proper care of children, and in general is in bad shape, it is important for them to report this to the relevant agency.

When leadership uses the media to speak in one clear and truthful voice it helps calm the population. For example, during the first Gulf war (Operation

Desert) in 1991, Israeli citizens were considered under threat of imminent attack with bio-chemical weapons. One public television news broadcaster rose to a status of a national icon and was crowned as "the national calmer" because of his ability to convey clear and friendly advice. While the information was found later to be inaccurate, at the time it was the best available and had a reassuring effect in a chaotic and frightening context.

To allow communities to recover, access to resources is critical. The skills of communities to cope with the effects of trauma and belief in their own ability to do so (i.e. community efficacy) are insufficient if there are no resources that allow them to actually act on these skills and beliefs. This is especially true in relation to communities that have limited resources and were socially and economically disadvantaged before the traumatic event because of poverty, minority status, or depleted resources (Hobfoll et al., 2007b). For example, after hurricane Katrina, the more affluent neighborhoods of New Orleans in addition to superior material resources also had the human capital (i.e. educated, well-connected community members and strong advocacy groups) that allowed them to maximize benefiting from resources which were made available, whereas the Lower Ninth failed to exhaust resources that were potentially coming to them (Rich, 2012).

One important resource is the availability of a cadre of individuals who can provide effective help. While in developed communities interventions to address the aftermath of collective trauma can be offered by professionals, in resource-challenged environments, the main carriers of the recovery efforts are local figures, such as the village teacher or priest, who lack appropriate training. Therefore, it is of utmost importance to develop and make available to these service providers intervention strategies that are resilient, robust, and do not require lengthy preparation (NATO, 2012).

In addition to recovery strategies, community-focused preparedness plans are also useful. For example, protocols for warning, plans for evacuation routes and organized relocation to safe zones that maximizes keeping the community intact, and mutual plans for hosting and support among communities and emergency tactics for access to resources all instill a sense of mastery, which is crucial in trauma exposure, and reduces the stress created by the need to develop solutions in the middle of a crisis.

Like individual and family-focused interventions, activities that target the restoration and rehabilitation of communities after a traumatic exposure must be culturally informed. To secure that rituals and actions are compatible with the religious, cultural, and social norms of the community, working in collaboration with local leaders and key figures, such as the priest or village elders, is of utmost importance. Such collaborative work also strengthens and validates the self-recovering potential of the community and thus its autonomy and pride.

In addition to strategies designed to address traumatic events and their aftermath, interventions to facilitate community resilience are also needed. Norris and colleagues (2008) identified five main strategies designed to achieve this goal. First, because the chain is only as strong as its weakest link, reducing of inequities, particularly attending to the safety of poor neighborhoods and the most vulnerable groups, and developing communities' economic resources have been strongly recommended. The second strategy involves maximizing the mobilization of local capacities and reliance on local resources and strengths rather than external experts, which leads to empowering the affected community, enhancing its self-confidence, often lost to the traumatic exposure, and benefiting from the expertise and connections of community members. Third, coalitions built on previously existing relationships with a history of working together and mutual trust offer useful vehicles for promoting the community's ability to bounce back. Fourth, reinforcement of natural social support systems can help people to receive information and encouragement to guide their efforts to recover. Finally, maintaining a balance between developing plans and the flexibility to change them as needed rather than rigidly sticking to an existing strategy allows exhaustion of available resources and maximizing their effective use.

Sample Programs for Interventions in Traumatized Communities

The model based on the Linking Human Systems Approach (LHSA) to help traumatized families (Landau, Mittal & Wieling, 2008) is applicable to communities that experience mass trauma, and has been implemented in diverse traumatized communities around the world. The main tenet of the model in its community application, called LINC, is the idea that, like individuals and families, communities are intrinsically competent and thus, with appropriate guidance, can access their inherent resilience to resolve their own problems. According to this model, extended familial, social, professional, and communal support systems are engaged as change agents that reconnect people with each other and with their community's history of managing traumas, as well as with outside professionals, in order to identify and mobilize resources for addressing the stressful event and its aftermath. This is done while maintaining intact the community's traditions and sense of pride. Being reconnected and building on the resilience of past generations are anticipated to provide support and encouragement as well as allow access to collective strengths for healing the community and those within it. Building on these strengths enhances community members' sense of self-efficacy and solidarity, as well as helping to gain access to tangible and intangible resources. These processes combined are believed to enhance people's inherent resilience and ability to successfully address a traumatic experience (Landau, 2010).

Implementing the model includes assessment of existing resources, the awareness (or lack thereof) of community members of their availability and the degree to which they have been mobilized, the balance between stressors and resources, and the degree of disruption of connections among people and within the community's legacy and history. Based on this assessment, a multi-level intervention plan is developed that targets individual leaders, groups of families, and/or the community as a whole. Groups consisting of diverse sections of the population are formed and work to conceptualize goals and identify resources, leaders, feasible tasks, and strategies to achieve them. The model especially emphasizes enhancing connectedness on all levels as a crane for change.

The Victims of Violence (VOV) Program developed the Community Crisis Response Team (CCRT) model (Harvey, Mondesir & Aldrich, 2007). This model was created in 1988 and is designed to address the impact of violent crimes including rape, family violence, child and elder abuse, hate crime, sexual or physical assault, school violence, and murder on communities and on service providers. It uses neighborhood activists, community leaders, professionals and volunteers of diverse disciplines, racial and cultural backgrounds and agency affiliation, such as social workers and police officers specializing in the fields of victimization, crisis intervention, and the treatment of trauma, with expertise with certain population groups including children, the elderly, and immigrants. The model follows six steps. First, a request from an affected community initiates the activation of the intervention. One possible critique is that communities that are badly devastated may not be organized enough to ask for help and thus may not be able to benefit from the services. Next, staff members and community representatives collaboratively discuss the nature of the event and the requests of the community, then map available resources, identifying gaps and formulating services that CCRT can offer to address community needs. Once agreement is reached relating to what should be done, the intervention is implemented and eventually evaluated based on feedback from community members and organizations. The interventions may include consultation of local agencies in developing their strategies for action and mobilizing their own crisis response resources, direct involvement in co-facilitating community meetings, coordination of interventions, assessment of needs and referrals relating to mental health issues, and providing a modified version of traumatic stress debriefing that focuses on creating a safe space, psychoeducation, and fostering of self-care.

Ajdukovic (2004), a psychologist from the University of Zagreb, Croatia suggested a similar three-phase model that emphasizes the elements of mutual and public recognition of losses suffered by all groups, encouraging the rebuilding of social relationships among enemies, looking for common ground among sub-groups as a process towards reconciliation and building of trust. The model combines providing treatment to traumatized individuals, empowerment of care providers to allow them to perform their role effectively, teaching about strategies for conflict management, and re-establishing of social norms. In addition a message of tolerance and social reconstruction is enhanced by creating opportunities for people from opposite sides of the conflict to meet and have a dialogue such that mutual demonizing is challenged and they gradually learn about their mutual perceptions and feelings, and work to develop a situation where they can live together though may not agree on many issues. One example of such efforts are workshops conducted with Jewish and Arab youths in Israel designed to bring together members of social groups that are part of a conflict and create conditions conducive to the development of mutual familiarity, trust, and revision of social and self-perceptions to enhance preparedness for addressing stressful events (Berger & Gelkopf, 2011).

Also successful are various Community-Based Disaster Preparedness (CBDP) approaches, which share respect for local social and cultural knowledge and build on local capacities and resources, including social capital, to make a significant and long-lasting contribution to reducing vulnerability and strengthening adaptive community coping. One example is the Community Readiness Model (CRM), which is an assessment, capacity building, and sustaining stage-based tool, developed by the Tri-Ethnic Center for Prevention Research at Colorado State University to provide an issue-specific, culturally congruent approach to facilitate planning and mobilize community change. It is informed by the availability and accessibility of efforts, programs, and policies to address a collective issue, community members' knowledge about and attitudes towards the issue, and the efforts to address it, and community formal and informal leadership support. Because enhancing linkage across systems, and mutual trust and collaboration, which are the cornerstones of the model, contribute to a community's ability to cope and heal following a collective trauma, this approach has shown to be effective following natural disasters (Ersing & Kost, 2012).

References

Adams, R. E. & Boscarino, J. A. (2006). Predictors of PTSD and delayed PTSD after disaster: The impact of exposure and psychosocial resources. *The Journal of Nervous and Mental Disease, 194*(7), 485–493.

Adams, R. E., Boscarino, J. A. & Figley, C. R. (2009). Compassion fatigue and psychological distress among social workers: A validation study. *American Journal of Orthopsychiatry, 76*(1), 103–108.

Adger, W. N. (2000). Social and ecological resilience: Are they related? *Progress in Human Geography, 24*(3), 347–364.

Affleck, G., Tennen, H., Croog, S. & Levine, S. (1987). Causal attribution, perceived benefits, and morbidity after a heart attack: An 8-year study. *Journal of Consulting and Clinical Psychology, 55*(1), 29–35.

Ajdukovic, D. (2004). Social context of trauma and healing. *Medicine, Conflict and Survival, 20*(2), 120–135.

Aldrich, D. P. (2011). The externalities of strong social capital: Post-tsunami recovery in Southeast India. *Journal of Civil Society, 7*(1) 81–99.

Aldwin, C. M. (1994). *Stress, coping and development: An integrative perspective.* New York: Guilford Press.

Alem, A., Jacobsson, L. & Hanlon, C. (2008). Community-based mental health care in Africa: Mental health workers' views. *World Psychiatry, 7*(1), 54–57.

Alexander, J. C., Eyerman, R., Giesen, B., Smelser, N. J. & Sztompka, P. (2004). *Cultural trauma and collective identity.* London, Los Angeles: University of California Press.

Alisic, E., van der Schoot, T. A. W., van Ginkel, J. R. & Kleber, R. J. (2008). Looking beyond posttraumatic stress disorder in children: Posttraumatic stress reactions, posttraumatic growth, and quality of life in a general population sample. *Journal of Clinical Psychiatry, 69*(9), 1455–1461.

Alkhatib, A., Regan, J. & Barrett, D. (2007). The silent victims: Effects of war and terrorism on child development. *Psychiatric Annals, 37,* 586–589.

Almli, L. M., Fani, N., Smith, A. & Ressler, K. (2014). Genetic approaches to understanding post-traumatic stress disorder. *The International Journal of Neuropsychopharmacology, 17*(2), 355–370.

Amaya-Jackson, L., Reynolds, V., Murray, M. C., McCarthy, G., Nelson, A., Cherney, M. S., Lee, R., Foa, E. & March, J. S. (2003). Cognitive–behavioral treatment for pediatric posttraumatic stress disorder: Protocol and application in school and community settings. *Cognitive & Behavioral Practice, 10,* 204–213.

American Psychiatric Association (APA) (1980). *Diagnostic and statistical manual of mental disorders* (DSM-III). Washington, DC: APA

American Psychiatric Association (APA) (1994). *Diagnostic and statistical manual of mental disorders* (DSM-IV). Washington, DC: APA

American Psychiatric Association (APA) (2000). *Diagnostic and statistical manual of mental disorders* (DSM-IV-R). Washington, DC: APA.

American Psychiatric Association (APA) (2013). *Diagnostic and statistical manual of mental disorders* (DSM-V). Washington, DC: APA.

American Psychological Association (2009). Children and trauma: Report of the task force on post-traumatic stress disorder and trauma in children and adolescents. Washington, DC: APA.

Amirkhan, J. H. & Greaves, H. (2003). Sense of coherence and stress: The mechanics of a healthy disposition. *Psychology & Health, 18*(1), 31–62.

Anderson, K. (1994). Family sense of coherence: As collective and consensus in relation to family quality of life after illness diagnosis. In H. McCubbin, E. Thompson, A. Thompson & J. Fromer (Eds.), *Sense of coherence and resiliency* (pp.169–188). Madison, WI: University of Wisconsin.

Angell, R. C. (1936). *The family encounters the depression.* New York: Charles Scribner's Sons.

Antoni, M., Lehman, J., Kilbourn, K., Boyers, A., Culver, J., Alferi, S. . . . Carver, C. (2001). Cognitive-behavioral stress management intervention decreases the prevalence of depression and enhances benefit finding among women under treatment for early-stage breast cancer. *Health Psychology: Official Journal of the Division of Health Psychology, American Psychological Association, 20*(1), 20–32.

Antonovsky, A, (1979). *Health, stress, and coping.* San Francisco, CA: Jossey-Bass.

Antonovsky, A. (1998). The sense of coherence: An historical and future perspective. In H. I. McCubbin, E. A. Thompson, A. I. Thompson & J. E. Fromer (Eds.), *Stress, coping, and health in families: Sense of coherence and resiliency* (pp. 3–21). Thousand Oaks, CA: Sage.

Antonovsky, A. & Sourani, T. (1988). Family sense of coherence. *Journal of Marriage and the Family, 50*(1), 79–92.

Armagan, E., Engindeniz, Z., Devay, A. O., Erdur, B. & Ozcakir, A. (2006). Frequency of post-traumatic stress disorder among relief force workers after the tsunami in Asia: Do rescuers become victims? *Pre-hospital and Disaster Medicine, 21*(3), 168–172.

Arnold, D., Calhoun, L. G., Tedeschi, R. & MacCann, A. (2005). Vicarious posttraumatic growth in psychotherapy. *Journal of Humanistic Psychology, 45*(2), 239–263.

Aronson, B. & Kahn, G. B. (2004). Group interventions for treatment of traumatized adolescents. In *Group Interventions for Treatment of Psychological Trauma* (Module 3, 89–114). Washington, DC: American psychological Association.

Arvay, M. J. (2001). Secondary traumatic stress among trauma counselors: What does the research say? *International Journal for the Advancement of Counselling, 23*(4), 283–293.

Arvidson, J., Kinniburgh, K., Howard, K., Spinazzola, J., Strothers, H., Evans, M. . . . Blaustein, M. E. (2011). Treatment of complex trauma in young children: Developmental and cultural considerations in application of the ARC intervention model. *Journal of Child & Adolescent Trauma, 4*(1), 34–51.

Barakat, L. P., Aldefer, M. A. & Kazak, A. E. (2006). Posttraumatic growth in adolescent survivors of cancer and their mothers and fathers. *Journal of Pediatric Psychology, 31*(4), 413–419.

Barr, P. (2011). Posttraumatic growth in parents of infants hospitalized in a neonatal intensive care unit. *Journal of Loss and Trauma: International Perspectives on Stress & Coping, 16*, 117–134.

Bates, G. W., Trajstman, S. A. & Jackson, C. A. (2004). Internal consistency, test-retest reliability and sex differences on the posttraumatic growth inventory in an Australia sample with trauma. *Psychological Reports, 94*(3), 793–794.

Batten, S. V. & Orsillo, S. M. (2002). Therapist reactions in the context of collective trauma. *The Behavior Therapist, 25*, 36–40.

Baum, N. & Ramon, S. (2010). Professional growth in turbulent times. *Journal of Social Work, 10*(2), 139–156.

Beardslee, W., Lester, P., Klosinski, L., Saltzman, W., Woodward, K., Nash, W., Mogil, C., Koffman, R. & Leskin, G. (2011). Family-centered preventive intervention for military families: Implications for implementation science. *Prevention Science: The Official Journal of the Society for Prevention Research, 12*(4), 339–348.

Beauchesne, M. A., Kelley, B. R., Patsdaughter, C. A. & Pickard, J. (2002). Attack on America: Children's reactions and parents' responses. *Journal of Pediatric Health Care, 16*(5), 213–221.

Beavers, W. R. & Hampson, R. B. (2000). The Beavers systems model of family functioning. *Journal of Family Therapy, 22*(2), 128–143.

Belgrave, F. Z., Chase-Vaughn, G., Gray, F., Addison, J. D. & Cherry, V. R. (2000). The effectiveness of a culture- and gender-specific intervention for increasing resiliency among African American preadolescent females. *Journal of Black Psychology, 26*(2), 133–147.

Belizzi, K. M. & Blank, T. O. (2006). Predicting posttraumatic growth in breast cancer survivors. *Journal of Health Psychology, 25*(1), 47–56.

Ben Arzi, N., Solomon, Z. & Dekel, R. (2000). Secondary traumatization among wives of PTSD and post-concussion casualties: Distress, caregiver burden and psychological separation. *Brain Injury, 14*(8), 725–36.

Ben-David, A. & Lavee, Y. (1992). Families in the sealed room: Interaction patterns of Israeli families during SCUD missile attacks. *Family Process, 31*(1), 35–44.

Benight, C. C., Ruzek, J. I. & Waldrep, E. (2008). Internet interventions for traumatic stress: A review and theoretically based example. *Journal of Traumatic Stress, 21*(6), 513–520.

Benner, A. D. & Su Yeong, K. (2010). Understanding Chinese American adolescents' developmental outcomes: Insights from the Family Stress Model. *Journal of Research on Adolescence, 20*(1), 1–12.

Benzies, K. & Mychasiuk, R. (2009). Fostering family resiliency: A review of the key protective factors. *Child & Family Social Work, 14*, 103–114.

Berger, R. (1996). Group Work with immigrant adolescents. *Journal of Child and Adolescent Group Therapy, 6*(4), 169–179.

Berger, R. (2005). It takes a community to raise an adolescent: Community-based clinical services for immigrant adolescents. In A. Lightburn & P. Sessions (Eds.), *Community based clinical practice* (pp. 441–458). NY: Oxford University Press.

Berger, R. (2008). Fostering posttraumatic growth in adolescent immigrants. In L. Liebenberg & M. Ungar (Eds.), *Resilience in action: Working with youth across cultures and contexts* (pp. 87–110). Toronto: Toronto University press.

Berger, R. (2010a). EBP: Practitioners in search of evidence. *Journal of Social Work, 10*, 175–191.

Berger, R. (2010b). Encounter of a racially mixed group with stressful situations. *Groupwork, 19*, 28–41.

Berger, R. & Gelkopf, M. (2011). An intervention for reducing secondary traumatization and improving professional self-efficacy in well baby clinic nurses following war and terror: A random control group trial. *International Journal of Nursing Studies, 48*(5), 601–610.

Berger, R. & Joyce, P. A. (2010). From research to practice: Developing and delivering a culturally competent trauma curriculum for child welfare practitioners after 9/11. *Journal of Child and Adolescent Trauma, 3,* 25–35.

Berger, R. & Weiss, T. (2006). Posttraumatic Growth in Latina immigrants. *Journal of Immigrant and Refugee Studies, 4,* 55–72.

Berger, R. & Weiss, T. (2008). The posttraumatic growth model: An expansion to the family system. *Traumatology, 15,* 63–74.

Berger, R. & Weiss, T. (2010). Posttraumatic growth in US Latinos. In T. Weiss & R. Berger (Eds.), *Posttraumatic growth and culturally competent practice: Lessons learned from around the globe* (pp. 113–128). Hoboken, NJ: Wiley.

Berger, R., Joyce, P. A., Lynn, M. & Gregg, G. (2002). Working with the effects of trauma in "at risk" families. Protocol developed for NYC Administration for Children Services/Project Liberty.

Berger, R., Pat-Horenczyk, R. & Gelkopf, M. (2007). School-based intervention for prevention and treatment of elementary students' terror-related distress in Israel: A quasi-randomized controlled trial. *Journal of Traumatic Stress, 20*(4), 541–551.

Berger, R., Paul, M. S. & Henshaw, L. A. (2013). Women's experience of infertility: A multi-systemic perspective. *International Journal of Women Issues, 54*(1), 54–68.

Berkowitz, S. J., Stover, C. & Marans, S. R. (2011). The Child and Family Traumatic Stress Intervention: Secondary prevention for youth at risk of developing PTSD. *Journal of Child Psychology & Psychiatry, 52*(6), 676–685.

Berntsen, D., Johannessen, K. B., Thomsen, Y. D., Bertelsen, M., Hoyle, R. H. & Rubin, D. C. (2012). Peace and war: Trajectories of posttraumatic stress disorder symptoms before, during, and after military deployment in Afghanistan. *Psychological Science, 3*(12), 1557–1165.

Betancourt, T. S., Speelman, L., Onyango, G. & Bolton, P. (2009). A qualitative study of mental health problems among children displaced by war in Northern Uganda. *Transcultural Psychiatry, 46,* 238–256.

Bethany, B. L., Myrick, A. C. , Lowenstein, R. J., Classen, C. C., Laminus, R., McNary, S. W., Pain, C. & Putnam, F. W. (2011). A survey of practices and recommended treatment interventions among expert therapists treating patients with dissociative identity disorder and dissociative disorder not otherwise specified. *Psychological Trauma: Theory, Research, Practice, and Policy, 5,* no pagination specified.

Bichescu, D., Neuner, F., Schauer, M. & Elbert, T. (2007). Narrative exposure therapy for political imprisonment related chronic posttraumatic stress disorder and depression. *Behaviour Research and Therapy, 45*(9), 2212–2220.

Bisson, J. I. & Andrew, M. (2007). Psychological treatment of posttraumatic stress disorder (PTSD). *Cochrane database of systematic reviews.* Issue 3. Art. No: CD003388.

Bisson, J. I., Tavakoly, B., Witteveen, A, B., Ajdukovic, D., Jehel, L., Joahnsen, V. J., Nordanger, D., Garcia, F. O., Punamäki, R-L., Schnyder, U., Sezgin, A. U., Wittman, L. & Olff, M. (2010). TENTS guidelines: Development of post-disaster psychosocial care guidelines through a Delphi process. *The British Journal of Psychiatry, 196*(1), 69–74.

Black, K. & Lobo, M. (2008). A conceptual review of family resilience factors. *Journal of Family Nursing, 14*(1), 33–55.

Blanchard, E. B., Jones-Alexander, J., Buckley, T. C. & Forneris, C. A. (1996a). Psychometric properties of the PTSD Checklist (PCL). *Behavioral research and Therapy, 34*(8), 669–673.

Blanchard, E. B., Hickling, E. J., Taylor, A. E., Loos, W. R., Fomeris, C. A. & Jaccard, J. (1996b). Who develops PTSD from motor vehicle accidents? *Behaviour Research and Therapy, 34*, 1–10.

Board on Population Health and Public Health Practice (2008). *Treatment of posttraumatic stress disorder: An assessment of the evidence*. Washington, DC: National Academies Press.

Bodenmann, G. (1995). A systemic-transactional conceptualization of stress and coping in couples. *Swiss Journal of Psychology, 54*, 34–49.

Bodenmann, G. & Randall, A. K. (2012). Common factors in the enhancement of dyadic coping. *Behavior Therapy, 43*(1), 88–98.

Boehm, A., Enosh, G. & Shamai, M. (2010). Expectations of grassroots community leadership in times of normality and crisis. *Journal of Contingencies and Crisis Management, 18*(4), 184–194.

Boelen, P. A. & van den Bout, J. (2008). Complicated grief and uncomplicated grief are distinguishable constructs. *Psychiatry Research, 157*(1), 311–314.

Bokszczanin, A. (2008). Parental support, family conflict, and overprotectiveness: Predicting PTSD symptom levels of adolescents 28 months after a natural disaster. *Anxiety, Stress & Coping, 21*(4), 325–335.

Bonanno, G. A. (2004). Loss, trauma, and human resilience: Have we underestimated the human capacity to thrive after extremely aversive events? *American Psychologist, 59*(91), 20–28.

Bonanno, G. A. & Mancini, A. D. (2008). The human capacity to thrive in the face of potential trauma. *Pediatrics, 121*(2), 369–375.

Bonanno, G. A., Brewin, C. R., Kaniasty, K. & La Greca, A. M. (2010). Weighing the costs of disaster: Consequences, risks, and resilience in individuals, families and communities. *Psychological Science in the Public Interest, 11*(11), 11–49.

Boss, P. G. (1980). Normative family stress: Family boundary changes across the lifespan. *Family Relations, 29*(4), 445–450.

Boss, P. (2002). *Family stress management: A contextual approach*. Thousand Oaks, CA: Sage.

Boss, P. (2007). Ambiguous Loss Theory: Challenges for scholars and practitioners. *Family Relations, 56*(2), 105–111.

Boss, P., Beaulieu, L., Wieling, E., Turner, W. & LaCruz, S. (2003). Healing loss, ambiguity and trauma: A community-based intervention with families of union workers missing after the 9/11 attack in New York City. *Journal of Marital & Family Therapy, 29*(4), 455–467.

Bowler, R. M., Han, H., Gocheva, V., Nakagawa, S., Alper, H., DiGrande, L. & Cone, J. E. (2010). Gender differences in probable posttraumatic stress disorder among police responders to the 2001 World Trade Center terrorist attack. *American Journal of Industrial Medicine, 53*(12), 1186–1196.

Bradbury, T. N., Fincham, F. D. & Beach, S. H. (2000). Research on the nature and determinants of marital satisfaction: A decade in review. *Journal of Marriage and Family, 62*(4), 964–980.

Bradley, R., Greene, J., Russ, E., Dutra, L. & Westen, D. (2005). A multidimensional meta-analysis of psychotherapy for PTSD. *American Journal of Psychiatry, 162*(2), 214–227.

Bradshaw, R. A., Cook, A. & McDonald, M. J. (2011). Observed and experiential integration (OEI): Discovery and development of a new set of trauma therapy techniques. *Journal of Psychotherapy Integration, 21*(2), 104–171.

Braun-Lewensohn, O. & Sagy, S. (2011). Salutogenesis and culture: Personal and community sense of coherence among adolescents belonging to three different cultural groups. *International Review of Psychiatry, 23*(6), 533–541.

Breslau, N., Davis, G. C., Andreski, P. & Peterson, E. (1991). Traumatic events and post-traumatic stress disorder in an urban population of young adults. *Archives of General Psychiatry, 48*(3), 216–222.

Breslau, N., Lucia, V. C. & Davis, G. C. (2004). Partial PTSD versus full PTSD: An empirical examination of associated impairment. *Psychological Medicine, 34*(7), 1205–1214.

Breslau, N., Kessler, R. C., Chilcoat, H. D., Schultz, L. R., Davis, G. C. & Andreski, P. (1998). Post-traumatic stress disorder following disasters: A systematic review. *Archives of General Psychiatry, 55*, 626–632. 10.1001/archpsyc.55.7.6269672053.

Breton, M. (2001). Neighbourhood resiliency. *Journal of Community Practice, 19*(1), 21–36.

Brewin, C. R., Andrews, B. & Valentine, J. D. (2000). Meta-analysis of risk factors for posttraumatic stress disorder in trauma-exposed adults. *Journal of Consulting and Clinical Psychology, 68*(5), 748–766.

Bride, B. E. (2007). Prevalence of secondary traumatic stress among social workers. *Social Work, 52*(1), 63–70.

Bride, B. E. & Figley, C. R. (2009). Secondary trauma and military veteran caregivers. *Smith College Studies of Social Work, 79*(3–4), 314–329.

Bristol, M. M. (1987). Mothers of children with autism or communication disorders: Successful adaptation and the Double ABCX model. *Journal of Autism and Developmental Disorders, 17*, 469–486.

Bristol, M. M., Gallagher, J. J. & Schopler, E. (1988). Mothers and fathers of young developmentally disabled and nondisabled boys: Adaptation and spousal support. *Developmental Psychology, 24*, 441–451.

Brockhouse, R., Msetfi, R. M., Cohen, K. & Joseph, S. (2011). Vicarious exposure to trauma and growth in therapists: The moderating effects of sense of coherence, organizational support, and empathy. *Journal of Traumatic Stress, 24*(6), 735–742.

Brody, J. E. (2011). For a doctor, survival and transformation. *New York Times*, Science Times, 10 October, D7.

Bromet, E., Havenaar, J. & Guey, L. (2011). A 25-year retrospective review of the psychological consequences of the Chernobyl accident. *Clinical Oncology (Royal College of Radiologists), 23*(4), 297–305.

Bruneau, M., Chang, S. E., Eguchi, R. T., Lee, G. C., O'Rourke, T. D., Reinhorn, A. M., Masanobu, S., Tierney, K., Wallace, W. A. & von Winterfeldti, D. (2003). A framework to quantitatively assess and enhance the seismic resilience of communities. *Earthquake Spectra, 19*(4), 733–752.

Brunsma, D. & Picou, J. S. (2008). Disasters in the twenty-first century: Modern destruction and future instruction. *Social Forces, 87*(2), 983–991.

Bryant, R. A., Moulds, M. L., Guthrie, R. M., Dang, S. T., Mastrodomenico, J., Nixon, R.D.V., Felmingham, K. L. & Hopwood, S. (2008). A randomized controlled trial of exposure therapy and cognitive restructuring for posttraumatic stress disorder. *Journal of Consulting and Clinical Psychology, 76*(4), 695–703.

Bryant, R. A., Sackville, T., Dang, S. T., Moulds, M. & Guthrie, R. (1999). Treating Acute Stress Disorder: An evaluation of cognitive behavior therapy and counseling techniques. *American Journal of Psychiatry, 156*(11), 1780–1786.

Burr, W. R. & Klein, S. (1994). *Reexamining family stress: New theory and research.* Thousand Island, CA: Sage.

Busuttil, W. (2006). The development of a 90-day residential program for the treatment of Complex Posttraumatic Stress Disorder. *Journal of Aggression, Maltreatment & Trauma, 12*(1/2), 29–55.

Butler, L. D., Blasey, C. M., Garlan, R. W., McCaslin, S. E., Azarow, J., Chen, X, A., Desjardins, J. C., DiMiceli, S., Seagraves, D. A., Hastings, T. A., Kraemer, H. C. & Spiegel, D. (2005). Posttraumatic growth following the terrorist attacks of September 11, 2001: Cognitive, coping, and trauma symptom predictors in an internet convenience sample. *Traumatology, 11*(4), 247–267.

Caldera, T., Palma, L., Penayo, U. & Kullgren, G. (2001). Psychological impact of hurricane Mitch in Nicaragua in a one-year perspective. *Social Psychiatry & Psychiatric Epidemiology, 36*(3), 108–114.

Calhoun, L. G. & Tedeschi, R. G. (Eds.) (2006). *Handbook of posttraumatic growth: Research and practice.* Mahwah, NJ: Erlbaum.

Calhoun, L. G. & Tedeschi, R. G. (2013). *Posttraumatic growth in clinical practice.* NY: Routledge.

Calhoun, L. G., Cann, A. & Tedeschi, R. G. (2010). The posttraumatic growth model: Sociocultural considerations. In T. Weiss & R. Berger (Eds.), *Posttraumatic growth and culturally competent practice: Lessons learned from around the globe* (pp. 1–14). Hoboken, NJ: Wiley.

Calhoun, L. G., Cann, A., Tedeschi, R. G. & McMillan, J. (2000). A correlational test of the relationship between posttraumatic growth, religion, and cognitive processing. *Journal of Traumatic Stress, 13*(3), 521–527.

Callahan, R. J. & Callahan, J. (2000). *Stop the nightmares of trauma: Thought Field Therapy.* Chapel Hill, NC: Professional Press.

Campbell, C. L. & Demi, A. S. (2000). Adult children of fathers missing in action (MIA): An examination of emotional distress, grief, and family hardiness. *Family Relations, 49*(3), 267–278.

Campbell, J. & McCrystal, P. (2005). Mental health social work and the troubles in Northern Ireland: A study of practitioner experiences. *Journal of Social Work, 5*(2), 173–190.

Canive, J. M. & Castillo, D. (1997). Latino veterans diagnosed with PTSD: Assessment and treatment issues. *NCP Clinical Quarterly, 7*(1), 12–15.

Caplan, G. (1964). *Principles of preventive psychiatry.* New York: Basic Books.

Caplan, G. (1970). *The theory and practice of mental health consultation.* New York: Basic Books.

Cardeña, E. & Nijenhuis, E. (2000). Embodied sorrow. Special issue on somatoform dissociation. *Journal of Trauma and Dissociation, 1*(4), 1–5.

Carrion, A. (2010). Factors identified by Latino middle school students and their parents as contributors to academic success. Unpublished dissertation. Adelphi University, School of Social Work, 3448160.

Carver, C. S. & Antoni, M. H. (2004). Finding benefit in breast cancer during the year after diagnosis predicts better adjustment 5 to 8 years after diagnosis. *Health Psychology, 23*(6), 595–598.

Cary, C. E. & McMillen, J. (2012). The data behind the dissemination: A systematic review of trauma-focused cognitive behavioral therapy for use with children and youth. *Children & Youth Services Review, 34*(4), 748–757.

Catani, C., Gewirtz, A. H., Wieling, E., Schauer, E., Elbert, T. & Neuner, F. (2010). Tsunami, war, and cumulative risk in the lives of Sri Lankan schoolchildren. *Child Development, 81*(4), 1176–1191.

Cavan Shone, R. & Ranck Howland, K. (1938). *The Family and the depression: A study of one hundred Chicago families.* Chicago, IL: The University of Chicago Press.

Chapman, C., Mills, K., Slade, T., McFarlane, A. C., Bryant, R. A., Creamer, M., Silove, D. & Teesson, M. (2012). Remission from post-traumatic stress disorder in the general population. *Psychological Medicine, 42*(8), 1695–1703.

Chimienti, G. & Abu Nasr, J. (1992). Children's reactions to war related stress II. The influence of gender, age, and the mother's reaction. *International Journal of Mental Health, 21*(4), 72–86.

Chimienti, G., Abu Nasr, J. A. & Khalifeh, I. (1989). Children's reactions to war-related stress: Affective symptoms and behavior problems. *Social Psychiatry and Psychiatric Epidemiology, 24*, 282–287.

Clauss-Ehlers, C. S. (2008). Sociocultural factors, resilience, and coping: Support for a culturally sensitive measure of resilience. *Journal of Applied Developmental Psychology, 29*(3), 197–212.

Clauss-Ehlers, C. S. & Lopez Levi, L. (2002). Violence and community, terms in conflict: An ecological approach to resilience. *Journal of Social Distress and the Homeless, 11(4)*, 265–278.

Cloitre, M., Courtois, C. A., Charuvastra, A., Carapezza, R., Stolbach, B. C. & Green, B. L. (2011). Treatment of complex PTSD: Results of the ISTSS expert clinician survey on best practices. *Journal of Traumatic Stress, 24*(6), 615–627.

Cloitre, M., Petkova, E., Wang, J. & Lu (Lassell), F. (2012). An examination of the influence of a sequential treatment on the course and impact of dissociation among women with PTSD related to childhood abuse. *Depression and Anxiety, 29*(8).

Cloitre, M., Stovall-McClough, K., Chase, K., Nooner, K., Zorbas, P., Cherry, S., Jackson, C. L., Weijin, G. & Petkova, E. (2010). Treatment for PTSD related to childhood abuse: A randomized controlled trial. *American Journal of Psychiatry, 167*(8), 915–924.

Cobb, A. R., Tedeschi, R. G., Calhoun, L.G. & Cann, A. (2006). Correlates of posttraumatic growth in survivors of intimate partner violence. *Journal of Traumatic Stress, 19*(6), 895–903.

Cohan, C. L., Cole, S. W. & Schoen, R. (2009). Divorce following the September 11 terrorist attacks. *Journal of Social & Personal Relationships, 26*(4), 512–530.

Cohen, J. A., Berliner, L. & March, J. S. (2000). Treatment of children and adolescents. In E. B. Foa, T. M. Keane & M. J. Friedman (Eds.), *Effective treatments for PTSD* (pp. 106–138). New York: The Guilford Press.

Cohen, J. A., Mannarino, A. P. & Staron, V. (2006). Modified cognitive behavioral therapy for childhood traumatic grief (CBT-CTG): A pilot study. *Journal of the American Academy of Child and Adolescent Psychiatry, 45*(12), 1465–1473.

Cohen, J. A., Jaycox, L., Walker, D., Mannarino, A., Langley, A. & DuClos, J. (2009). Treating traumatized children after Hurricane Katrina: Project Fleur-de Lis. *Clinical Child & Family Psychology Review, 12*(1), 55–64.

Cohen, K. & Collens, P. (2013). The impact of trauma work on trauma workers: A meta-synthesis on vicarious trauma and vicarious posttraumatic growth. *Psychological Trauma: Theory, Research, Practice, and Policy, 5*(6), 570–580.

Cohen, M. (2008). Acute stress disorder in older, middle-aged and younger adults in reaction to the second Lebanon war. *International Journal of Geriatric Psychiatry, 23*(1), 34–40.

Cohen Silver, R., Holman, A., McIntosh, D. N., Poulin, M. & Gil-Rivas, V. (2002). Nationwide longitudinal study of psychological responses to September 11. *Journal of the American Medical Association, 288*, 1235–1244.

Coll, C. G. & Lamberty, G. (1996). An integrative model for the study of developmental competencies in minority children. *Child Development, 67*(5), 1891–1914.

Comer, J. S. & Kendall, P. C. (2007). Terrorism: The psychological impact on youth. *Clinical Psychology: Science and Practice, 14*, 179–212.

Comer, J. S., Furr, J. M., Beidas, R. S., Weiner, C. L. & Kendall, P. C. (2008). Children and terrorism-related news: Training parents in coping and media literacy. *Journal of Consulting and Clinical Psychology, 76*(4), 568–578.

Conger, R. D. & Donnellan, M. B. (2007). An interactionist perspective on the socio-economic context of human development. *Annual Review of Psychology, 58*(1), 175–199.

Conger, R. D., Wallace, L. E., Sun, Y., Simons, R. L., McLoyd, V. C. & Brody, G. H. (2002). Economic pressure in African American families: A replication and extension of the Family Stress Model. *Developmental Psychology, 38*(2), 179–193.

Copeland, W. E., Keeler, G., Angold, A. & Costello, E. J. (2007). Traumatic events and posttraumatic stress disorder in childhood. *Archives of General Psychiatry, 64*, 577–584.

Cordova, M. J., Cunningham, L. L., Carlson, C. R. & Andrykowski, M. A. (2001). Posttraumatic growth following breast cancer: A controlled comparison study. *Health Psychology, 20*, 176–185.

Cornille, T. A. & Woodard Meyers, T. (1999). Secondary traumatic stress among child protective service workers: Prevalence, severity and predictive factors. *Traumatology, 5*(1), 15–31.

Cougle, J. R., Resnick, H. & Kilpatrick, D. G. (2011). Factors associated with chronicity in posttraumatic stress disorder: A prospective analysis of a national sample of women. *Psychological Trauma: Theory, Research, Practice, and Policy*, no Pagination Specified.

Courtois, C. A. (2008). Complex trauma, complex reactions: Assessment and treatment. *Psychological Trauma: Theory, Research, Practice, and Policy, S*(1), 86–100.

Courtois, C. A., Ford, J. D. & Cloitre, M. (2009). Best practices in psychotherapy for adults. In C. A. Courtois & J. D. Ford (Eds.), *Treating complex traumatic stress disorders: An evidence-based guide* (pp. 82–103). NY: Guilford.

Coyle, J. P., DeWit, D., Macdonald, S., Maguin, E., Nochajski, T. & Safyer, A. (2009). An exploratory study of the nature of family resilience in families affected by parental alcohol abuse. *Journal of Family Issues, 30*(12), 1606–1623.

Craig, C. & Sprang, G. (2010). Compassion satisfaction, compassion fatigue, and burn-out in a national sample of trauma treatment therapists. *Anxiety, Stress, and Coping, 23*(3), 319–339.

Creamer, M. & Parslow, R. (2008). Trauma exposure and posttraumatic stress disorder in the elderly: A community prevalence study. *The American Journal of Geriatric Psychiatry, 16* (10), 853–856.

Creamer, M., Burgess, P. & McFarlane, A. C. (2001). Post-traumatic stress disorder: Findings from the Australian national survey of mental health and well-being. *Psychological Medicine, 31*(7), 1237–1247.

Crenshaw, D. A. & Hardy, K. V. (2007). The crucial role of empathy in breaking the silence of traumatized children in play therapy. *International Journal of Play Therapy, 16*(2), 160–175.

Cryder, C. H., Kilmer, R. P., Tedeschi, R. G. & Calhoun, L. G. (2006). An exploratory study of posttraumatic growth in children following a natural disaster. *American Journal of Orthopsychiatry, 76*(1), 65–69.

Cukor, J., Wyka, K., Mello, B., Olden, M., Jayasinghe, N., Roberts, J. . . . Difede, J. (2011). The longitudinal course of PTSD among disaster workers deployed to the World Trade Center following the attacks of September 11th. *Journal of Traumatic Stress, 24*(5), 506–514.

Culver, L., Fincham, D. & Seedat, S. (2009). Posttraumatic stress in AIDS-orphaned children exposed to high levels of trauma: The protective role of perceived social support. *Journal of Traumatic Stress, 22*(2), 106–112.

Culver, L. M., McKinney, B. L. & Paradise, L. V. (2011). Mental health profession-als' experiences of vicarious traumatization in post-hurricane Katrina New Orleans. *Journal of Loss & Trauma, 16*(1), 33–42.

Cunningham, M. (1999). The impact of sexual abuse treatment on the sexual abuse clinician. *Child and Adolescent Social Work Journal, 16*, 277–290.

Curran, P. S. (1988). Psychiatric aspects of terrorist violence: Northern Ireland 1969–1987. *British Journal of Psychiatry, 153*(4), 470–475.

D'Andrea, W., Ford, J., Stolbach, B., Spinazzola, J. & van der Kolk, B. A. (2012). Understanding interpersonal trauma in children: Why we need a developmentally appropriate trauma diagnosis. *American Journal of Orthopsychiatry, 82*(2), 187–200.

Danieli, Y. (1985). The treatment and prevention of long-term effects and intergenerational transmission of victimization: A lesson from Holocaust survivors and their children. In C. R. Figley (Ed.), *Trauma and its wake: The study and treatment of posttraumatic stress disorder* (pp. 248–313). New York: Bruner/Mazel.

Darling, C., Hill, E. & McWey, L. M. (2004). Understanding stress and quality of life for clergy and clergy spouses. *Stress & Health: Journal of the International Society for the Investigation of Stress, 20*(5), 261–277.

Davis, C. G., Nolen-Hoeksema, S. & Larson, J. (1998). Making sense of loss and benefiting from the experience: Two construals of meaning. *Journal of Personality and Social Psychology, 75*(2), 561–574.

Davis, C. G., Wortman, C. B., Lehman, D. R. & Silver, R. (2000). Searching for meaning in loss: Are clinical assumptions correct? *Death Studies, 24*(6), 497–540.

Deblinger, E., Behl, L. E. & Clickman, A. R. (2012). Trauma-focused cognitive-behavioral therapy for children who have experienced sexual abuse. In P. Kendall (Ed.), *Child and adolescent therapy: Cognitive-behavioral procedures* (pp. 345–375). New York: Guilford Press.

de Jong, J. T. V. M. (Ed.) (2002). *Trauma, war, and violence: Public mental health in socio-cultural context*. New York: Kluwer Academic/Plenum.

Dekel, R. (2007). Posttraumatic distress and growth among wives of prisoners of war: The contribution of husbands' posttraumatic stress disorder and wives' own attachment. *American Journal of Orthopsychiatry, 77*(3), 419–426.

Dekel, R. & Baum, N. (2010). Intervention in a shared traumatic reality: A new challenge for social workers. *British Journal of Social Work, 40*(6), 1927–1944.

Dekel, R. & Goldblatt, H. (2008). Is there intergenerational transmission of trauma? The case of combat veterans' children. *American Journal of Orthopsychiatry, 78*(3), 281–289.

Dekel, R. & Monson, C. M. (2010). Military-related post-traumatic stress disorder and family relations: Current knowledge and future directions. *Aggression and Violent Behavior, 15*(4), 303–309.

Dekel, R., Goldblatt, H., Keidar, M., Solomon, Z. & Polliack, M. (2005). Being a wife of a veteran with posttraumatic stress disorder. *Family Relations, 54*(1), 24–36.

Dekel, R., Hantman, S., Ginzburg, K. & Solomon, Z. (2007). The cost of caring? Social workers in hospitals confront ongoing terrorism. *British Journal of Social Work, 37*(7), 1247–1261.

Dekel, S., Ein-Dor, T. & Solomon, Z. (2012). Posttraumatic growth and posttraumatic distress: A longitudinal study. *Psychological Trauma: Theory, Research, Practice, and Policy, 4*, 94–101.

DeRosa, R. & Pelcovitz, D. (2008). Group treatment for chronically traumatized adolescents: Igniting SPARCS of change. In D. Brom, R. Pat-Horenczyk & J. D. Ford (Eds.), *Treating traumatized children: Risks, resilience and recovery* (pp. 225–239). London: Routledge.

DiMaggio, C. & Galea, S. (2006). The mental health and behavioral consequences of terrorism. In R. Davis, A. Lurigio & S. Herman (Eds.), *Victims of crime* (pp. 147–160). London: Sage.

Dobrof, R. (2002). From the editor. *Journal of Gerontological Social Work, 37*(1), 1–2.

Dohrenwend, B. P., Turner, J., Turse, N. A., Adams, B. G., Koenen, K. C. & Marshall, R. (2006). The psychological risks of Vietnam for US veterans: A revisit with new data and methods. *Science, 313*(5789), 979–982.

Dougall, A., Herberman, H., Delahanty, D., Inslicht, S. & Gaum, A. (2000). Similarity of prior trauma exposure as a determinant of chronic stress responding to an airline disaster. *Journal of Counseling and Clinical psychology, 68*(2), 290–295.

Drummond, J., Kysela, G. M., McDonald, L. & Query, B. (2002). The family adaptation model: Examination of dimensions and relations. *Canadian Journal of Nursing Research, 34*(1), 29–46.

Dubow, E. F., Huesmann, L. R. & Boxer, P. (2009). A social-cognitive-ecological framework for understanding the impact of exposure to persistent ethnic-political violence on children's psychosocial adjustment. *Clinical Child Family Psychology Review, 12*(2), 113–126.

Dunst, C., Trivette, C. & Cross, A. (1986). Mediating influences of social support: Personal, family, and child outcomes. *American Journal of Mental Deficiency, 90*, 403–417.

Ehlers, A., Mayou, R. A. & Bryant, B. (1998). Psychological predictors of chronic posttraumatic stress disorder after motor vehicle accidents. *Journal of Abnormal Psychology, 107*(3), 508–519.

Ehntholt, K. A. & Yule, W. (2006). Practitioner review: Assessment and treatment of refugee children and adolescents who have experienced war-related trauma. *Journal of Child Psychology and Psychiatry, 47*(12), 1197–1210.

Eidelson, R. J., D'Alessio, G. R. & Eidelson, J. I. (2003). The impact of September 11 on psychologists. *Professional Psychology: Research and Practice, 34*(2), 144–50.

Elbert, T., Schauer, M., Schauer, E., Huschka, B., Hirth, M. & Neuner, F. (2009). Trauma-related impairment in children: A survey in Sri Lankan provinces affected by armed conflict. *Child Abuse & Neglect, 33*, 238–246.

Ellis, B. H., Fogler, J., Hansen, S., Forbes, P., Navalta, C. P. & Saxe, G. (2011). Trauma Systems Therapy: 15-month outcomes and the importance of effecting environmental change. *Psychological Trauma: Theory, Research, Practice, and Policy*. Advance online publication, doi: 10.1037/a0025192.

Ellwood, L. S., Mott, J., Lohr, J. M. & Galovski, T. E. (2011). Secondary trauma symptoms in clinicians: A critical review of the construct, specificity, and implications for trauma-focused treatment. *Clinical Psychology Review, 31*(1), 25–36.

ElZein, H. L. & Ammar, D. F. (2010). Parent and teacher perceptions of assessing Lebanese children's reaction to war-related stress: A survey of psychological and behavioral functioning. *Journal of Child & Adolescent Trauma, 3*(4), 255–278.

Engel, S. M., Berkowitz, G. S., Wolff, M. S. & Yehuda, R. (2005). Psychological trauma associated with the World Trade Center attacks and its effect on pregnancy outcome. *Paediatric & Perinatal Epidemiology, 19*(5), 334–341.

Erbes, C. R., Arbisi, P. A., Kehle, S. M., Ferrier-Auerbach, A. G., Barry, R. A. & Polusny, M. A. (2011). The distinctiveness of hardiness, positive emotionality, and negative emotionality in National Guard soldiers. *Journal of Research in Personality, 45*(5), 508–512.

Erikson, E. H. (1963). *Childhood and society*. New York: Norton.

Ersing, R. L. & Kost, K. A. (Eds.) (2012). *Surviving disaster: The role of social networks*. Chicago, IL: Lyceum Press.

Espié, E., Gaboulaud, V., Baubet, T., Casas, G., Mouchenik, Y., Yun, O., Grais, R. F. & Rose Moro, M. (2009). Trauma-related psychological disorders among Palestinian children and adults in Gaza and the West Bank, 2005–2008. *International Journal of Mental Health Systems, 3*, 21–25.

Evans, W., Marsh, S. C. & Weigel, D. J. (2010). Promoting adolescent sense of coherence: Testing models of risk, protection, and resiliency. *Journal of Community & Applied Social Psychology, 20*(1), 30–43.

Everly, G. S. & Mitchell, J. T. (2000). The debriefing "controversy" and crisis intervention: A review of lexical and substantive issues. *International Journal of Emergency Mental Health. 2*(4), 211–225.

Falsetti, S. A., Resick, P. A. & Davis, J. L. (2003). Changes in religious beliefs following trauma. *Journal of Traumatic Stress, 16*(4), 391–398.

Farhood, L. (2004). The impact of high and low stress on the health of Lebanese families. *Research and Theory for Nursing Practice, 18*(2–3), 197–212.

Fazel, M. & Stein, A. (2003). Mental health of refugee children. *British Medical Journal, 327*(7407), 134.

Fazel, M., Doll, H. & Stein, A. (2009). A school-based mental health intervention for refugee children: An exploratory study. *Clinical Child Psychology and Psychiatry, 14*(2), 297–309.

Feldman, R. & Vengrober, A. (2011). Posttraumatic stress disorder in infants and young children exposed to war-related trauma. *Journal of the American Academy of Child & Adolescent Psychiatry, 50*(7), 645–658.

Figley, C. R. (1989). *Helping traumatized families*. San Francisco, CA: Jossey-Bass.

Figley, C. R. (1995). *Compassion fatigue: Coping with secondary traumatic stress disorder in those who treat the traumatized*. New York: Brunner/Mazel.

Flensborg-Madsen, T., Ventegodt, S. & Merrick, J. (2005). Sense of coherence and physical health: A review of previous findings. *Scientific World Journal, 5*, 665–673.

Florian, V., Mikulincer, M. & Taubman, O. (1995). Does hardiness contribute to mental health during a stressful real-life situation? The roles of appraisal and coping. *Journal of Personality and Social Psychology, 68*(4), 687–695.

Foa, E. B. & Kozak, M. J. (1986). Emotional processing of fear: Exposure to corrective information. *Psychological Bulletin, 99*(1), 20–35.

Foa, E. B. & Rothbaum, B. A. (1998). *Treating the trauma of rape: Cognitive behavioral therapy for PTSD. New York: The Guilford Press.*

Foa, E. B., Cahill, S. P., Boscarino, J. A., Hobfoll, S. E., Lahad, M., McNally, R. J. & Solomon, Z. (2005). Social, psychological, and psychiatric interventions following terrorist attacks: Recommendations for practice and research. *Neuropsychopharmacology, 30*(10), 1806–1817.

Foa, E. B., Keane, T. M., Friedman, M. J. & Cohen, J. A. (2009). *Effective treatments for PTSD: Practice guidelines from the International Society for Traumatic Stress Studies*. New York: The Guilford Press.

Folkman, S. & Lazarus, R. (1980). An analysis of coping in a middle-aged community sample. *Journal of Health and Social behavior, 21*(3), 219–239.

Forbes, A. & Roger, D. (1999). Stress, social support and fear of disclosure. *British Journal of Health Psychology, 4*(1359107), 165–165.

Forbes, D., Creamer, M., Bisson, J. I., Cohen, J. A., Crow, B. E., Foa, E. B., Friedman, M. J., Keane, T. M., Kudler, H. S. & Ursano, R. J. (2010). A guide to guidelines for the treatment of PTSD and related conditions. *Journal of Traumatic Stress, 23*(5), 537–552.

Ford, J. D. (2009). Neurobiological and developmental research. In C. A. Courtois & J. D. Ford (Eds.), *Treating complex traumatic stress disorders: An evidence-based guide* (pp. 31–58). New York: Guilford.

Ford, J. D. & Courtois, C. A. (2009). Defining and understanding complex trauma and complex traumatic stress disorder. In C. A. Courtois & J. D. Ford (Eds.), *Treating complex traumatic stress disorders: An evidence-based guide* (pp. 23–30). New York: Guilford.

Ford, J. D., Fallot, R. D. & Harris, M. (2009). Group therapy. In C. A. Courtois & J. D. Ford (Eds.), *Treating complex traumatic stress disorders: An evidence-based guide* (pp. 415–440). New York: Guilford.

Formoso, D., Gonzales, N. A., Barrerra, M., Jr. & Dumka, L. E. (2007). Interparental relations, maternal employment, and fathering in Mexican American families. *Journal of Marriage and Family, 69*(1), 26–39.

Franciskovič, T., Stevanović, A., Jelusić, I., Roganović, B., Klarić, M. & Grković, J. (2007). Secondary traumatization of wives of war veterans with posttraumatic stress disorder. *Croatian Medical Journal, 48*(2), 177–184.

Fraser, M. W., Richman, J. M. & Galinsky, M. J. (1999). Risk, protection and resilience: Toward a conceptual framework for social work practice. *Social Work Research, 23*(3), 131–143.

Frazier, P., Conlon, A. & Glaser, T. (2001). Positive and negative life changes following sexual assault. *Journal of Consulting and Clinical Psychology, 69* (6), 1048–1055.

Frazier, P., Tennen, H., Gavian, M., Park, C., Tomich, P. & Tashiro, T. (2009). Does self-reported posttraumatic growth reflect genuine positive change? *Psychological Science 20*(7), 912–919.

Friedman, M. J., Resick, P. A., Bryant, R. A. & Brewin, C. R. (2011). Considering PTSD for DSM-5. *Depression & Anxiety, 28*(9), 750–769.

Fromm, G. (Ed.) (2012). *Lost in transmission: Studies of trauma across generations.* London: Karnac.

Fullerton, C. S., Ursano, R. J. & Wang, L. (2004). Acute stress disorder, post-traumatic stress disorder, and depression in disaster or rescue workers. *American Journal of Psychiatry, 161*(8), 1370–1376.

Furr, J. M., Comer, J. S., Edmunds, J. M. & Kendall, P. C. (2010). Disasters and youth: A meta-analytic examination of posttraumatic stress. *Journal of Consulting and Clinical Psychology, 78*(6), 765–780.

Gabert-Quillen, C. A., Fallon, W. & Delahanty, D. L. (2011). PTSD after traumatic injury: An investigation of the impact of injury severity and peritraumatic moderators. *Journal of Health Psychology, 16*(4), 678–687.

Galea, S., Ahern, J., Resnick, H., Kilpatrick, D., Bucuvalas, M., Gold, J. & Vlahov, D. (2002). Psychological sequelae of the September 11 terrorist attacks in New York City. *New England Journal of Medicine, 346*(13), 982–987.

Galovski, T. & Lyons, J. A. (2004). Psychological sequelae of combat violence: A review of the impact of PTSD on the veteran's family and possible interventions. *Aggression & Violent Behavior, 9*(5), 477–501.

Gamble, W. C. (1994). Perceptions of controllability and other stressor event characteristics as determinants of coping among young adolescents and young adults. *Journal of Youth and Adolescence, 23*(1), 65–84.

Gammonley, D. & Dziegielewski, S. F. (2006). Crisis intervention responses to children victimized by terrorism: Children are not little adults. *Brief Treatment and Crisis Intervention, 6*(1), 22–35.

Ganor, M. & Ben-Lavy, Y. (2003). Community resilience: Lessons derived from Gilo under fire. *Journal of Jewish Communal Service, 79*(2/3), 105–108.

Garbarino, J., Dubrow, N., Kostelny, K. & Pardo, C. (1998). *Children in danger: Coping with the consequences of community violence.* San Francisco, CA: Jossey-Bass.

Garmezy, N. (1994). Reflections and commentary on risk, resilience, and development. In R. J. Haggerty, L. R. Sherrod, N. Garmezy & M. Rutter (Eds.), *Stress, risk and resilience in children and adolescents: Processes, mechanisms and interventions.* New York, Cambridge University Press.

Garmezy, N. & Rutter, M. (1983). *Stress, coping and development in children.* New York: McGraw-Hill/Cambridge University Press.

Garwick, A., Detzner, D. & Boss, P. (1994). Family perceptions of living with Alzheimer's disease. *Family Process, 33*(3), 327–340.

Gerin, W., Milner, D., Chawla, S. & Pickering, T. G. (1995). Social support as a moderator of cardiovascular reactivity in women: A test of the direct effects and buffering hypotheses. *Psychosomatic Medicine, 57*(1), 16–22.

Geron, Y., Malkinson, R. & Shamai, M. (2005). Families in the war zone: Narratives of "Me" and the "Other" in the course of therapy. *AFTA Monograph Series, 1*(1), 17–25.

Gershoff, E. T., Aber, J. L., Ware, A. & Kotler, J. A. (2010). Exposure to 9/11 among youth and their mothers in New York City: Enduring associations with mental health and sociopolitical attitudes. *Child Development, 81*(4), 1142–1160.

Gewirtz, A., Forgatch, M. & Wieling, E. (2008). Parenting practices as potential mechanisms for child adjustment following mass trauma. *Journal of Marital and Family Therapy, 34*(2), 177–192.

Gibson, L. E. (2007). *Acute Stress Disorder.* Washington, DC: US Department of Veterans Affairs. Retrieved from http://www.ptsd.va.gov/professional/pages/acute-stress-disorder.asp

Gidron, Y., Gal, R., Freedman, S. A., Twiser, I., Lauden, A., Snir, Y. & Benjamin, J. (2001). Translating research findings to PTSD prevention: Results of a randomized-controlled pilot study. *Journal of Traumatic Stress, 14*(4), 773–780.

Gidron, Y. & Nyklicek, I. (2009). Experimentally testing Taylor's stress, coping and adaptation framework. *Anxiety, Stress & Coping, 22,* 525–535.

Ginzburg, K., Solomon, Z. & Bleich, A. (2002). Repressive coping style, acute stress disorder and posttraumatic stress disorder after myocardial infarction. *Psychosomatic Medicine, 64*(5), 748–745.

Gist, R. & Woodall, S. (2000). There are no simple solutions to complex problems. In J. M. Violanti & P. Douglas (Eds.), *Posttraumatic stress interventions: Challenges, issues and perspectives* (pp. 81–95). Springfield, IL: Charles C. Thomas.

Glantz, M. D. & Johnson, J. L. (1999). *Resilience and development: Positive life adaptations.* New York: Kluwer Academic/Plenum Publishers.

Godeau, E., Vignes, C., Navarro, F., Iachan, R., Ross, J., Pasquier, C. & Guinard, A. (2005). Effects of a large-scale industrial disaster on rates of symptoms consistent with posttraumatic stress disorders among schoolchildren in Toulouse. *Archives of Pediatrics & Adolescent Medicine, 159*(6), 579–584.

Goenjian, A. K., Karavan, I., Pynoos, R. S., Minassian, D., Najarian, L. M., Steinberg, A. M. & Fairbanks, L. A. (1997). Outcomes of psychotherapy among early adolescents after trauma. *American Journal of Psychiatry, 154*(4), 536–542.

Greenberg, J., Seltzer, M., Krauss, M. & Kim, H. (1997). The differential effects of social support on the psychological well-being of aging mothers of adults with mental illness or mental retardation. *Family Relations, 46*(4), 383–394.

Grubaugh, A. L. & Resick, P. A. (2007). Posttraumatic growth in treatment-seeking female assault victims. *Psychiatric Quarterly, 78*(2), 145–155.

Guo, Y., Chen, C., Lu, M., Tan, H., Lee, H. & Wang, T. (2004). Posttraumatic stress disorder among professional and non-professional rescuers involved in an earthquake in Taiwan. *Psychiatry Research, 127*(1/2), 35–41.

Haen, C. (2005). Rebuilding security: Group therapy with children affected by September 11. *International Journal of Group Psychotherapy, 55*(3), 391–414.

Hafstad, G. S., Gil-Rivas, V., Kilmer, R. P. & Raeder, S. (2010). Parental adjustment, family functioning, and posttraumatic growth among Norwegian children and adolescents following a natural disaster. *American Journal of Orthopsychiatry, 80*(2), 248–257.

Haggerty, R. J., Sherrod, L. R., Garmezy, N. & Rutter, M. (Eds.) (1994). *Stress, risk, and resilience in children and adolescents: Processes, mechanisms, and interventions.* Cambridge, CT: Cambridge University press.

Halpern, J. & Tramontin, M. (2007). *Disaster mental health: Theory and practice.* Canada: Thompson Brooks/Cole.

Hammermeister, J. & Burton, D. (2001). Stress, appraisal, and coping revisited: Examining the antecedents of competitive state anxiety with endurance athletes. *The Sport Psychologist, 15*, 66–90.

Harper, M. (2012). Taming the amygdala: An EEG analysis of exposure therapy for the traumatized. *Traumatology, 18*(2), 61–74.

Harris, T. B., Carlisle, L. L., Sargent, J. & Primm, A. B. (2010). Trauma and diverse child populations. *Child and Adolescent Psychiatric Clinics of North America, 19*(4), 869–887.

Harrison, R. L. & Westwood, M. J. (2009). Preventing vicarious traumatization of mental health therapists: Identifying protective practices. *Psychotherapy Theory, Research, Practice, Training, 46*(2), 203–219.

Harvey, J., Barnett, K. & Rupe, S. (2006). Posttraumatic growth and other outcomes of major loss in the context of complex family lives. In L. G. Calhoun & R. G. Tedeschi (Eds.), *Handbook of posttraumatic growth* (pp. 100–117). Mahwah, NJ: Lawrence Erlbaum.

Harvey, M. R., Mondesir, A. V. & Aldrich, H. (2007). Fostering resilience in traumatized communities: A community empowerment model of intervention. *Journal of Aggression, Maltreatment & Trauma, 14*(1/2), 265–285.

Hastings, R. P. & Taunt H. M. (2002). Positive perceptions in families of children with developmental disabilities. *American Journal on Mental Retardation, 107*(2), 116–127.

Hawker, D. M., Durkin, J. & Hawker, D. J. (2011). To debrief or not to debrief our heroes: That is the question. *Clinical Psychology & Psychotherapy, 18*(6), 453–463.

Hawley, D. R. (2000). Clinical implications of family resilience. *The American Journal of Family Therapy, 28*(2), 101–116.

Hawley, D. R. & DeHaan, L. (1996). Towards a definition of family resilience. *Family Process, 35*(3), 283–298.

Hayes, S. C., Luoma, J. B., Bond, F. W., Masuda, A. & Lillis, J. (2006). Acceptance and Commitment Therapy: Model, processes and outcomes. *Behaviour Research and Therapy, 44*(1), 1–25.

Heath, N. M., Hall, B. J., Russ, E. U., Canetti, D. & Hobfoll, S. E. (2012). Reciprocal relationships between resource loss and psychological distress following exposure to political violence: An empirical investigation of COR theory's loss spirals. *Anxiety, Stress & Coping, 25*(6), 679–695.

Hee-Kyung, K., Rueter, M. A., Seonju, K., Sun Wha, O. & Mi-Sook, L. (2003). Marital relationships following the Korean economic crisis: Applying the Family Stress Model. *Journal of Marriage & Family, 65*(2), 316–325.

Helgeson, V. S., Reynolds, K.A. & Tomich, P. L. (2006). A meta-analytic review of benefit finding and growth. *Journal of Consulting and Clinical Psychology, 74*(5), 797–816.

Herek, G. M., Capitanio, J. P. & Widman, K. F. (2002). HIV-related stigma and knowledge in the United States: Prevalence and trends, 1991–1999. *American Journal of Public Health, 92*(3), 371–377.

Herman, J. L. (1992a). *Trauma and Recovery*. New York: Basic Books.

Herman, J. L. (1992b). Complex PTSD: A syndrome in survivors of prolonged and repeated trauma. *Journal of Traumatic Stress, 5*(3), 377–391.

Hernandez, P., Gangsei, D. & Engstrom, D. (2007). Vicarious resilience: A new concept in work with those who survive trauma. *Family Process, 46*(2), 229–241.

Hesse, A. R. (2002). Secondary trauma: How working with trauma survivors affects therapists. *Clinical Social Work Journal, 30*(3), 293–309.

Hicks, M. M. & Conner, N. E. (2014). Resilient ageing: A concept analysis. *Journal of Advanced Nursing, 70*(4), 744–755.

Hildon, Z., Montgomery, S. M., Wiggins, R. D. & Netuveli, G. (2010). Examining resilience of quality of life in the face of health-related and psychosocial adversity at older ages: What is "right" about the way we age? *The Gerontologist, 50*(1), 36–47.

Hill, J. S., Lau, M. Y. & Sue, D. W. (2010). Integrating trauma psychology and cultural psychology: Indigenous perspectives on theory, research, and practice *Traumatology, 16*(4), 39–47.

Hill, R. (1949). *Families under stress: Adjustment to the crisis of war separation and reunion*. New York: Harper & Row.

Hill, R. (1958). Social stress on the family. *Social Case Work, 49*, 139–150.

Hiskey, S. (2012). Psychological responses to trauma in older people. *Mental Health Practice, 16*(3), 12–16.

Hobfoll, S. E. (1989). Conservation of resources: A new attempt at conceptualizing stress. *American Psychologist, 44*(3), 513–524.

Hobfoll, S. E. & Lilly, R. S. (1993). Resource conservation as a strategy for community psychology. *Journal of Community Psychology, 21*(2), 128–148.

Hobfoll, S. E. & Vaux, A. (1993). Social support: Social resources and social context. In L. Goldberger & S. Breznitz (Eds.), *Handbook of stress* (pp. 685–705). New York: Free Press.

Hobfoll, S. E., Hall, B. J., Canetti-Nisim, D., Galea, S., Johnson, R. J. & Palmieri, P. A. (2007a). Refining our understanding of traumatic growth in the face of terrorism: Moving from meaning cognitions to doing what is meaningful. *Applied Psychology: An International Review, 56*(3), 345–366.

Hobfoll, S. E., Watson, P., Bell, C. C., Bryant, R. A., Brymer, M. J., Friedman, M. J., Friedman, M., Gersons, B. P., de Jong, J. T., Layne, C. M., Maguen, S., Neria, Y., Norwood, A. E., Pynoos, R. S., Reissman, D., Ruzek, J. I., Shalev, A. Y., Solomon, Z., Steinberg, A. M. & Ursano, R. J. (2007b). Five essential elements of immediate and mid-term mass trauma intervention: Empirical evidence. *Psychiatry, 70*(4), 283–315.

Holmes, T. H. & Rahe, R. H. (1967). The Social Readjustment Rating Scale. *Journal of Psychosomatic Research, 11*(2), 213–221.

Hooper, L. M. & DePuy, V. (2010). Mediating and moderating effects of differentiation of self on depression symptomatology in a rural community sample. *The Family Journal, 18*(4), 358–368.

Horwitz, A. V. (2007). Transforming normality into pathology: The "DSM" and the outcomes of stressful social arrangements. *Journal of Health and Social Behavior*, 48(3), 211–222.

Hoven, C. W., Duarte, C. S., Wu, P., Doan, T., Syngh, N., Mandell, D. J., Bin, F., Teichman, Y., Teichman, M., Wicks, J., Musa, G. & Coghen, P. (2009). Parental exposure to mass violence and child mental health: The First Responder and WTC Evacuee Study. *Clinical Child and Family Psychology Review, 12*, 95–112.

Howard, S., Dryden, J. & Johnson, B. (1999). Childhood resilience: Review and critique of literature. *Oxford Review of Education, 25*(3), 307–323.

Ibbotson, G. & Williamson, A. (2010). Treatment of post-traumatic stress disorder using trauma-focused hypnosis.*Contemporary Hypnosis, 27*(4), 257–267.

Inter-Agency Standing Committee (2007). *IASC guidelines on mental health and psychosocial support in emergency settings.* Geneva, Switzerland: Author.

Institute of Medicine (2007). *Treatment of posttraumatic stress disorder: An assessment of the evidence.* Washington, DC: National Academy Press.

Ireland, S., Gilchrist, J., & Maconochie, I. (2008). Debriefing after failed paediatric resuscitation: A survey of current UK practice. *Emergency Medicine Journal, 25*(6), 328–330.

Jackson, C., Nissenson, K. & Cloitre, M. (2009). Cognitive behavior therapy. In C. A. Courtois & J. D. Ford (Eds.), *Treating complex traumatic stress disorders: An evidence-based guide* (pp. 243–263). New York: Guilford.

Jacobs, J., Horne-Moyer, H. L. & Jones, R. (2004). The effectiveness of critical incident stress debriefing with primary and secondary trauma victims. *International Journal of Emergency Mental Health, 6*(1), 5–14.

Janet, P. (1889). *L'Automatisme psychologie.* Paris: Alcan.

Janoff-Bulman, R. (1992). *Shattered assumptions: Towards a new psychology of trauma.* New York: Free Press.

Janoff-Bulman, R. & Sheikh, S. (2006). From national trauma to moralizing nation. *Basic and Applied Social Psychology, 28*(4), 325–332.

Jaycox, L. H., Cohen, J. A., Mannarino, A. P., Walker, D. W., Langley, A. K., Gegenheimer, K. L., Scott, M. & Schonlau, M. (2010). Children's mental health care following Hurricane Katrina: A field trial of trauma-focused psychotherapies. *Journal of Traumatic Stress, 23*(2), 223–231.

Jehel, L., Paternity, S., Brunet, A., Duchet, C., & Guelfi, J. D. (2003). Predictions of the occurrence and intensity of post-traumatic stress disorder in victims 32 months after bomb attack. *European Journal of Psychiatry, 18*(4), 172–176.

Johnson, R. J., Hobfoll, S. E., Hall, B. J., Canetti-Nisim, D., Galea, S. & Palmieri, P. A. (2007). Posttraumatic growth: Action and reaction. *Applied Psychology, 56*(3), 428–436.

Johnston, J. H., Bailey, W. A. & Wilson, G. (2014). Mechanisms for fostering multigenerational resilience. *Contemporary Family Therapy, 36*(1), 148–161.

Jones, E. M. & Landreth, G. (2002). The efficacy of intensive individual play therapy for chronically ill children. *International Journal of Play Therapy, 11*(1), 117–140.

Jordans, M. D., Komproe, I. H., Tol, W. A., Kohrt, B. A., Luitel, N. P., Macy, R. D. & de Jong, J. M. (2010). Evaluation of a classroom-based psychosocial intervention in conflict-affected Nepal: A cluster randomized controlled trial. *Journal of Child Psychology & Psychiatry, 51*(7), 818–826.

Jordans, M. D., Tol, W. A. & Komproe, I. H. (2011). Mental health interventions for children in adversity: Pilot-testing a research strategy for treatment selection in low-income settings. *Social Science & Medicine, 73*(3), 456–466.

Jordans, M. D., Komproe, I. H., Tol, W. A., Susanty, D., Vallipuram, A., Ntamatumba, P., Labusa, A. C. & de Jong, J. T. V. M. (2011). Practice-Driven Evaluation of a Multi-layered Psychosocial Care Package for Children in Areas of Armed Conflict. *Community Mental Health Journal, 47*(3), 267–277.

Jovanovic, T. & Ressler, K. J. (2010). How the neurocircuitry and genetics of fear inhibition may inform our understanding of PTSD. *American Journal of Psychiatry, 167*(6), 648–662.

Joyce, P. & Berger, R. (2007). Which language does PTSD Speak? The Westernization of Mr. Sanchez. *Journal of Trauma Practice, 5*(4), 53–67.

Kaiser, E., Gillette, C. S. & Spinazzola, J. (2010). A controlled pilot-outcome study of sensory integration (SI) in the treatment of complex adaptation to traumatic stress. *Journal of Aggression, Maltreatment & Trauma, 19*(7), 699–720.

Kaniasty, K. & Norris, F. H. (2004). Social support in the aftermath of disasters, catastrophes, and acts of terrorism: Altruistic, overwhelmed, uncertain, antagonistic, and patriotic communities. In R. Ursano, A. Norwood & C. Fullerton (Eds.), *Bioterrorism: Psychological and public health interventions* (pp. 200–229). Cambridge: Cambridge University Press.

Kardiner, A. & Spiegel, H. (1947). *War stress and neurotic illness.* New York: Hoeber.

Karlin, B. E., Ruzek, J. I., Chard, K. M., Eftekhari, A., Monson, C. M., Hembree, E. A., Resick, P. A. & Foa, E. B. (2010). Dissemination of evidence-based psychological treatments for posttraumatic stress disorder in the Veterans Health Administration. *Journal of Traumatic Stress, 23*(6), 663–673.

Karney, B. R. & Bradbury, T. N. (1995). The longitudinal course of marital quality and stability: A review of theory, method, and research. *Psychological Bulletin, 118*, 3–34.

Kearns, M. C., Ressler, K. J., Zatzick, D. & Rothbaum, B. O. (2012). Early interventions for PTSD: A review. *Depression and Anxiety, 29*(10), 833–842.

Kendall-Tackett, K. (2002). The health effects of childhood abuse: Four pathways by which abuse can influence health. *Child Abuse and Neglect, 6/7*, 715–730

Kennedy, J. E., Davis, R. C. & Taylor, B. G. (1998). Changes in spirituality and well-being among victims of sexual assault. *Journal for the Scientific Study of Religion, 37*(2), 322–328.

Kent, M., Davis, M. C. & Reich, J. W. (2014). Introduction. In M. Kent, M. C. Davis & J. W. Reich (Eds.), *The resilience handbook: Approaches to stress and trauma* (pp. xii–xix). New York: Routledge/Taylor and Francis.

Kessler, R. C., Sonnega, A., Bromet, E., Hughes, M. & Nelson, C. B. (1995). Posttraumatic stress disorder in the national comorbidity survey. *Archive of General Psychiatry, 52*(12), 1048–1060.

Kiliç, C. & Ulusoy, M. (2003). Psychological effects of the November 1999 earthquake in Turkey: An epidemiological study. *Acta Psychiatrica Scandinavia, 108*(3), 232–238.

Killian, K. D. (2008). Helping till it hurts? A multimethod study of compassion fatigue, burnout, and self-care in clinicians working with trauma survivors. *Traumatology, 14*(2), 32–44.

Kilmer, R. & Gil-Rivas, V. (2010). Exploring posttraumatic growth in children impacted by Hurricane Katrina: Correlates of the phenomenon and developmental considerations. *Child Development, 81*(4), 1210–1226.

Kim-Cohen, J. & Turkewitz, R. (2012). Resilience and measured gene-environment interactions. *Development & Psychopathology, 24*(4), 1297–1306.

Kimhi, S. & Shamai, M. (2004). Community resilience and the impact of stress: Adult response to Israel's withdrawal from Lebanon. *Journal of Community Psychology, 32*(4), 439–451.

Kimhi, S., Eshel, Y., Zysberg, L. & Hantman, S. (2010). Post-traumatic growth and symptoms of stress among adolescents. In F. Azaiza, N. Nachmias & M. Cohen (Eds.), *Health, education, and welfare services in times of crisis: Lessons learned from the Second Lebanon War* (pp. 145–163). Haifa, Israel: Pardes Publications.

Kira, I. A. (2010). Etiology and treatment of post-cumulative traumatic stress disorders in different cultures. *Traumatology, 16*(4), 128–141.

Kiser, L. J., Donohue, A., Hodgkinson, S., Medoff, D. & Black, M. M. (2010). Strengthening family coping resources: The feasibility of a multifamily group intervention for families exposed to trauma. *Journal of Traumatic Stress, 23*(6), 802–807.

Kleim, B. & Ehlers, A. (2009). Evidence for a curvilinear relationship between post-traumatic growth and posttrauma depression and PTSD in assault survivors. *Journal of Traumatic Stress, 22*(1), 45–52.

Klein, T. P., Devoe, E. R., Miranda-Julian, C. & Linas, K. (2009). Young children's response to September 11th: The New York City experience. *Infant Mental Health Journal, 30*, 1–22.

Knipe, J. (2010). The method of constant installation of present orientation and safety (CIPOS). Eye movement desensitization and reprocessing (EMDR) scripted protocols: Special populations. In M. Luber (Ed.), *Eye movement desensitization and reprocessing (EMDR) scripted protocols: Special populations* (pp. 235–241). New York: Springer Publishing.

Kobasa, S. C. (1979). Stressful life events, personality and health: An inquiry into hardiness. *Journal of Personality and Social Psychology, 37*(1), 1–11.

Koos, E. L. (1946). *Families in trouble.* New York: King's Crown Press.

Koplewicz, H. S., Vogel, J. M., Solanto, M. V., Morrissey, R. F., Alonso, C. M., Abikoff, H., Gallagher, R. & Novick, R. M. (2002). Child and parent responses to the 1993 World Trade Center bombing. *Journal of Traumatic Stress, 15*(1), 77–85.

Koren, D., Arnon, I. & Klein, E. (1999). Acute stress response and posttraumatic stress disorder in traffic accident victims: A one-year prospective, follow-up study. *American Journal of Psychiatry, 156*(3), 367–373.

Kouneski, E. (2000). Circumplex model and FACES: Review of literature. Retrieved from www.faces.IV.com

Krohne, H. W. (1996). Individual differences in coping. In M. Zeidner & N. S. Endler (Eds.), *Handbook of coping: Theory, research, applications* (pp. 381–409). New York: Wiley.

Kronenberg, M. E., Hansel, T. C., Brennan, A. M., Osofsky, H. J., Osofsky, J. D. & Lawrason, B. (2010). Children of Katrina: Lessons learned about post-disaster symptoms and recovery patterns. *Child Development, 81*(4), 1241–1259.

Kulka, R. A., Schlenger, W. E., Fairbank, J. A., Hough, R. L., Jordan, B. K., Marmar, C. R. & Weiss, D. S. (1990). *Trauma and the Vietnam War generation.* New York: Brunner/Mazel.

Lahad, M. & Ben Nesher, U. (2008) Community coping: Resilience models for preparation, intervention and rehabilitation in man-made and Natural Disasters. In K. Gow & D. Paton (Eds.), *Resilience: The phoenix of natural disasters* (pp. 195–208). New York: Nova Science Publishers.

Lambert, J. E., Engh, R., Hasbun, A. & Holzer, J. (2012). Impact of posttraumatic stress disorder on the relationship quality and psychological distress of intimate partners: A meta-analytic review. *Journal of Family Psychology, 26*(5), 729–737.

Landau, J. (2007). Enhancing resilience: Families and communities as agents for change. *Family Process, 46*, 351–365.

Landau, J. (2010). Communities That Care for Families: The LINC Model for Enhancing Individual, Family, and Community Resilience. *American Journal of Orthopsychiatry, 80*(4), 516–524.

Landau, J., Mittal, M. & Wieling, E. (2008). Linking human systems: Strengthening individuals, families, and communities in the wake of mass trauma. *Journal of Marital & Family Therapy, 34*(2), 193–209.

Lapp, L. K., Agbokou, C. & Ferreri, F. (2011). PTSD in the elderly: the interaction between trauma and aging. *International Psychogeriatrics, 23*(6), 858–868.

Laufer, A. & Solomon, Z. (2009). Gender differences in PTSD in Israeli youth exposed to terror attacks. *Journal of Interpersonal Violence, 24*(6), 959–976.

Laufer, A. & Solomon, Z. (2010). Posttraumatic growth in Israeli Jews. In T. Weiss & R. Berger (Eds.), *Posttraumatic growth and culturally competent practice: Lessons learned from around the globe* (pp. 15–29). Hoboken, NJ: Wiley.

Lavee, J., McCubbin, H. & Olson, D. (1987). The effects of stressful life events and transitions on family functioning and well-being. *Journal of Marriage and the family, 49*(4), 857–873.

Lavee, Y., McCubbin, H. I. & Patterson, J. M. (1985). The Double ABCX Model of Family Stress and Adaptation: An empirical test by analysis of structural equations with latent variables. *Journal of Marriage & Family, 47*(4), 811–825.

Layne, C. M., Pynoos, R. S., Saltzman, W. S., Arslanagic, B., Black, M. & Savjak, N. (2001). Trauma/grief-focused group psychotherapy: School-based post-war intervention with traumatized Bosnian adolescents. *Group Dynamics: Theory, Research, and Practice, 5*(4), 277–290.

Layne, C. M., Saltzman, W. R., Poppleton, L., Burlingame, G. M., Pašalić, A., Durakovicć, E., Music, M., Nihada, A., Dapo, N., Arslanagic, B., Steinberg, A. M. & Pynoos, R. S. (2008). Effectiveness of a school-based group psychotherapy program for war-exposed adolescents: A randomized controlled trial. *Journal of the American Academy of Child & Adolescent Psychiatry, 47*(9), 1048–1062.

Lazarus, R. S. (1966). *Psychological stress and the coping process.* New York: McGraw-Hill.

Lazarus, R. S. (1991). *Emotion and adaptation.* New York: Oxford University Press.

Lazarus, R. S. (1993). Coping theory and research: Past, present, and future. *Psychosomatic Medicine, 55*(3), 234–247.

Lazarus, R. S. & Folkman, S. (1984). *Stress, appraisal and coping.* New York: Springer.

Lechner, S., Antoni, M. H. & Carver, C. S. (2006). Curvilinear associations between benefit finding and psychosocial adjustment to breast cancer. *Journal of Consulting and Clinical Psychology, 74*(5), 828–840.

Leek Openshaw, L. (2011). School-based support groups for traumatized students. *School Psychology International, 32*(2), 163–178.

Lengua, L. J., Long, A. C., Smith, K. I. & Meltzoff, A. N. (2005). Pre-attack symptomatology and temperament as predictors of children's responses to the September 11 terrorist attacks. *Journal of Child Psychology and Psychiatry and Allied Disciplines, 46*(6), 631–645.

Lepore, S. J. & Revenson, T. A. (2006). Resilience and posttraumatic growth: Recovery, resistance and reconfiguration. In L. Calhoun & R. Tedeschi (Eds.), *Handbook of posttraumatic growth: Research and practice* (pp. 24–46). Mahwah, NJ: Lawrence Erlbaum.

Lev-Wiesel, R., Goldblatt, H., Eisikovits, Z. & Admi H. (2008). Growth in the shadow of war: The case of social workers and nurses working in a shared war reality. *The British Journal of Social Work, 21,* 1–2.

Levine, P. (1997). *Waking the tiger: Healing trauma.* Berkeley, CA: North Atlantic Books.

Lewis, K. L. & Grenyer, B. F. S. (2009). Borderline personality or complex posttraumatic stress disorder? An update on the controversy. *Harvard Review of Psychiatry, 17*(5), 322–328.

Lietz, C. A. (2006). Uncovering stories of family resilience: A mixed methods study of resilient families, Part 1. *Families in Society: The Journal of Contemporary Social Services, 87*(4), 575–582.

Lietz, C. A. (2007). Uncovering stories of family resilience: A mixed methods study of resilient families, Part 2. *Families in Society: The Journal of Contemporary Social Services, 88*(1), 147–155.

Lindsay, J. (2007). The impact of the 2nd Intifada: An exploration of the experiences of Palestinian psychosocial counselors and social workers. *Illness, Crisis & Loss, 15*(2), 137–153.

Lindemann, E. (1944). Symptomatology and management of acute grief. *American Journal of Psychiatry, 101*, 141–48.

Linley, P. A. & Joseph, S. (2004). Positive change following trauma and adversity. *Journal of Traumatic Stress, 17*, 11–21.

Linley, P. A., Joseph, S. & Goodfellow, B. (2008). Positive changes in outlook following trauma and their relationship to subsequent posttraumatic stress, depression and anxiety. *Journal of Social & Clinical Psychology, 27*(8), 877–891.

Linneroth, P. J., Mrdjenovich, A. J. & Moore, B. A. (2011). Professional burnout in clinical military psychologists: Recommendations before, during, and after deployment. *Professional Psychology, Research & Practice, 42*(1), 87–93.

Little, S. G., Akin-Little, A. & Somerville, M. P. (2011). Response to trauma in children: An examination of effective intervention and post-traumatic growth. *School Psychology International, 32*(5), 448–463.

Litz, B. T., Gray, M. J., Bryant, R. A. & Adler, A. B. (2002). Early intervention for trauma: Current status and future directions. *Clinical Psychology: Science and Practice, 9*(2), 112–134.

Llabre, M. M. & Hadi, F. (2009). War-related exposure and psychological distress as predictors of health and sleep: A longitudinal study of Kuwaiti children. *Psychosomatic Medicine, 71*, 776–783.

Longstaff, P. (2005). *Security, resilience, and communication in unpredictable environments such as terrorism, natural disasters, and complex technology.* Cambridge, MA: Center for Information Policy Research. Harvard University.

Ludwig, K., Imberti, P., Rodriguez, R. & Torrens, A. (2006). Healing trauma and loss through a community-based multi-family group with Latino immigrants. *Social Work with Groups, 29*(4), 45–59.

Lustig, C. D. & Akey, T. (1999). Adaptation in families with adult children with mental retardation: Impact of family strengths and appraisal. *Education and Training in Mental Retardation and Developmental Disabilities, 34*(3), 26–270.

Luthar, S. S. & Brown, P. J. (2007). Maximizing resilience through diverse levels of inquiry: Prevailing paradigms, possibilities, and priorities for the future. *Development and Psychopathology, 19*(3), 931–955.

Luthar, S. S., Cicchetti, D. & Becker, B. (2000). The construct of resilience: A critical evaluation and guidelines for future work. *Child Development, 71*(3), 543–562.

Luthar, S. S., Sawyer, J. A. & Brown, P. J. (2006). Conceptual issues in studies of resilience. *Annals of the New York Academy of Sciences, 1094*(1), 105–115.

Lykes, M. (1994). Terror, silencing and children: International, multidisciplinary collaboration with Guatemalan Maya communities. *Social Science & Medicine, 38*(4), 543–552.

Mackey, R. & Fisher, R. (2010, January 27). Problems with food distribution in Haiti. *The New York Times*, p. 1.

Maddi, S., Khoshaba, D., Harvey, R., Fazel, M. & Resurreccion, N. (2010). The personality construct of hardiness: Relationships with the construction of existential meaning in life. *Journal of Humanistic Psychology, 51*(3), 369–388.

Maercker, A. & Zoellner, T. (2004). The Janus face of self-perceived growth: Toward a two-component model of posttraumatic growth. *Psychological Inquiry, 15*(1), 41–48.

Maercker, A., Brewin, C. R., Bryant, R. A., Cloitre, M., Reed, G. M., van Ommeren, M., Humayun, A., Jones, L. M., Kagee, A., Llosa, A. E., Rousseau, C., Somasundaram, D. J., Souza, R., Suzuki, Y., Weissbecker, I., Wessely, S. C., First, M. B. & Saxena, S. (2013). Proposals for mental disorders specifically associated with stress in the International Classification of Diseases-11. *The Lancet, 381*(9878), 1683–1685.

Maguen, S., Lucenko, B. A., Reger, M. A., Gahm, G. A., Litz, B. T., Seal, K. H., Knight, S. J. & Marmar, C. R. (2010). The impact of reported direct and indirect killing on mental health symptoms in Iraq war veterans. *Journal of Traumatic Stress, 23*(1), 86–90.

Magyar, J. & Theophilos, T. (2010). Review article: Debriefing critical incidents in emergency departments. *Emergency Medicine Australia, 22*(6), 499–506.

Makhashvili, N., Tsiskarishvili, L. & Drožđek, B. (2010). Door to the unknown: On large-scale public mental health interventions in post-conflict zones-experiences from Georgia. *Traumatology, 16*, 63–72.

Malekoff, A. (2008). Transforming Trauma and Empowering Children and Adolescents in the Aftermath of Disaster through Group Work. *Social Work with Groups, 31*(1), 29–52.

Mancini, A. & Bonanno, G. (2006). Resilience in the face of potential trauma: Clinical practices and illustrations. *Journal of Clinical Psychology, 62*(8), 971–985.

Mannarino, A. P. & Cohen, J. (2011). Traumatic loss in children and adolescents. *Journal of Child & Adolescent Trauma, 4*(1), 22–33.

Manne, S., Ostroff, J., Winkel, G., Goldstein, L., Fox, K. & Grana, G. (2004). Posttraumatic growth after breast cancer: Patient, partner and couple perspectives. *Psychosomatic Medicine, 66*, 442–454.

Manning, M., Wainwright, L. & Bennett, J. (2011). The double ABCX model of adaptation in racially diverse families with a school-age child with autism. *Journal of Autism & Developmental Disorders, 41*(3), 320–331.

Marmar, C., Weiss, D., Schlenger, W. & Fairbank, J. (1994). Peritraumatic dissociation and posttraumatic stress in male Vietnam theatre veterans. *American Journal of Psychiatry, 151*(6), 902–907.

Marsella, A. J. (2010). Ethnocultural aspects of PTSD: An overview of concepts, issues, and treatments. *Traumatology, 16*(4), 17–26.

Marsella, A. J., Friedman, M. J. & Spain, E. H. (1996). Ethnocultural aspects of PTSD: An overview of issues and research directions. In A. Marsella, M. Friedman, E. Gerrity & R. Scurfield (Eds.), *Ethnocultural aspects of PTSD: Issues, research, and clinical applications* (pp. 105–129). Washington, DC: American Psychological Association.

Masten, A. S. & Narayan, A. J. (2012). Child development in the context of disaster, war, and terrorism: Pathways of risk and resilience. *Annual Review of Psychology, 63*(1), 227–257.

Masten, A. S. & Obradovic, J. (2008). Disaster preparation and recovery: Lessons from research on resilience in human development. *Ecology & Society, 13*(1), 1–16.

Masten, A., Best, K. & Garmezy, N. (1990) Resilience and development: Contributions from the study of children who overcome adversity. *Development and Psychopathology, 2*, 425–444.

McCann, L. & Pearlman, L. A. (1999). Vicarious traumatization: A framework for understanding the psychological effects of working with victims. In M. J. Horowitz (Ed.), *Essential papers on posttraumatic stress disorder* (pp. 498–517). New York: New York University Press.

McCormack, L., Hagger, M. S. & Joseph, S. (2011). Vicarious growth in wives of Vietnam veterans: A phenomenological investigation into decades of "lived" experience. *Journal of Humanistic Psychology, 51*(3), 273–290.

McCubbin, H. I. & McCubbin, M. A. (1988). Typologies of resilient families: Emerging roles of Social Class and Ethnicity. *Family Relations, 37*(3), 247–255.

McCubbin, H. I. & Patterson, J. M. (1983). The family stress process: The Double ABCX model of adjustment and adaptation. In H. I. McCubbin, M. B. Sussman & J. M. Patterson (Eds.), *Social stress and the family: Advances and developments in family stress theory and research* (pp. 7–37). New York: Haworth Press.

McCubbin, H. I., Cauble, A. E. & Patterson, J. M. (Eds.) (1982). *Family stress, coping, and social support*. Springfield, IL: Charles C. Thomas.

McCubbin, H., Thompson, A. & McCubbin, M. (1996). *Family assessment: Resiliency, coping and adaptation – inventories for research and practice*. Madison, WI: University of Wisconsin System.

McDermott, B. M.C. & Palmer, L. J. (1999). Post-disaster service provision following proactive identification of children with emotional distress and depression. *Australian and New Zealand Journal of Psychiatry, 33*(6), 855–863.

McFarlane, A. C. & Norris, F. (2006). Definitions and concepts in disaster research. In F. Norris, S. Galea, M. Friedman & P. Watson (Eds.), *Methods for disaster mental health research* (pp.3–19). New York: Guilford Press.

McFarlane, A. C. & Van Hooff, M. (2009). Impact of childhood exposure to a natural disaster on adult mental health: 20-year longitudinal follow-up study. *British Journal of Psychiatry, 195*(2), 142–148.

McLay, R. N., Graap, K., Spira, J., Perlman, K., Johnston, S., Rothbaum, B. O., Difede, J. A., Deal, W., Oliver, D., Baird, A., Bordnick, P. S., Spitalnick, J., Pyne, J. M. & Rizzo, A. (2012). Development and testing of virtual reality exposure therapy for post-traumatic stress disorder in active duty service members who served in Iraq and Afghanistan. *Military Medicine, 177*(6), 635–642.

McLeigh, J. D. (2010). What are the policy issues related to the mental health? *American Journal of Orthopsychiatry, 80*(2), 177–182.

McMillen, J., Smith, E. M. & Fisher, R. H. (1997). Perceived benefit and mental health after three types of disaster. *Journal of Consulting & Clinical Psychology, 65*(5), 733–739.

McNamee, A. & Mercurio, M. L. (2006). Picture books: Can they help caregivers create an "illusion of safety" for children in unsafe times? *Perspectives on Urban Education, 4*(2), 1–13.

Meichenbaum, D. (1985). *Stress inoculation training*. New York: Pergamon.

Meldrum, L., King, R. & Spooner, D. (2002). Secondary traumatic stress in case managers working in community mental health services. In C. R. Figley (Ed.), *Treating compassion fatigue* (pp. 85–106). New York: Brunner-Routledge.

Meyerson, D. A., Grant, K. E., Carter, J. & Kilmer, R. P. (2011). Posttraumatic growth among children and adolescents: A systematic review. *Clinical Psychology Review, 31*(6), 949–964.

Michultka, D., Blanchard, E. B. & Kalous, T. (1998). Responses to civilian war experiences: Predictors of psychological functioning and coping. *Journal of Traumatic Stress, 11*(3), 571–577.

Mikulincer, M., Florian, V. & Solomon Z. (1995). Marital intimacy, family support, and secondary traumatization: A study of wives of veterans with combat stress reaction. *Anxiety, Stress, and Coping, 8*(3), 203–213.

Milam, J. (2004). Posttraumatic growth among HIV/AIDS patients. *Journal of Applied Social Psychology, 34*(11), 2353–2376.

Milam, J. (2006). Posttraumatic Growth and HIV disease progression. *Journal of Consulting & Clinical Psychology, 74*(5), 817–827.

Milam, J. E., Ritt-Olson, A. & Unger, J. B. (2004). Posttraumatic Growth among adolescents. *Journal of Adolescent Research, 19*(2), 192–204.

Miller, S. M. (1980). When is a little information a dangerous thing? Coping with stressful events by monitoring versus blunting. In S. Levine & H. Ursin (Eds.), *Health and coping* (pp. 145–169). New York: Plenum.

Minuchin, S. (1974). *Families and family therapy.* Cambridge, MA: Harvard University Press.

Monson, C. M., Fredman, S. J. & Taft, C. T. (2011a). Couple and family issues and interventions for veterans of the Iraq and Afghanistan wars. In J. I. Ruzek, P. P. Schnurr, J. J. Vasterling & M. J. Friedman (Eds.) (pp. 151–169). Washington, DC: American Psychological Association.

Monson, C. M., Fredman, S. J., Adair, K. C., Stevens, S. P., Resick, P. A., Schnurr, P. P., MacDonald, H. Z. & Macdonald, A. (2011b). Cognitive-behavioral conjoint therapy for PTSD: Pilot results from a community sample. *Journal of Traumatic Stress, 24*(1), 97–101.

Monson, C. M., Schnurr, P. P., Resick, P. A., Friedman, M. J., Young-Xu, Y. & Stevens, S. P. (2006). Cognitive processing therapy for veterans with military-related posttraumatic stress disorder. *Journal of Consulting and Clinical Psychology, 74*(5), 898–907.

Moore, A. M., Gamblin, C., Geller, D., Youssef, M., Hoffman, K., Gemmell, L., Likumahuwa, S., Bovbjerg, D., Marsland, A. & Steel, J. (2011). A prospective study of posttraumatic growth as assessed by self-report and family caregiver in the context of advanced cancer. *Psycho-Oncology, 20*(5), 479–487.

Morland, L. A., Hynes, A. K., Mackintosh, M., Resick, P. A. & Chard, K. M. (2011). Group cognitive processing therapy delivered to veterans via telehealth: A pilot cohort. *Journal of Traumatic Stress, 24*(4), 465–469.

Morsette, A., Swaney, G., Stolle, D., Schuldberg, D., van den Pol, R. & Young, M. (2009). Cognitive Behavioral Intervention for Trauma in Schools (CBITS): School-based treatment on a rural American Indian reservation. *Journal of Behavior Therapy & Experimental Psychiatry, 40*(1), 169–178.

Mulia, N., Schmidt, L., Bond, J., Jacobs, L. & Korcha, R. (2008). Stress, social support and problem drinking among women in poverty. *Addiction, 103*(8), 1283–1293.

Musallam, N., Ginzburg, K., Lev-Shalem, L. & Solomon, Z. (2005). The psychological effects of Intifada Al Aqsa: Acute stress disorder and distress in Palestinian-Israeli students. *Israeli Journal of Psychiatry and Related Sciences, 42*(2), 96–105.

Nachshen, J. S. & Minnes, P. (2005). Empowerment in parents of school-aged children with and without developmental disabilities. *Journal of Intellectual Disability Research, 49*, 889–904.

Nadeau, J. W. (2001). Meaning making in family bereavement: A family systems approach. In M. S. Stroebe, R. O. Hansson, W. Stroebe & H. Schut (Eds.), *Handbook of bereavement research: Consequences, coping and care* (pp. 329–347). Washington, DC: American Psychological Association.

Najavits, L. M. (2001). *Seeking safety: A treatment manual for PTSD and substance abuse.* New York: Guildford Press.

Nasar Sayeed Khan, M., Alam, S., Hameed Warris, S. H. & Mujtaba, M. (2007). Frequency of post-traumatic stress disorder and its association with types of physical injuries and depression in earthquake victims. *Pakistan Journal of Medical Science, 23*(3), 386–389.

National Institute of Mental Health (2002). *Mental health and mass violence: Evidence-based early psychological intervention for victims/survivors of mass violence. A workshop to reach consensus on best practices*. NIH Publication No. 02–5138, Washington, DC: US Government Printing Office.

NATO (2012). *Reaching vulnerable populations worldwide: Applying evidence-based training and core psychological change processes to disseminate effective services for trauma survivors*. Amsterdam: The NATO Science for Peace and Security Programme.

Nelson Goff, B. S. & Smith, D. (2005). Systemic traumatic stress: The Couple Adaptation to Traumatic Stress Model. *Journal of Marital and Family Therapy, 31*, 145–157.

Nelson Goff, B. S., Crow, J. R., Reisbig, A. J. & Hamilton, S. (2007). The impact of individual trauma symptoms of deployed soldiers on relationship satisfaction. *Journal of Family Psychology, 21*(3), 344–353.

Neria, Y., Nandi, A. & Galea, S. (2008). Post-traumatic stress disorder following disasters: A systematic review. *Psychological Medicine, 38*(4), 467–480.

Neuner, F., Schauer, M., Klaschik, C., Karunakara, U. & Elbert, T. (2004). A comparison of narrative exposure therapy, supportive counseling, and psychoeducation for treating Posttraumatic Stress Disorder in an African refugee settlement. *Journal of Consulting and Clinical Psychology, 72*(4), 579–587.

Newman, C. L & Motta, R. W. (2007). The effect of aerobic exercise on childhood PTSD, anxiety, and depression. *International Journal of Emergency Mental Health, 9*(2), 133–158.

Nijdam, M. J., Baas, M. A. M., Olff, M. & Gersons, B. P. R. (2013). Hotspots in trauma memories and their relationship to successful trauma-focused psychotherapy: A pilot study. *Journal of Traumatic Stress, 26*(1), 38–44.

Nishith, P., Mechanic, M. B. & Resick, P. A. (2000). Prior interpersonal trauma: The Contribution to current PTSD Symptoms in female rape victims. *Journal of Abnormal Psychology, 109*(1), 20–25.

Norris, F., Phifer, J. & Kaniasty, K. (1994). Individual and community reactions to the Kentucky floods: Findings from a longitudinal study of older adults. In R. Ursano, B. McCaughey & C. Fullerton (Eds.), *Individual and community responses to trauma and disaster: The structure of human chaos* (pp. 378–400). Cambridge: Cambridge University Press.

Norris, F., Friedman, M. J., Watson, P. I., Bryne, C. M., Diaz, E. & Kaniasty, K. (2002). 60,000 disaster victims speak: Part I. An empirical review of the empirical literature, 1981–2001. *Psychiatry: Interpersonal & Biological Processes, 65*(3), 207–239.

Norris, F. H., Murphy, A. D., Baker, C. K. & Perilla, J. L. (2004). Postdisaster PTSD over four waves of a panel study of Mexico's 1999 flood. *Journal of Traumatic Stress, 17*(4), 283–292.

Norris, F. H., Stevens, S. P., Pfefferbaum, B., Wyche, K. F. & Pfefferbaum, R. L. (2008). Community resilience as a metaphor, theory, set of capacities, and strategy for disaster readiness. *American Journal of Community Psychology, 41*(1–2), 127–150.

North, C. S., Suris, A. M., Davis, M. & Smith, R. P. (2009). Toward validation of the diagnosis of posttraumatic stress disorder. *American Journal of Psychiatry, 166*(1), 34–41.

North, C. S., Tivis, L., McMillen, J., Pfefferbaum, B., Cox, J., Spitznagel, E. L., Bunch, K., Schorr, J. & Smith, E. M. (2002). Coping, functioning, and adjustment of rescue workers after the Oklahoma City bombing. *Journal of Traumatic Stress, 15*(3), 171–176.

Obrist, B., Pfeiffer, C. & Henley, R. (2010). Multi-layered social resilience: A new approach in mitigation research. *Progress in Development Studies, 10*(4), 283–293.

Ohtani, T., Iwanami, A., Kasai, K., Yamasue, H., Kato, T., Sasaki, T. & Kato, N. (2004). Post-traumatic stress disorder symptoms in victims of the Tokyo subway attack: A 5-year follow-up study. *Psychiatry and Clinical Neurosciences, 8*, 624–629.

Olson, D. H. (1991). Commentary: Three-dimensional (3-D) Circumplex model and revised scoring of FACES III. *Family Process, 30*(1), 74–79.

Olson, D. H. (2011). FACES IV and the Circumplex model validation study. *Journal of Marital and Family Therapy, 37*(1), 64–80.

Olson, D. H. & Gorall, D. M. (2003). Circumplex model of marital and family systems. In F. Walsh (Ed.), *Normal family processes* (pp. 514–547). New York: Guilford.

Olson, D., Russell, C. & Sprenkle, D. (1983). Circumplex model of marital and family systems: VI. Theoretical update. *Family Process, 22*, 69–83.

Olson, D., Sprenkle, D. & Russell, C. (1979). Circumplex model of marital and family systems: I. Cohesion and adaptability dimensions, family types and clinical applications. *Family Process, 18*, 3–28.

Orcutt, H. K., Erickson, D. J. & Wolfe, J. (2004). The course of PTSD symptoms among Gulf War veterans: A growth mixture modeling approach. *Journal of Traumatic Stress, 17*(3), 195–202.

Owens, G. P., Baker, D. G., Kasckow, J., Ciesla, J. A. & Mohamed, S. (2005). Review of assessment and treatment of PTSD among elderly American armed forces veterans. *International Journal of Geriatric Psychiatry, 20*(12), 1118–1130.

Palinkas, L. A., Downs, M. A., Petterson, J. S. & Russell, J. (1993). Social, cultural, and psychological impacts of the Exxon Valdez oil spill. *Human Organization, 52*(1), 1–12.

Panter-Brick, C., Eggerman, M., Gonzalez, V. & Safdar, S. (2009). Violence, suffering, and mental health in Afghanistan: A school-based survey. *The Lancet, 9692*, 807–816.

Park, C. L. & Fenster, J. R. (2004). Stress-related growth: Predictors of occurrence and correlates with psychological adjustment. *Journal of Social and Clinical Psychology, 23*(2), 195–215.

Park, C. L., Cohen, L. H. & Murch, R. L. (1996). Assessment and prediction of stress-related growth. *Journal of Personality, 64*(1), 71–105.

Park, C. L., Riley, K. E. & Snyder, L. B. (2012). Meaning making, coping, making sense, and post-traumatic growth following the 9/11 terrorist attacks. *Journal of Positive Psychology, 7*(3), 198–207.

Pastor, L. H. (2004). Culture as causality: Examining the causes and consequences of collective trauma. *Psychiatric Annals, 34*(8), 616–622.

Paton, D. & Johnston, D. M. (2001). Disasters and communities: Vulnerability, resilience and preparedness. *Disaster Prevention and Management, 10*(4), 270–277.

Patterson, J. M. (2002a). Integrating family resilience and family stress theory. *Journal of Marriage and the Family, 64*(2), 349–361.

Patterson, J. M. (2002b). Understanding family resilience. *Journal of Clinical Psychology, 58*(3), 233–246.

Patterson, J. M. & Garwick, A. W. (1994). Levels of meaning making in family stress theory. *Family Process, 33*(3), 287–304.

Patterson, J. M., Budd, J., Goetz, D. & Warwick, W. J. (1993). Family correlates of a 10-year pulmonary health trend in Cystic Fibrosis. *Pediatrics, 91*(2), 383–389.

Pattwell, S. S., Duhoux, S., Hartley, C. A., Johnson, D. C., Jing, D., Elliot, M. D., Ruberry, E. J., Powers, A., Mehta, N., Yang, R. R., Soliman, F., Glatt, C. E., Casey, B. J., Ninan, I. & Lee, F. S. (2012). Altered fear learning across development in both mouse and human. *Proceeding of the National Academy of Sciences of the U S A, 109*(40), 16318–16323.

Pearlman, L. A. & Caringi, J. (2009). Living and working self-reflectively to address vicarious trauma. In C. A. Courtois & J. D. Ford (Eds.), *Treating complex traumatic stress disorders: An evidence-based guide* (pp. 202–224). New York: Guilford Press.

Pearlman, L. A. & Mac Ian, P. S. (1995). Vicarious trauma: An empirical study of the effects of trauma work on trauma therapists. *Professional Psychology: Research and Practice, 26*, 558–565.

Penza, K. M., Heim, C. C. & Nemeroff, C. B. (2003). Neurobiological effects of childhood abuse: Implications for the pathophysiology of depression and anxiety. *Archives of Women's Mental Health, 6*(1), 15–23.

Perlman, R. & Warren, R. (1977). *Families in the energy crisis: Impacts and implications for theory and policy.* Cambridge, MA: Ballinger.

Perrin, M. A., DiGrande, L. C., Wheeler, L. T., Farfel, M. & Brackbill, R. (2007). Differences in PTSD prevalence and associated risk factors among World Trade Center disaster rescue and recovery workers. *American Journal of Psychiatry, 164*(9), 1385–1394.

Perry, B. D. (2009). Examining child maltreatment through a neurodevelopmental lens: Clinical applications of the neurosequential model of therapeutics. *Journal of Loss & Trauma, 14*(4), 240–255.

Picou, J., Marshall, B. K. & Gill, D. A. (2004). Disaster, litigation, and the corrosive community. *Social Forces, 82*(4), 1493–1522.

Pietrzak, R. H., Goldstein, R. B., Southwick, S. M. & Grant, B. F. (2012). Psychiatric comorbidity of full and partial posttraumatic stress disorder among older adults in the United States: Results from wave 2 of the national epidemiological survey on alcohol and related conditions. *The American Journal of Geriatric Psychiatry, 20*(5), 380–390.

Pine, D. S. & Cohen, J. A. (2002). Trauma in children and adolescents: Risk and treatment of psychiatric sequelae. *Biological Psychiatry, 51*(7), 519–531.

Pirutinsky, S., Rosmarin, D. H. & Pargament, K. I. (2009). Community attitudes towards culture-influenced mental illness: Scrupulosity vs. non-religious OCD among orthodox Jews. *Journal of Community Psychology, 37*(8), 949–958.

Pisula, E. & Kossakowska, Z. (2010). Sense of coherence and coping with stress among mothers and fathers of children with autism. *Journal of Autism & Developmental Disorders, 40*(12), 1485–1494.

Polatinsky, S. & Esprey, Y. (2000). An assessment of gender differences in the perception of benefit resulting from the loss of a child. *Journal of Traumatic Stress, 13*(4), 709–718.

Possick, C., Sadeh, R. A. & Shamai, M. (2008). Parents' experience and meaning construction of the loss of a child in a national terror attack. *American Journal of Orthopsychiatry, 78*, 93–102.

Powell, S., Rosner, R., Butollo, W., Tedeschi, R. G. & Calhoun, L. G. (2003). Posttraumatic growth after war: A study with former refugees and displaced people in Sarajevo. *Journal of Clinical Psychology, 59*(1), 71–83.

Powers, M. B., Halpern, J. M., Ferenschak, M. P., Gillihan, S. J. & Foa, E. B. (2010). A meta-analytic review of prolonged exposure for posttraumatic stress disorder. *Clinical Psychology Review, 30*(6), 635–641.

Priebe, S., Bogic, M., Ajdukovic, D., Franciskovic, T., Galeazzi, G. M., Kucukalic, A., Lecic-Tosevski, D., Morina, N., Popovski, M., Wang, D. & Schützwohl, M. (2010). Mental disorders following war in the Balkans: A study in five countries. *Archive of General Psychiatry, 67*(5), 518–528.

Prigerson, H. G., Horowitz, M. J., Jacobs, S. C., Parkes, C. M., Aslan, M., Goodkin, K., Raphael, B., Marwit, S. J., Wortman, C., Neimeyer, R. A., Bonanno, G., Block, S. D., Kissane, D., Boelen, P., Maercker, A., Litz, B. T., Johnson, J. G., First, M. B. & Maciejewski, P. K. (2009). Prolonged grief disorder: Psychometric validation of criteria proposed for *DSM–V* and *ICD-11*. *PLOS Medicine, 6*(8), e1000121.

Punamäki, R. J. (2002). The uninvited guest of war enters childhood: Developmental and personality aspects of war and military violence. *Traumatology, 8*(3), 181–204.

Qouta, S., Punamäki, R. J. & El Sarraj, E. (2008). Child development and family mental health in war and military violence: The Palestinian experience. *International Journal of Behavioral Development, 32*(4), 310–321.

Quenqua, D. (2012, 7 December). Children can usually recover from emotional trauma. *New York Times*, Science Times, p. 1.

Quiros, L. & Berger, R. (2013). Trauma-informed practice. *Loss and trauma*. Retrieved from tandfonline.com/doi/full/10.1080/15325024.2013.836353#. UvLJ5WJdVwg

Randall, A. K. & Bodenmann, G. (2009). The role of stress in close relationships and marital satisfaction. *Clinical Psychology Review, 29*(2), 105–115.

Rapoport, L. (1962). The state of crisis: Some theoretical considerations. *Social Service Review, 36*(2), 211–217.

Rassiger, C. (2011). Student–teacher relationships and academic success in at-risk Latino and black middle school students. Unpublished Dissertation, Adelphi University, School of Social Work, 3455591.

Reich, J. W. (2006). Three psychological principles of resilience in natural disasters. *Disaster Prevention and Management, 15*, 793–798.

Reiss, D. (1981). *The family construction of reality*. Cambridge, MA: Harvard University press.

Resick, P. A., Bovin, M. J., Calloway, A. L., Dick, A. M., King, M. W., Mitchell, K. S., Suvak, M. K., Wells, S. Y., Stirman, S. W. & Wolf, E. J. (2012). A critical evaluation of the complex PTSD literature: Implications for DSM-5. *Journal of Traumatic Stress, 25*(3), 241–251.

Resick, P. A., Nishith, P., Weaver, T. L., Astin, M. C. & Feuer, C. A. (2002). A comparison of cognitive-processing therapy with prolonged exposure and a waiting condition for the treatment of chronic posttraumatic stress disorder in female rape victims. *Journal of Consulting and Clinical Psychology, 70*(4), 867–879.

Revenson, T. A. & DeLongis, A. (2011). Couples coping with chronic illness. In S. Folkman (Ed.), *The Oxford handbook of stress, health, and coping* (pp. 101–123). New York: Oxford University Press.

Rhodes, R. D., Harrison, D. W. & Demaree, H. A. (2002). Hostility as a moderator of physical reactivity and recovery to stress. *International Journal of Neuroscience, 112*(2), 167–186.

Rich, N. (2012). Jungleland: The Lower Ninth ward in New Orleans gives new meaning to 'urban growth'. *The New York Time Magazine*, March 12.

Roberts, A. L., Gilman, S. E., Breslau, J., Breslau, M. & Koenen, K. C. (2011). Race/ethnic differences in exposure to traumatic events, development of post-traumatic stress disorder, and treatment seeking for post-traumatic stress disorder in the United States. *Psychological Medicine, 41*(1), 71–83.

Roberts, A. R. (2002). Assessment, crisis intervention, and trauma treatment: The integrative ACT intervention model. *Brief Treatment Crisis Intervention, 2*(1), 1–22.

Roberts, N. P., Kitchiner, N. J., Kenardy, J. & Bisson, J. I. (2010). Multiple-session early psychological interventions for the prevention of post-traumatic stress disorder. *Cochrane Database of Systematic Reviews*, Issue 3. Art. No: CD006869.

Roca, V. & Freeman, T. W. (2002). Psychosensory symptoms in combat veterans with posttraumatic stress disorder. *Journal of Neuropsychiatry and Clinical Neurosciences, 14*(2), 185–189.

Rolland, J. S. (2003). Mastering family challenges in serious illness and disability. In F. Walsh (Ed.), *Normal family processes: Growing diversity and complexity* (3rd ed.) (pp. 460–491). New York: Guilford Press.

Ronen, T., Rahav, G. & Rosenbaum, M. (2003). Children's reactions to a war situation as a function of age and sex. *Anxiety, Stress & Coping, 16*(1), 59–69.

Rose, S. C., Bisson, J., Churchill, R. & Wessely, S. (2002). Psychological debriefing for preventing post-traumatic stress disorder (PTSD). *Cochrane Database of Systematic Reviews*, Issue 2. Art. No: CD000560.

Rosenheck, R. & Nathan, P. (1985). Secondary traumatization in children of Vietnam veterans. *Hospital and Community Psychiatry, 36*(5), 538–539.

Rowe, C. L. & Liddle, H. A. (2008). When the levee breaks: Treating adolescents and families in the aftermath of Hurricane Katrina. *Journal of Marital & Family Therapy, 34*(2), 132–148.

Rowland-Klein, D. (2004). The transmission of trauma across generations: Identification with parental trauma in children of Holocaust survivors. In D. R. Catherall (Ed.), *Handbook of stress, trauma and the family* (pp. 117–136). New York: Brunner-Mazel.

Rubin, G. J., Brewin, C. R., Greenberg, N., Simon, J. & Wessley, S. (2005). Psychological and behavioural reactions to the bombings in London on 7 July 2005: Cross-sectional survey of a representative sample of Londoners. *British Medical Journal, 331*(7517), 606–611.

Ruden, R. A. (2011). *When the past is always present: Emotional traumatization, causes, and cures.* New York: Routledge/Taylor & Francis.

Ruggiero, K. J., Resnick, H. S., Acierno, R., Carpenter, M. J., Kilpatrick, D. G., Coffey, S. F., Ruscio, A. M., Stephens, R. S., Stasiewicz, P. R., Roffman, R. A., Bucuvalas, M. & Galea, S. (2006). Internet-based intervention for mental health and substance use problems in disaster-affected populations: A pilot feasibility study. *Behavior Therapy, 37*, 190–205.

Rutter, M. (1987). Psychosocial resilience and protective mechanisms. *American Journal of Orthopsychiatry, 57*, 316–331.

Rutter, M. (2007). Resilience, competence, and coping. *Child Abuse & Neglect, 31*(3), 205–209.

Ruzek, J. I., Hoffman, J., Robert, C., Prins, A. & Gahm, G. (2011). Bringing internet-based education and intervention into mental health practice: afterdeployment.org. *European Journal of Psychotraumatology, 2*, 7278.

Ryn, Z. (1990). The evolution of mental disturbances in the concentration camp syndrome (KZ-syndrome). *Genetic, Social & General Psychology Monographs, 116*(1), 23–36.

Rynearson, E. K. (2001). *Retelling violent death.* Philadelphia, PA: Brunner Routledge.

Sagi-Schwartz, A. (2008). The well-being of children living in chronic war zones: The Palestinian-Israeli case. *International Journal of Behavioral Development, 32*, 322–336.

Sagy, S. & Antonovsky, A. (1992). The family sense of coherence and the retirement transition. *Journal of Marriage & Family, 54*(4), 983–993.

Sakai, C. E., Connoly, S. M. & Oas, P. (2010). Treatment of PTSD in Rwandan child genocide survivors using Though Field Therapy. *International Journal of Emergency Mental Health, 12*(1), 41–50.

Salloum, A., Carter, P., Burch, B., Garfinkel, A. & Overstreet, S. (2011). Impact of exposure to community violence, Hurricane Katrina, and Hurricane Gustav on post-traumatic stress and depressive symptoms among school-age children. *Anxiety, Stress & Coping, 24*(1), 27–42.

Salloum, A., Garside, L. W., Irwin, C., Anderson, A. D. & Francois, A. H. (2009). Grief and trauma group therapy for children after hurricane Katrina. *Social Work with Groups, 32*(1/2), 64–79.

Saloviita, T., Itälinna, M. & Leinonen, E. (2003). Explaining the parental stress of fathers and mothers caring for a child with intellectual disability: A Double ABCX Model. *Journal of Intellectual Disability Research, 47*(4–5), 300–312.

Salter, E. & Stallard, P. (2004). Posttraumatic growth in child survivors of a road traffic accident. *Journal of Traumatic Stress, 17*(4), 335–340.

Saltzman, W., Layne, C., Steinberg, A., Arslanagic, B. & Pynoos, R. (2003). Developing a culturally and ecologically sound intervention program for youth exposed to war and terrorism. *Child and Adolescent Psychiatric Clinics of North America, 12*(2), 319–342.

Samardzic, R. R. (2012). P-977 – Posttraumatic depression: Issue of comorbidity. *European Psychiatry, 27*(1), Supplement, 1–11.

Sandler, I. N., Ma, Y., Tein, J.-Y., Ayers, T. S., Wolchik, S., Kennedy, C. & Millsap, R. (2010). Long-term effects of the family bereavement program on multiple indicators of grief in parentally bereaved children and adolescents. *Journal of Consulting and Clinical Psychology, 78*(2), 131–143.

Sattler, D. N., DeAlvarado, A. M., DeCastro, N. B., Male, R. V., Zetino, A. M. & Vega, R. (2006). El Salvador earthquakes: Relationships among acute stress disorder symptoms, depression, traumatic event exposure, and resource loss. *Journal of Traumatic Stress, 20*(6), 879–893.

Sayers, S. L., Farrow, V., Ross, J. & Oslin, D. W. (2009). Family problems among recently returned military veterans. *The Journal of Clinical Psychiatry, 70*(2), 163–170.

Schlenger, W. E., Caddell, J. M., Ebert, L., Jordan, B. K., Rourke, K. M., Wilson, D., Thalji, L., Dennis, J. M., Fairbank, J. A. & Kulka, R. A. (2002). Psychological reactions to terrorist attacks: Findings from the National Study of Americans' Reactions to September 11. *The Journal of the American Medical Association, 288*(5), 581–588.

Schonfeld, D. J. (2002). Supporting adolescents in times of national crisis: Potential roles for adolescent health care providers. *Journal of Adolescent Health, 30*, 302–307.

Schroevers, M. J., Helgeson, V. S., Sanderman, R. & Ranchor, A. V. (2010). Type of social support matters for prediction of posttraumatic growth among cancer survivors. *Psycho-Oncology, 19*(1), 46–53.

Schuettler, D. & Boals, A. (2011). The path to posttraumatic growth versus posttraumatic stress disorder: Contributions of event centrality and coping. *Journal of Loss and Trauma, 16*, 180–194.

Schuman, J. A., Vranceanu, A.-M. & Hobfoll, S. E. (2004). The ties that bind: Resources caravans and losses among traumatized families. In D. R. Catherall (Ed.), *Handbook of stress, trauma and the family* (pp. 33–50). New York: Brunner-Mazel.

Schuster, M. A., Stein, B. D., Jaycox, L. H., Collins, R. L., Marshall, G. N., Elliott, M. N., Zhou, A. J., Kanouse, D. E., Morrison, J. L. & Berry, S. H. (2001). A national survey of stress reactions after the September 11, 2001, terrorist attacks. *New England Journal of Medicine, 345*(20), 1507–1512.

Scully, P. J. (2011). Taking care of staff: A comprehensive model of support for paramedics and emergency medical dispatchers. *Traumatology, 17*, 35–42.

Seery, M. D., Holman, E. & Silver, R. (2010). Whatever does not kill us: Cumulative lifetime adversity, vulnerability, and resilience? *Journal of Personality & Social Psychology, 99*(6), 1025–1041.

Seidler, G. H. & Wagner, F. E. (2006). Comparing the efficacy of EMDR and trauma-focused cognitive-behavioral therapy in the treatment of PTSD: A meta-analytic study. *Psychological Medicine, 36*(11), 1515–1522.

Selye, H. (1976). *The stress of life.* New York: McGraw Hill.

Senol-Durak, E. & Ayvasik, H. (2010). Factors associated with posttraumatic growth among myocardial infarction patients: Perceived social support, perception of the event and coping. *Journal of Clinical Psychology in Medical Settings, 17*(2), 150–158.

Shakespeare-Finch, J. & Morris, B. (2010). Posttraumatic growth in Australian populations. In T. Weiss & R. Berger (Eds.), *Posttraumatic growth and culturally competent practice: Lessons learned from around the globe* (pp. 157–172). Hoboken, NJ: Wiley.

Shalev, A., Tuval, R., Frenkiel-Fishman, S., Hadar, H. & Eth, S. (2006). Psychological responses to continuous terror: A study of two communities in Israel. *American Journal of Psychiatry, 163*(4), 667–673.

Shamai, M. (2012). *Couples in the line of fire.* Paper presented at the International Conference on Trauma through the Life Cycle from a Strength Based Perspective, Jerusalem, January 9.

Shamai, M. (forthcoming). *Systemic interventions in situations of collective and national trauma.* New York/London: Routledge.

Shamai, M. & Ron, P. (2009). Helping direct and indirect victims of national terror: Experiences of Israeli social workers. *Qualitative Health Research, 19*(1), 42–54.

Shamai, M., Kimhi, S. & Enosh, G. (2007) Social systems and personal reactions to threats of war and terror. *Journal of Social and Personal Relationships, 24*(5), 747–764.

Shapiro, F. & Laliotis, D. (2011). EMDR and the adaptive information processing model: Integrative treatment and case conceptualization. *Clinical Social Work Journal, 39*(2), 191–200.

Sharabi, A., Levi, U. & Margalit, M. (2012). Children's loneliness, sense of coherence, family climate, and hope: Developmental risk and protective factors. *Journal of Psychology, 146*(1/2), 61–83.

Sharpless, B. A. & Barber, J. P. (2011). A clinician's guide to PTSD treatments for returning veterans. *Professional Psychology: Research and Practice, 42*(1), 8–15.

Shaw, A., Joseph, S. & Linley, P. A. (2005). Religion, spirituality, and posttraumatic growth: A systematic review. *Mental Health, Religion and Culture, 8*(1), 1–11.

Shin, J. Y. & Crittenden, K. S. (2003). Well-being of mothers of children with mental retardation: An evaluation of the Double ABCX model in cross cultural context. *Asian Journal of Social Psychology, 6*(3), 171–184.

Shmotkin, D. & Litwin, H. (2009). Cumulative adversity and depressive symptoms among older adults in Israel: The differential roles of self-oriented versus other-oriented events of potential trauma. *Social Psychiatry and Psychiatric Epidemiology, 44*(11), 989–997.

Shmotkin, D., Shrira, A. & Palgi, Y. (2011). Does trauma linger into old-old age? Using the Holocaust experience as a paradigm. In L. W. Poon & J. Cohen-Mansfield (Eds.), *Understanding well-being in the oldest old* (pp. 81–95). New York: Cambridge University Press.

Shrira, A. (2012). The effect of lifetime cumulative adversity on change and chronicity in depressive symptoms and quality of life in older adults. *International Psychogeriatrics, 24*(12), 1988–1997.

Shu-Li, L. (2000). Coping and adaptation in families of children with cerebral palsy. *Exceptional Children, 66*(2), 201–219.

Silver, R. L. & Wortman, C. B. (1980). Coping with undesirable life events. In J. Garber and M. E. P. Seligman (Eds.), *Human helplessness* (pp. 279–375). New York: Academic Press.

Slone, M., Shoshani, A. & Paltieli, T. (2009). Psychological consequences of forced evacuation on children: Risk and protective factors. *Journal of Traumatic Stress, 22*(4), 340–343.

Solomon, E. P. & Heide, K., M. (1999). Type III trauma: Towards more effective conceptualization of psychological trauma. *International Journal of Offender Therapy and Comparative Criminology, 43*(2), 202–210.

Solomon, Z., Gelkopf, M. & Bleich, A. (2005). Is terror gender-blind? Gender differences in reaction to terror events. *Social Psychiatry and Psychiatric Epidemiology, 40*(12), 947–954.

Somasundaram, D. (2004). Short- and long-term effects on the victims of terror in Sri Lanka. *Journal of Aggression, Maltreatment & Trauma, 9*(1/2), 215–228.

Somasundaram, D. & Sivayokan, S. (2013). Rebuilding community resilience in a post-war context: Developing insight and recommendations – a qualitative study in Northern Sri Lanka. *International Journal of Mental Health Systems, 7*(1), 1–24.

Somer, E., Buchbinder, E., Peled-Avram, M. & Ben-Yizhack, Y. (2004). The stress and coping of Israeli emergency room social workers following terrorist attacks. *Qualitative Health Research, 14*(8), 1077–1093.

Song, S. J., Tol, W. & de Jong, J. (2014). Indero: Intergenerational trauma and resilience between Burundian former child soldiers and their children. *Family Process, 53*(2), 239–251.

Spilka, B. (1993). *Spirituality: Problems and directions in operational zing – a fuzzy concept.* Paper presented at the American Psychological Association annual conference, Toronto, Canada.

Stein, B. D., Jaycox, L. H., Kataoka, S. H., Wong, M., Tu, W., Elliott, M. N. & Fink, A. (2003). A mental health intervention for schoolchildren exposed to violence: A randomized control trial. *Journal of the American Medical Association, 290*(5), 603–611.

Steinberg, K. S. & Rooney, P. M. (2005). America gives: A survey of Americans' generosity after September 11th. *Nonprofit and Voluntary Sector Quarterly, 34*(1), 110–135.

Stuber, J., Resnick, H. & Galea, S. (2006). Gender disparities in posttraumatic stress disorder after mass trauma. *Gender Medicine, 3*(1), 54–67.

Stuber, J., Galea, S., Pfefferbaum, B., Vandivere, S., Moore, K. & Fairbrother, G. (2005). Behavior problems in New York City's children after the September 11, 2001, terrorist attacks. *American Journal of Orthopsychiatry, 75*(2), 190–200.

Suárez-Orozco, C., Hee Jin, B. & Ha Yeon, K. (2011). I felt like my heart was staying behind: Psychological implications of family separations and reunifications for immigrant youth. *Journal of Adolescent Research, 26*(2), 222–257.

Swick, S. D., Dechant, E., Jellinek, M. S. & Belluck, J. (2002). Children of victims of September 11th: A perspective on the emotional and developmental challenges they face and how to help meet them. *Journal of Developmental and Behavioral Pediatrics, 23*(5), 378–384.

Sztompka, P. (2000). Cultural trauma: The other face of social change. *European Journal of Social Theory, 3*(4), 449–467.

Taylor, S. E. (1995). *Health psychology* (3rd ed.). Singapore: McGraw-Hill.

Taylor, S. E., Asmundson, G. J. & Carleton, R. N. (2006). Simple versus complex PTSD: A cluster analytic investigation. *Journal of Anxiety Disorders, 20*(4), 459–472.

Tedeschi, R. G. & Calhoun, L. G. (1996). The Posttraumatic Growth Inventory: Measuring the Positive Legacy of Trauma. *Journal of Traumatic Stress, 9*(3), 455–471.

Tedeschi, R. G. & McNally, R. J. (2011). Can We Facilitate Posttraumatic Growth in Combat Veterans? *American Psychologist, 66*(1), 19–24.

Tehrani, N. (2007). The cost of caring: The impact of secondary trauma on assumptions, values, and beliefs. *Counselling Psychology Quarterly, 20*(4), 325–339.

Teichman, Y., Berger, R., Ziv, D. & Balamuth, R. (1987). Family Evaluation: The Circumplex model (primary data), *Sichot, 1*, 16–26 (Hebrew).

Terr, L. C. (1991). Childhood traumas: An outline and overview. *American Journal of Psychiatry, 148*(1), 10–20.

Thabet, A., Vostanis, P. & Karim, K. (2005). Group crisis intervention for children during ongoing war conflict. *European Child & Adolescent Psychiatry, 14*(5), 262–269.

The European Network for Traumatic Stress (TENTS) (2009). *Guidelines on interventions in the aftermath of disasters.* Cardiff, UK: Cardiff University Press.

Thiel de Bocanegra, H. & Brickman, E. (2004). Mental health impact of the World Trade Center attacks on displaced Chinese workers. *Journal of Traumatic Stress, 17*(1), 55–62.

Thoits, P. A. (1983). Dimensions of life events that influence psychological distress: An evaluation and synthesis of the literature. In H. B. Kaplan (Ed.) (1983). *Psychosocial stress: Trends in theory and research* (pp. 33–103). New York: Academic Press.

Thomas, V. & Lewis, R. A. (1999). Observational couple assessment: A cross-model comparison. *Journal of Family Therapy, 21*(1), 78–95.

Tonkins, S. & Lambert, M. J. (1996). A treatment outcome study of bereavement groups for children. *Child & Adolescent Social Work Journal, 13*(1), 3–21.

Tomich, P. L. & Helgeson, V. S. (2004). Is finding something good in the bad always good? Benefit finding among women with breast cancer. *Health Psychology, 23*(1), 16–23.

Tomoda, A., Navalta, C. P., Polcari, A., Sadato, N. & Teicher, M. H. (2009). Childhood sexual abuse is associated with reduced gray matter volume in visual cortex of young women. *Biological Psychiatry, 66*(7), 642–648.

Tornstam, L. (2011). Maturing into transcendence. *Journal of Transpersonal Psychology, 43*(2), 166–180.

Traupman, E., Smith, T., Florsheim, P., Berg, C. & Uchino, B. (2011). Appraisals of spouse affiliation and control during marital conflict: Common and specific cognitive correlates among facets of negative affectivity. *Cognitive Therapy & Research, 35*(3), 187–198.

Trickett, P. K., Noll, J. G., Susman, E. J, Shenk, C. E. & Putnam, F. W. (2010). Attenuation of cortisol across development for victims of sexual abuse. *Development and Psychopathology, 22*(1), 165–175.

Trickey, D., Siddaway, A. P., Meiser-Stedman, R., Serpell, L. & Field A. P. (2012). A meta-analysis of risk factors for post-traumatic stress disorder in children and adolescents. *Clinical Psychology Review, 32*(2), 122–138.

Tuohy, R. & Stephens, C. (2012). Older adults' narratives about a flood disaster: Resilience, coherence and personal identity. *Journal of Aging Studies, 26*(1), 26–34.

Tyhurst, J. S. (1951). Individual reactions to community disaster. *American Journal of Psychiatry, 107*, 764–769.

Uehara, E. S., Morelli, P. T. T. & Abe-Kim, J. (2001). Somatic complaint and social suffering among survivors of the Cambodian killing fields. *Journal of Human Behavior in the Social Environment, 3*(3/4), 243–262.

Ungar, M. (2004). *Nurturing hidden resilience in troubled youth.* Toronto: University of Toronto Press.

Ungar, M. (2011). The social ecology of resilience: Addressing contextual and cultural ambiguity of a nascent construct. *American Journal of Orthopsychiatry, 81*(1), 1–17.

Ungar, M. (2013). Resilience, trauma, context, and culture. *Trauma, violence, & abuse, 14*(3), 255–266.

Updegraff, J. A. & Taylor, S. E. (2000). From vulnerability to growth: Positive and negative effects of stressful life events. In J. H. Harvery & E. D. Miller (Eds.), *Loss and Trauma: General and close relationship* perspectives (pp. 3–28). Philadelphia: Brunner-Routledge.

Updegraff, J. A., Taylor, S. E, Kemeny, M. E. & Wyatt-Gail, E. (2002). Positive and negative effects of HIV infection in women with low socioeconomic resources. *Personality and Social Psychology Bulletin, 28*(3), 382–394.

van der Kolk, B. A. (1994). The body keeps the score: Memory and the evolving psychobiology of posttraumatic stress. *Harvard Review of Psychiatry, 1*(5), 253–265.

van der Kolk, B. A. (2003). The neurobiology of childhood trauma and abuse. *Child and Adolescent Psychiatric Clinic of North America, 12*(2), 293–317.

van der Kolk, B. A. & Pynoos, R. S. (2009). *Proposal to include a developmental trauma disorder diagnosis for children and adolescents in DSM-V.* Retrieved from http://www.traumacenter. org/announcements/DTD_papers_Oct_09.pdf

van der Kolk, B. A., Roth, S., Pelcovitz, D., Sunday, S. & Spinazzola, J. (2005). Disorders of extreme stress: The empirical foundation of a complex adaptation to trauma. *Journal of Traumatic Stress, 18*(5), 389–399.

van der Kolk, B., Spinazzola, J., Blaustein, M. E., Hopper, J. W., Hopper, E. K., Korn, D. L. & Simpson, W. B. (2007). A randomized clinical trial of EMDR, fluoxetine and pill placebo in the treatment of PTSD: Treatment effects and long-term maintenance. *Journal of Clinical Psychiatry, 68*(1), 37–46.

van der Oord, S., Lucassen, S. S., Van Emmerik, A. P. & Emmelkamp, P. G. (2010). Treatment of post-traumatic stress disorder in children using cognitive behavioural writing therapy. *Clinical Psychology & Psychotherapy, 17*(3), 240–249.

van Emmerik, A. A. P., Kamphuis, J. H. & Emmelkamp, P. M. G. (2008). Treating acute stress disorder and posttraumatic stress disorder with cognitive behavioral therapy or structured writing therapy: A randomized controlled trial. *Psychotherapy and Psychosomatics, 77*(2), 93–100.

van Hook, M. P. (2008). *Social work practice with families: A resiliency-based approach.* Chicago, IL: Lyceum Books.

van IJzendoorn, M. H., Bakermans-Kranenburg, M. J. & Sagi-Schwartz, A. (2003). Are children of Holocaust survivors less well-adapted? No meta-analytic evidence for secondary traumatization. *Journal of Traumatic Stress, 16*, 459–469.

Verger, P., Dab, W., Lamping, D. L., Loze, J.-Y., Deschaseaux-Voinet, C. & Abenhaim, L. (2004). The psychological impact of terrorism: An epidemiologic study of posttraumatic stress disorder and associated factors in victims of the 1995–1996 bombings in France. *The American Journal of Psychiatry, 161*(8), 1384–1389.

Wagner, B. & Maercker, A. (2010). Trauma and posttraumatic growth in Germany. In T. Weiss & R. Berger (Eds.), *Posttraumatic Growth and Culturally Competent Practice: Lessons Learned from Around the Globe* (pp. 73–84). Hoboken, NJ: Wiley.

Wagner, B., Schultz, W. & Knaevelsrud, C. (2011). Efficacy of an internet-based intervention for posttraumatic stress disorder in Iraq: A pilot study. *Psychiatry Research, 195*, 85–88.

Walsh, F. (2003). Family resilience: A framework for clinical practice. *Family Process, 42*(1), 1–18.

Webb, N. B. (2011). Play therapy for bereaved children: Adapting strategies to community,school, and home settings. *School Psychology International, 32*(2), 132–143.

Wei, M., Vogel, D. L., Ku, T.-Y. & Zakalik, R. A. (2005). Adult attachment, affect regulation, negative mood and interpersonal problems: The mediating roles of emotional reactivity and emotional cutoff. *Journal of Counseling Psychology, 52*, 14–24.

Weine, S., Becker, D., McGlashan, T. H., Vojvodka, D., Hartman, S. & Robbins, J. P. (1995). Adolescent survivors of "ethnic cleansing": Observations on the first year in America. *Journal of the American Academy of Child and Adolescent* Psychiatry, *34*(9), 1153–1159.

Weiner, D. A., Schneider, A. & Lyons, J. S. (2009). Evidence-based treatments for trauma among culturally diverse foster care youth: Treatment retention and outcomes. *Children & Youth Services Review, 31*(11), 1199–1205.

Weingarten, K. (2004). Witnessing the effects of political violence in families: Mechanisms of intergenerational transmission and clinical interventions. *Journal of Marital and Family Therapy, 30*(1), 45–59.

Weinrib, A. Z., Rothrock, N. E., Johnson, E. E. L. & Lutgendorf, S. K. (2006). The assessment and validity of stress-related growth in a community-based sample. *Journal of Consulting and Clinical Psychology, 74*(5), 851–858.

Weiss, D. S. (2012). PTSD: Constructs, diagnoses, disorders, syndromes, symptoms, and structure. *Journal of Traumatic Stress, 25*(3), 237–238.

Weiss, T. (2002). Posttraumatic growth in women with breast cancer and their husbands: An intersubjective validation study. *Journal of Psychosocial Oncology, 20*(2), 65–80.

Weiss, T. (2004). Correlates of posttraumatic growth in husbands of breast cancer survivors. *Psycho-Oncology, 13*(4), 260–268.

Weiss, T. & Berger, R. (Eds.) (2010). *Posttraumatic growth and culturally competent practice: Lessons learned from around the globe.* Hoboken, NJ: Wiley.

Wells, M. E. (2006). Psychotherapy for families in the aftermath of a disaster. *Journal of Clinical Psychology, 62*(8), 1017–1027.

Werner, E. E. & Smith, R. S. (1992). *Overcoming the odds: High risk children from birth to adulthood.* Ithaca, NY: Cornell University Press.

Westphal, M. & Bonanno, G. A. (2007). Posttraumatic growth and resilience to trauma: Different sides of the same coin or different coins? *Applied Psychology: An International Review, 56*(3), 417–427.

Wexler, I. D., Branski, D. & Kerem, E. (2006). War and children. *Journal of the American Medical Association, 296*, 579–581.

Wickrama, K. A. S. & Kaspar, V. (2007). Family context of mental health risk in Tsunami-exposed adolescents: Findings from a pilot study in Sri Lanka. *Social Science & Medicine, 64*(3), 713–723.

Wieling, E. & Mittal, M. (2008). Developing evidence-based systemic interventions for mass trauma. *Journal of Marital and Family Therapy, 34*(2), 127–131.

Wiesel, E. (1960). *Night.* New York: Hill & Wang.

Williams, R. (2007). The psychological consequences for children of mass violence, terrorism and disasters. *International Review of Psychiatry, 19*(3), 263–277.

Windle, G. (2010). What is resilience? A review and concept analysis. *Reviews in Clinical Gerontology, 21*(2), 152–169.

Wittouck, C., van Autreve, S. & De Jaegere, E. (2011). The prevention and treatment of complicated grief: A meta-analysis. *Clinical Psychology Review, 31*(1), 69–78.

Wolmer, L., Hamiel, D. & Laor, N. (2011). Preventing children's posttraumatic stress after disaster with teacher-based intervention: A controlled study. *Journal of the American Academy Of Child & Adolescent Psychiatry, 50*(6), 340–348.

Wolpe, J. (1958). *Psychotherapy by reciprocal inhibition.* Stanford: Stanford University Press.

Wong, M. L., Cavanaugh, C. E., MacLeamy, J. B., Sojourner-Nelson, A. & Koopman, C. (2009). Posttraumatic growth and adverse long-term effects of parental cancer in children. *Families, Systems, and Health, 27*(1), 53–63.

Wooding, S. & Raphael, B. (2004). Psychological impact of disasters and terrorism on children and adolescents: Experiences from Australia. *Prehospital and Disaster Medicine, 19*(1), 10–20.

Wortman, C. B. (2004). Posttraumatic growth: Progress and problems. *Psychological Inquiry, 15*(1), 81–90.

Yahav, R. (2011). Exposure of children to war and terrorism: A review. *Journal of Child & Adolescent Trauma, 4*(2), 90–108.

Yahav, R. & Cohen, M. (2007). Symptoms of acute stress in Jewish and Arab Israeli citizens during the second Lebanon war. *Social Psychiatry and Psychiatric Epidemiology, 42*, 830–836.

Yehuda, R., Schmeidler, J., Giller, E., Siever, L. & Binder-Byrnes, K. (1998). Relationship between posttraumatic stress disorder characteristics of Holocaust survivors and their adult offspring. *American Journal of Psychiatry, 155*(6), 841–843.

Yellow Horse Brave Heart, M. (2003). The historical trauma response among natives and its relationship with substance abuse: A Lakota illustration. *Journal of Psychoactive Drugs, 35*(1), 7–13.

Zahradnik, M., Stewart, S., Stevens, D. & Wekerle, C. (2009). Knowledge translation in community-based study of the relations among violence exposure, post-traumatic stress and alcohol misuse in Mi'kmaq youth. *First People's Child and Family Review, 4*(2), 106–117.

Zautra, A., Hall, J. S., & Murray, K. E. (2008). Community development and community resilience: An integrative approach. *Community Development, 39*(3), 130–147. Retrieved from http://www.fncfcs.com/sites/default/files/online-journal/

Zöllner, T. & Maercker, A. (2006). Post-traumatic growth in clinical psychology: A critical review and introduction of a two-component model. *Clinical Psychology Review, 26*(5), 626–653.

Index